That Miss Hobhouse

Emily Hobhouse

JOHN FISHER

That Miss Hobhouse

Secker & Warburg · London

First published in England 1971 by
Martin Secker & Warburg Limited
14 Carlisle Street, London WIV 6NN

SBN 436 15702 0

Printed in Great Britain by
Willmer Brothers Limited, Birkenhead

Contents

List of Illustrations

Acknowledgements

My thanks are due to Mr Paul Hobhouse, Mrs Michael King (née Hobhouse) and to Mrs Henry Hobhouse, for their special kindness, and to other members of the Hobhouse family who, in varying degrees, have helped to unravel the intricacies of their expansive genealogy.

In Cornwall, where Emily spent the first thirty-five years of her life, I received valuable help from Mr P. L. Hull, the County Archivist, on the history of the Diocese of Truro, and Mr Paul Bolitho of the Cornwall County Library at Liskeard on the history of the country. The Editor of the *Cornish Times* at Liskeard was good enough to allow me to reproduce reports from that journal; the Reverend Geoffrey Perry, Rector of St Ive, and Mrs Wenmoth, who now lives in the former Rectory, put their knowledge of the history of the parish at my disposal. Mr W. H. Paynter was able to provide information on the local copper mines of the area, Miss Ethel Bennett, of Haddy's Row, St Ive Cross, a loyal partisan of the Hobhouse family, was able to show me some of Emily's early paintings. Mrs J. Sparkes of Highwood Pensilva was most helpful on farms and farm houses which formerly existed.

Emily herself followed the Cornish miners overseas and in this connection I received valuable guidance from Professor A. L. Rowse, and from Dr John Rowe of the History Faculty of Liverpool University. From Virginia, Minnesota, the city to which Emily migrated, I received liberal help from Mr J. Edward Pearsall, Mayor of the City, on city records. Mr Michael Brook, Head of the Minnesota Historical Society discovered traces of Emily's missionary activities, and Mr Everett Blomgren, Editor of the *Mesabi Daily News*, successfully undertook painstaking research into the files of earlier newspapers to trace details of her attachment to the City Mayor. Mrs Lillian Esala of the Virginia Public Library, Minnesota, looked into early records of the City Council and I am grateful to a number of other Virginians who provided authentic information on their city as it was when Emily lived there.

I am extremely grateful to Professor J. J. Oberholster of the History Faculty of the University of the Orange Free State for his practical help and wise advice, and to Mr Charles More of Pretoria for special inquiries made in that city. The valuable Steyn Collection in the Archives of the Orange Free State have been drawn on for extracts from several letters written during the last four years of Emily's life.

I am indebted to the librarian of the Peace Palace at The Hague for information on the history of the building, also to the South African Ambassador in London and his staff and to Dr Hofmeyr, Member of the South Africa Society, for the loan of books otherwise unobtainable.

The staff of the London Library, of the British Museum Reading Room, of the Royal Commonwealth Society and of the Society of Friends Library in Euston Road, London, have all been long-suffering.

Finally, I have to thank Miss Ann Hoffmann for her perceptive and rewarding research into a number of seemingly intractable but ultimately soluble historical conundrums.

The Author and Publishers also wish to express their appreciation for permission to quote from the following copyright material:

'A Cornish Emigrant's Song' from *A Cornish Anthology*, A. L. Rowse; Macmillan, London and Basingstoke, 1968

My Partnership by Beatrice Webb, Ed. Barbara Drake & Margaret Cole; London School of Economics and Political Science, first published by Logmans Green & Co, 1948

With Rimington by L. March Phillipps; Edward Arnold, 1902

Emily Hobhouse by A. Ruth Fry; Jonathan Cape, 1929

What I remember by Millicent Fawcett; T. Fisher Unwin, 1924

Millicent Garrett Fawcett by Ray Strachey; John Murray, 1931

Selections from the Smuts Papers, Ed. W. K. Hanocock & Jean Van der Poel; Cambridge University Press, 1966

Changes and Chances by Henry Nevinson; James Nisbet & Co Ltd, 1923

The War in South Africa by J. A. Hobson; George Allen & Unwin Ltd, 1900

Representative Verse of Charles Wesley, Ed. Frank Baker; Epworth Press, 1962.

I

Life in a Cornish Rectory

The year 1860 was a moderately eventful one for the warriors of the world. In Europe, Garibaldi's Red Shirts were freeing Naples and Sicily; in Peking, the British and French sacked the Empress's Summer Palace; in New Zealand the Maoris fought desperately to free themselves from White Power; in America the civil war over slavery was already threatening.

At home in England there was less military action, and the chief topic claiming attention round the tea table was an unusually cold and damp spring. However one event occurred which came to have a bearing on Britain's future military campaigns.

Emily Hobhouse was born on April 9th, Easter Monday, at the Rectory of St Ive, a small village about five miles northeast of Liskeard in East Cornwall. The hamlet prided itself on being pronounced Saint Eve by the *cognoscenti* and in having no connection with the better known artists' colony of St Ives on the other side of the county. It lay in a countryside dotted with 'holy wells' and Celtic crosses, and endowed with at least one lake into which King Arthur is said to have thrown his sword Excalibur.

Emily's childhood was spent amid a wild landscape that billows like a green tarpaulin in the wind, its folds bulging out unexpectedly here and there as if straining against the hempen cords of its cropped hedges. She grew up to shiver in the silence of Cornwall's ghostly mists, which rise like fine white gauze from the sea to blot out landmarks as high even as the pinnacled tower of St Ive church; and on her walks she battled against the west wind from the Atlantic which hurls trees and tiles to the ground and rooks across the skies from one side to the other. She knew and respected the reticence of Cornwall's countryside in which, with a few steps either way, one is lost to sight

11

as a lane writhes away downhill towards the nearest valley between tall banks dripping with ferns and Cornish moneywort, with only a rough granite gatepost between one and the sky.

As a child she had warmed to the Cornish folk, Anna Gane her nurse and Thomas Gane the gardener, for example, with their soft West country sing-song speech, their unpretentious humour, their cheefulness and their love of music at all times—even at funerals.

She was welcomed into their cottages, built often of waste slag from the copper mines or of clay mixed with chopped straw; she warmed herself over their turf fires at the open hearth, her chimney stool resting on a moorland granite hearthstone strewed for cleanliness with sand.

She knew their favourite dishes—which included pilchards chopped up with raw onions and salt, broth flavoured with pork, and pies which might hold anything from fish and apples to a cormorant or a still-born lamb flavoured with cream, herbs and salt. (It was said that the Devil himself was afeared to come to Cornwall lest he be cut up and put in a pie.)

For centuries Cornwall had remained England's most remote county, cut off from the rest of us by the wilderness of Dartmoor and the almost trackless waste of Bodmin Moor; and Cornwall had more in common with Brittany or Wales than with the Great Wen of London.

Superstitions flourished there like the fuchsia trees that still deck the walls of the cottage gardens. There had been witches in abundance and the 'piskies' had frolicked in the meadows by night and had ridden the farmers' horses till they dropped from exhaustion.

Mining, of course, was the dark side of Cornish life—for the miners. An hour's walk to work, for a night shift perhaps, in damp or smoke-filled air, always against the risk of floods, of a charge of dynamite exploding prematurely or of the collapse of a timber baulk that was supposed to hold up the roof of a gallery. Occasionally, accidents would happen even 'at grass'—i.e. ground level—as when the boiler in the engine room, which the men used to dry their clothes, burst or when the machinery strained and snapped the winding rope, sending the cage with the men in it crashing to the bottom of the shaft.

From this world of toil and hardship Emily and her family were far removed. The Hobhouses were wealthy and well connected. Henry Hobhouse II as a barrister flourished in the days of George III and bought the handsome ochre-fronted

12

family seat of Hadspen, which still stands today, with its fine avenue of trees, its lawns and its ha-ha, a few miles outside Castle Cary in Somerset. His son Henry III was a member of the Privy Council and Under-Secretary of State for Home Affairs and was given the delicate task of advising what action could be legitimately taken to prevent Queen Caroline from forcing her way into Westminster Abbey during the coronation of George IV. His grandson Henry V was Liberal MP for East Somerset. But the highly developed consciences of the Hobhouse family never seem to have become quite reconciled to the fact that Henry Hobhouse I, the Bristol merchant who founded the family fortunes, was engaged in the slave trade and managed ten sailing ships which plied between Bristol, Gaboon, Angola and the Caribbean, taking out copper, muskets, bugles, brandy, knives and looking-glasses, ferrying slaves in shackles across the Atlantic, and returning to Bristol with sugar and tobacco. And at least one Hobhouse believes that this may help to account for the strongly Liberal and radical cast of thought and action shown by some members of the family.

Emily was the grand-daughter of Henry Hobhouse III, the Privy Councillor; and her father, Reginald Hobhouse, was one of four sons whom the Privy Councillor had contrived to send to Eton and Balliol College Oxford. Three of them pulled together in the same college boat in the year of Queen Victoria's accession to the throne.

Henry Hobhouse III was also able to leave his surviving younger children legacies of rather more than £10,000 each but could not in addition relieve them altogether from the necessity to earn a living and in 1841 he made use of his position as a strong supporter of the Conservative party and of the Duke of Wellington to congratulate Sir Robert Peel on his return to power in his second ministry and to drop at the same time a hint that he would appreciate some preferment or Government appointment for one or more of his sons.

This may serve to explain why Reginald, who achieved a fourth class degree in Classics and a second class in Maths succeeded in 1854, the year of his father's death, to the living of St Ive with Pensilva, which was in the patronage of the Crown. He remained in the same parish until his death 51 years later.

After seven years' celibacy he married Miss Caroline Trelawny, third daughter of Sir William Trelawny Bt. of Harewood House, Calstock. The Trelawny family, one of the most famous in Cornwall, had long been noted for their independent spirit and one of them, Jonathan Trelawny, earned fame as one of the seven Bishops who went to prison for refusing to read James II's Act of Indulgence to Papists and Dissenters. At first the new bride had to squeeze into a minute cottage fit only for a bachelor but in time the rector built a new and more impressive dwelling placed on the brow of the hill. It was a remarkably long and narrow building, constructed of massive granite and slate with a steeply pitched slate roof. All the principal rooms faced south towards the English Channel and hardly any two windows were of equal size or shape. At one end was a turret, in which was installed a bell for summoning coachman or gardener to the house. Fifteen bells, each pendant on its coiled spring, warned the domestic staff in which quarter of the mansion their services were needed.

It was between these walls that Emily grew up. There are contrary views as to whether her childhood was happy or not —her own opinion and that of her relations. It is hard to know toward which verdict one should incline.

On the one hand Emily was one of a family of five—one older brother Alfred (born 1856), three elder sisters Caroline (1854), Blanche (1857), Maud (1858) and another brother Leonard (1864), four years younger than herself; and it is not to be supposed that they were less companionable or affectionate than other families of their day.

Leonard, to whom Emily was closest in intellect if not in years, believed that her recollections of her childhood as recorded by her first biographer, Ruth Fry, were too melancholy, and suggested that they were clouded by the very much less happy years she spent towards the close of her life. He pointed out that the family without exception could count on the loving care, not only of both parents but of devoted servants. He added that Emily's mother was a delightful and witty companion, who treated her children as equals rather than as juveniles and who took pleasure in reading not only Dickens to the children but French, German and Italian literature to herself.

Nor was it from her parents alone that Emily received kindness. Her father's younger brother Arthur Hobhouse, whose service to the Government in India earned him a peerage on the recommendation of Mr Gladstone, took the lead in organizing an annual family holiday at Charlton, Sir Edward Fry's country estate near Portishead in Somerset.

14

As Rachel Hobhouse, daughter of Henry Hobhouse V, and a cousin therefore of Emily, wrote of these holidays:

'It was like being plunged into another world with the old-fashioned more formal ways of the house and servants. I remember Aunt Mary reading aloud to us and how we drove the pair of carriage horses and played cricket with the butler and manservants. I remember picking mushrooms with Uncle Arthur and visiting the model dairy, the source of much Devonshire Cream, and the prospect of croquet and tennis and billiards and picnics added to the excitement of returning each year.'

From time to time Emily and one or more of her sisters would take off from Cornwall with their governess to stay in Bruton Street, Mayfair, with Lord and Lady Hobhouse, while their father and mother were wintering, for the Rector's health, in the South of France.

Emily aged seven received a Valentine card with the caption, 'Wherever I am I will always be missis,' and ever afterwards she was nicknamed the Missis not only by her family but by her friends, too, including Field Marshal Smuts.

Then there were family games of hide and seek, rallies of battledore and shuttlecock with the curate Mr Rogers, village concerts and amateur theatricals; gardening; chickens and rabbits to be looked after and the fun of haymaking, and seaside holidays at Bude.

But there was much to be set against this.

In the first place Emily suffered, when her mother was away, from a series of indifferent governesses who were totally unfitted, in her opinion at least, to give her the education she needed. When, at fifteen, she went to school for two terms she found the lessons stereotyped and uninspiring. Already she showed a trace of feminist envy at the advantages that boys at school and university enjoyed over girls.

Then one tragedy after another struck the family. In 1875, when Emily was fifteen, her sister Blanche, to whom she was especially close, caught consumption and, despite several visits for her health to the South of France, died, two years later, aged twenty, in Toulon.

In 1876 Caroline, Emily's eldest sister, married August Vansittart Thornton, a Deacon, son of Francis Vansittart Thornton, Rector of Southill with Callington, and flew from the nest.

Three years later Emily's mother, once the most vivacious

15

member of the family, died of a brain tumour and the following year her father was dangerously ill and had to be nursed.

Alfred, resisting his father's wish that he should enter the Church, left for New Zealand to become a school master. Leonard was at Balliol and already immersed in the problems of sociology.

For the nine years following her mother's death, Maud and Emily between them shared the work of the parish, encouraging the backsliders, visiting the poor, distributing food, clothing and literature, listening to the songs of some and the woes of many. She became acquainted with sickbeds and death. Parish work must have been a disheartening task, for Cornish folk were not on the whole enamoured of the ways of the church, which had neglected its people for so long. For 800 years Cornwall had remained in the diocese of Exeter, one of the largest and least controlled in the whole of the country. It was the haunt of sporting parsons, twenty of whom at one time kept packs of hounds within the diocese. Among them was the Perpetual Curate of Swymbridge, the former Rev. Jack Russell, later Vicar of Black Torrington near Hatherleigh, who kept a pack of foxhounds and three horses and thought nothing of riding fifty miles to hunt with a neighbouring pack on a day when his own had no fixture.

Many more clerics hunted several days a week and many a surplice was torn at the back because the vicar had taken the service once too often wearing spurs, and it was said that when Henry Philpotts, the Lord Bishop of Exeter, first came to his Diocese, and was traversing it in the episcopal coach, he saw a pack of foxhounds in full cry, pursued by a field composed largely of black-coated riders. So many were there that he supposed that some terrible catastrophe, as a token to which they were in mourning, had visited the country.

Later, as a wiser but no sadder Bishop, he was approached by one of his flock who remarked, 'I am told, my lord, that you object to my hunting.' 'Dear me,' answered the Bishop, with a ready smile, 'whoever could have told you that? What I object to is that you should ever do anything else.'

No wonder that when Thomas Hardy, as a young architect, visited St Juliot church in North Cornwall in 1870 to redesign the building, he found that the bells had been taken down from the tower and placed on the floor of the church, the benches had rotted and a mantle of ivy clothed the inner walls.

16

But those whom the Established Church neglected, the Dissenters sought out for salvation.

In the course of the 18th century John Wesley paid thirty-two visits to Cornwall including six to Liskeard and found there some of his most enthusiastic audiences. The first prayer house was set up in Liskeard in 1776 and travelling preachers visited the area about once every six weeks.

For the Cornish folk—lovers of religion, mystery plays and drama—found a special affinity in Wesley's teaching. They relished his appeal to those forgotten of men but precious in the sight of God. They welcomed his threats of hell fire for the sinner, his call for the blood of sacrifice, and his glorification of the converted, pierced through if not slain by the sword of the Lord.

Wesley rode through driving West Country rain and slept on bare boards to visit his flock and never lost an opportunity for making a convert. Alice Daniell, gathering honey in her cottage garden, was saved by the Lord after Wesley had asked her for a glass of water and spoke to her of 'truths sweeter than honey or the honeycomb'.

At Camelford, on Fair Day, his text (from Isaiah 55:1) was 'Come buy wine and milk without money and without price.' In Liskeard he spoke twice in one day, standing on a rock to which bulls had been tethered for baiting. Elsewhere he preached in backyards, in meadows or even on the sea shore.

Men who came to trifle or mock or even to throw eggs at his preachers, as at Quetiock, the next parish to St Ive, were often converted before the close of the first hymn and in June 1817 at St Cleer 'The Lord came down in such a powerful manner that our meeting was not concluded till one o'clock in the morning—Glory be to God.' The tinners of Gwennap woke Wesley between three and four in the morning, fearing that they would otherwise be too late to hear his words. Methodist hymns were sung at deep levels of the mines where indeed the vocalists all too often received a foretaste of the Hell that awaited backsliders.

Conversion in Wesley's view should be preceded by a strong conviction of sin and a lively apprehension of the consequences of eternal damnation, to be followed by spiritual turmoil and depression, from which the sufferer 'groaned to be set free' and could be liberated i.e. 'brought up out of the horrible pit and miry clay,' only by the knowledge that he was accepted by God. Methodist conversions were confirmed and strengthened by 'Love

17

Feasts' of plain cake and water, which participants consumed in witness of their love of God and of his love for them. Watchnight services were held at full moon as well as Bible Class meetings, and preaching services and private prayer was backed up by a quarterly fast.

Sports (even Cornish wrestling and hurling, i.e. hand football) were discouraged, as were theatre-going, card-playing and dancing, with its accompanying 'Devil's music' (a ban which extinguished many Cornish folk songs).

The original aim of Methodism had been to strengthen and deepen spiritual life within the established church and Wesley took parishioners of those areas he was visiting with him to Church before holding his own meetings afterwards outside the Church or in a nearby cottage. But the activities of Wesleyans were met too often with incomprehension, if not outright hostility by the pastors of the Established Church and the Wesleyans had to raise money for places of worship built in their own uncompromisingly severe and simple style. (At Lower Tremar the chapel was a cow-house with calico sheets hung from the rafters to hide the crib and manger from the worshippers.)

Eventually these chapels were licensed by the Bishop, Archdeacon or Justices of the Peace as places of worship for Protestant Dissenters and, in 1795, permission was given for the sacraments to be celebrated there. In 1836 the preachers were dignified by the title of Minister.

This was the situation facing Reginald Hobhouse when he succeeded to the living of St Ive with Pensilva in 1844. Methodism was no longer a movement for strengthening spiritual holiness within the Church of England, nor was it primarily a movement leading to repentance and conversion, it was a church which though not completely united, was capable of maintaining itself in independence indefinitely, and it was better organized than the Church of England to do so. Also—more disturbing—the Wesleyans tended to support Liberals rather than Tories.

Towards such a state of affairs there could, to Reginald Hobhouse's mind, be only one reply. A revival movement must be launched within the Church of England and especially in Cornwall and he was among the foremost in urging that the county should once again have its own Bishopric.

In 1876, when Emily was sixteen, the good news came. The Bishopric, in abeyance since before the Norman Conquest, was to be revived and placed, not at St Germans or at Bodmin as in the past, but at Truro. Its first Bishop was the remarkable

Edward White Benson, former Headmaster of Wellington and later 92nd Archbishop of Canterbury; though a doughty fighter in the cause of orthodoxy, he fully appreciated the achievement of the Methodists, who had cherished the sacred flame of religion in the days when most Cornishmen paid more attention to the price of bullocks. He knew that Wesley had helped to promote sobriety, morality, education and the sanctity of family life among Cornish folk. He was prepared accordingly to take over, if he could, what was best in Methodism and incorporate it into the episcopal corpus.

But this was not the way of Reginald Hobhouse, of whom his family wrote: 'His most striking characteristics were devotion to his clerical duties, his untiring industry and the minute care which he took to all matters he took in hand. He had a strong sense of humour and affection for his family but was rather inflexible and narrow in his views.'

In the Crockford's Clerical Directory of his day he is noted for having composed a special sermon on 'Ministerial Watchfulness', which scarcely suggests a spirit of innovation, and it was said of him that, after having been reproved by his brother Edmund, afterwards Bishop of Nelson in New Zealand, for reading a novel, he never again in his lifetime opened another.

He was highly respected, and his work in bringing about the revival of the Cornish Bishopric was recognized in 1878 when he was appointed Archdeacon of Bodmin.

He built at his own expense a day school for the children of his parishioners and he improved the 15th century pre-Reformation Church of St Ive in many other ways, adding a draught screen, a belfry screen and a chancel.

But he failed to establish communication, as the modern phrase goes, with his parishioners. His task was not easy for the parish had both miners and farmers, permanently at odds with each other. Tithe, too, an abomination to Cornishmen, was still payable up to 1890 and cannot have added to the rector's popularity, even though payment took place at the Butcher's Arms, St Ive.

The rector's sermons moreover were uninspiring compared with those delivered by intinerant Methodist preachers and when he departed from his set text to utter truths from the fullness of his heart, his emotions took control and he frequently broke down. His life was overshadowed by the family tragedies for, apart from his wife and daughter Blanche he had lost two children as infants, and this may partly have accounted for his relatively modest success in pastoral work.

Probably the clearest picture of the state of St Ive is provided by the return filled in by Reginald Hobhouse's successor in preparation for the visitation of the Bishop of Truro to the parish in 1896, the year after the death of Archdeacon Hobhouse. This describes the Dissenters in the parish as 'friendly' rather than 'indifferent' or 'aggressive' and they had held not a single outdoor preaching during the previous year, yet not one person during the previous four years had left them to join the Established Church.

The average number of communicants on Sundays in the St Ive Parish Church (capable of holding 200) was said in the return to be seven and at Pensilva sub-chapel nine, although the surrounding population was put at 900 souls. Twenty-six people in the whole parish, it was thought, could be regarded as communicants who received Holy Communion at least three times a year. To have grown up amid such an atmosphere of partial, if not total, failure cannot have been inspiring for Emily.

Moreover, for the parish, as for the whole of Cornwall, the years from 1840 onwards were a period of industrial and agricultural depression. Social and economic poverty added to the sense of loneliness and frustration of those who lived in the county. Already, in the days before Cornwall was properly served with roads, the railways had begun to act as a brain-drain and, though in 1895 the 9 a.m. from Waterloo took six and a half hours to reach Tavistock (from where it was three hours by coach to Liskeard), the consciousness of being able to reach London in a day inevitably detracted from the importance and authority of local opinion, as also from the attraction of local entertainments.

It was in these circumstances that Emily and Maud from 1880 between them carried on the work of the parish. Maud, the more timid, fought shy of long walks alone and took the calls nearest to the rectory and Emily, more self-confident, walked to the bounds of the parish, two or three miles in places, to visit more distant backsliders in lonely farms or miners' cottages, scattered, as is usual in Cornwall, in an apparently inconsequential manner across the countryside.

There, in the land of the supernatural, she was a 'white witch' to the cottagers—someone who could charm away warts, asthma or whooping cough. She would be told of the woman who was cured of a fever by a live pigeon cut in half and placed against

20

her feet. There she would find homes so poor that the children had to be sent upstairs naked while their only shift went into the wash tub. She would call at cottages where the front door was divided in two with an upper half to let in light and air while the lower half kept out the pigs and chickens. She would see the miners' families preparing the famous Hoggan or un-leavened dough, flavoured with a lump of green pork, which the Cornish labourer preferred to all else as his standby.

There would be walks across the green hills, scored with the purple furrows of the plough, streaked with golden gorse, and crossed here and there by a single line of stunted trees stalking into the wind.

At home to pass the time Emily learned to paint portraits and landscapes and studied the piano and violin. She took singing lessons and rendered drawing room ditties such as 'Lullaby'. She dressed up in Romany style to sing 'The Gypsie's Warning', and appeared in shoes decked with crystals to represent dewdrops on her feet when she performed 'Where the meadow dew is sweet'. There was choir practice at the piano—and practice too for 'Curls'—carols, in which around Christmas time Cornish voices made known that the King of Izeryhell had been born.

But all this fol-de-rol failed to make up for the generation gap between Emily and Maud, the two members of the family still at home, and their father. They respected him, loved him and occasionally shared family jokes with him. But they could not talk to him except impersonally and, since his wife's death, the light had gone out of his life.

After lunch and dinner the rector, who suffered almost perpetually from headaches, would retire to his study at the far end of the house, presumably to attend to Archidiaconal affairs, and could not thereafter be disturbed. Into his world Emily was never allowed to penetrate, and when her ally the Bishop of Truro (who thought about Dissenters much as she did) suggested that she should head a women's committee formed to raise money for the completion of Truro Cathedral, the Archdeacon, despite the fact that his daughter was now 24, used the parental veto.

Maud afterwards maintained—though with great good humour for the sisters were friends to the end of their days—that Emily was always rushing off to stay with her uncle and aunt and that it was she who had the ticking of the carriage clock for company after dinner.

This may have been so but not without cause, for Emily while in Venice suffered a severe accident (a slip perhaps on one of those treacherous marble staircases?) which compelled her to lie on her back and to rest for long periods. (Indeed a fall of this kind in the days when comparatively little was known about 'bad backs' and slipped discs would help to account for the crippling rheumatoid arthritis from which Emily suffered in later middle age.)

Neither Emily nor Maud was lucky in affairs of the heart. To the indignation of the Archdeacon Maud allowed herself to be courted by Ernest Hebblethwaite, Curate of St Ive, and a family row ensued. All communication between the two sweethearts was banned and for fifty-two weeks Maud had to send notes written for her by an intermediary. Her marriage took place in 1889 when Mr Hebblethwaite was appointed to the living of Poundstock (population 500), from which he derived a net income of £125 a year plus house. No promotion followed and no other living was offered to him when he left Poundstock in 1903, though his name continued to appear in Crockford's Clerical Directory with the Junior Oxford and Cambridge Club as his principal address.

For Emily, too, the cards would not run right. She became attracted to William John Barrett, called John by his family, who came to the rectory for choir practice and music lessons. John's father, Richard Barrett, farmed at Penquite, which lay on a bye-road overlooking the River Tiddy, nearly three miles from St Ive, but his brother Alfred farmed eight acres at Redwood, which was two miles nearer and provided a more convenient meeting place for John and Emily. The Barrett family was a sizeable one, there being three other brothers, Richard, Harry and Thomas. Moreover Richard's wife had worked at the Rectory. It was not long before Cornish tongues were a-wagging.

It is easy to suppose that this was a light-hearted affair belonging to Emily's 'romantic period' which would occur inevitably for a girl of strong feeling confined to the small world of a Cornish village. And indeed viewed by present-day standards, her attachment might have been little more than a flirtation. But of the two partners Emily was the elder and probably the initiator. Eventually, news of the association penetrated even the Archdeacon's ivory tower and an even more memorable family rumpus, lasting for some two hours, according to the most reliable estimates of the domestic staff, ensued behind locked doors. When we read Leonard Hobhouse's remark that a few words of reproof from the Archdeacon fell with the weight of tons, we can form some idea of the ordeal through which Emily must have passed. In the end she surrendered, realizing, perhaps, the scandal that in those times would have resulted from an association between the daughter of the Archdeacon and one of his choir, whose sister-in-law had been housemaid at the rectory.

Soon afterwards John Barrett left for America from where he returned only on brief visits, unmarried.

From 1889 onwards, after Maud's marriage, Emily alone looked after the rector and his parish. In 1892 illness forced him to resign his office as Archdeacon and she found herself in charge of a permanent invalid. It was she who took him for drives in the ponycart, she who waited after each service at the vestry door to give him her arm across the road—then mercifully free from traffic—which runs between the church and the rectory. She walked through sunshine and rain on her rounds and, to occupy her spare time even studied the unrewarding craft of illuminating manuscripts.

The year 1894 gave Emily a chance to shine, and to show powers of organization which no one had supposed her to possess. For in that year her father was to celebrate his fiftieth year as Rector of St Ive. Emily formed a Committee representing the clergy and parishioners, not only of St Ive and Pensilva, but also of Liskeard, Callington and other places where the Rector was known. Two hundred subscribers clubbed together to buy a two-handled silver goblet and salver decorated with a 'chased floral design' and the Rector's crest together with an inscription commemorating his services; the old man made a moving speech of retrospect in which he drew attention to the longevity of the clergy of East Cornwall (the Rev. J. R. P. Berkeley in the neighbouring parish of St Cleer had also held his living for fifty years) and recalled that Mr Andrew, the Churchwarden who had seen him inducted half a century before, was still hearty and still occupied the same post. Emily had arranged high tea at the Rectory, and, afterwards the Rev. H. Tomlinson photographed several groups. Evening service was held in the church, after which, according to the Cornish Times, 'the talented family of the Ven. R. Hobhouse gave a concert of vocal and instrumental music in the schoolroom, which was greatly appreciated.' The proceedings concluded with an attractive display of fireworks let off by Mr W. Huddy in Church Park, 'which, as a novelty at the village, was witnessed with interest and delight.'

But after this burst of celebration the shadows crept back again. The old man was still a handsome figure with his white hair and deeply marked features resembling somewhat the head of an eagle taken from one of his own lecterns. But, increasingly, his face was marked with pain from the growth that was to kill him.

In January 1895 in the midst of a bitter winter he died.

For Emily it was the end of ordinary family life within an ordinary family; but on the other hand no worthwhile career outside it was open to her. In an age which produced Octavia Hill, the founder of the National Trust, Annie Besant who became Chairman of the Indian National Congress, Elizabeth Garett Anderson, the first qualified woman doctor and the Pankhursts, Emily herself had accomplished nothing. At 35—and people aged more quickly in those days—she had passed no examinations, she had obtained no diplomas, and she was untrained to follow any calling. She had no roof to shelter her—although she could probably have had one to the end of her days if she had brought herself to ask her uncle for house-room. Already more than half her life had slipped away. She was no longer a young woman to be turned out into the world to fend for herself.

Yet within a fortnight she had left the village of her childhood and never to the end of her life returned to it.

And the way she occupied the next few years of her life showed marked originality.

2

A Man in Minnesota

'Oh! the eastern winds are blowing;
The breezes seem to say,
We are going, we are going,
To North Americay.

'There the merry bees are humming
Around the poor man's hive;
Parson Kingdon is not coming
To take away their tithe.

'There the yellow corn is growing
Free as the King's highway,
So we're going, we are going,
To North Americay

'Uncle Rab shall be churchwarden,
And Dick shall be the squire
And Jem, that lived at Norton,
Shall be leader of the quire;

'And I will be the preacher,
And preach three times a day
To every living creature,
In North Americay.'

Thus ran the song of the Cornish emigrants (of whom Emily
was soon to become one).

Most of those who left Cornwall in the last half of the
19th century were miners, for this was a branch of human activity
in which, for nearly a hundred years, Cornwall led the world.
And it was not only tin that they knew how to mine. During the
eighteenth and early nineteenth centuries, Cornish engineers
had continuously improved their pumps to a degree which made

it possible to clear a mine of water down to a depth of a third of a mile, and this in turn allowed the Cornish to mine copper on a large scale. Already in 1837 Cornwall produced about two-thirds of the world's copper and, at their peak in 1856, Cornish mines yielded more than 200,000 tons of copper a year.

But soon afterwards the days of expansion were over. In 1845 prospectors in Michigan had discovered rich lodes containing solid blocks of the metal, and from that time on the demand for Cornish copper fell sharply; by 1880, Cornwall produced only a fifth of the amount yielded a quarter of a century earlier. A few mine owners tried to exploit a second layer of tin which lay beneath the copper, but tin needed fewer miners than copper, and it was not long before this source of income vanished with the discovery of more easily mined alluvial deposits in Malaya.

Mine after mine shut down, the western mines first, then those developed more recently in the east of the county. Few mine owners had the reserves needed to weather a depression or to pump the water out of a mine that had been closed even temporarily. Whole villages were deserted, and the granite engine houses of the mines began to acquire their present-day mantle of ivy.

Leonard Courtney, lecturing to the Royal Institute of Cornwall in June 1897, reckoned that 230,000 miners would have left Cornwall by the end of the century, and statisticians estimated that the county lost a third of its population during the various depressions of the eighteen hundreds. Those that stayed behind tended to devote themselves to exporting fish, flowers, potatoes and broccoli and to importing tourists, especially after 1876 when the Great Western Railway took over the line through to Penzance.

Once abroad, however, the Cornish Jacks, as they were called, found that they were the world's greatest experts in deep mining. Many took part in the 1849 gold rush to California. Others went to Australia, Brazil or South Africa; or to Nevada, Montana, Colorado, Arizona, Idaho or Michigan. They were welcomed everywhere, and indeed it was said that all over the world, wherever there was a hole in the ground you would find a Cornishman at the bottom of it digging for metal.

They had their own system of piece work under which each job was a miniature contract estimated and bid for by individuals working under a mine captain, and the Captain as often as not had sent home for his team. The men had their own mining lingo (e.g. 'God-send' meaning a warning collapse of rock, and many other more technical terms). They had their own style of timber work in the mine that could be recognized at a glance. They had their own type of shovel, their own peculiar candlesticks. Even the plate-ties they used for the mine railways were in special Cornish style. They could work in extremes of hardship —temperatures in parts of the Wheal Clifford Mine at home in Cornwall had been known to rise at times to 125 degrees Fahrenheit. They had their own food; the Cornish pasty, re-heated in the mine on a Cornish stove—a shovel held over two candles.

The prospect of helping Cornish miners must obviously have appealed to Emily and she was no stranger to their life since mines were scattered about in several places near to her home. The Herodsfoot Mine, which lay in the upper valley of the Looe river, 3 miles south-west of Liskeard, was in production as late as 1904. There was the Wheal Ludcott mine a mile away from St Ive, and Wheal Wrey, Trebeigh, Butterdon, Wheal Gill and New Trelawny in the same area. In the north of the parish, near Pensilva, there were the mines on the moorland slope of Caradon Hill, from which copper was brought by horse railway via Liskeard en route for the Cornish port of Looe.

Furthermore, the Cornish Jacks sent home news from abroad in letters to their families, some of which were published in journals such as the *West Briton*. Often emigration was a local enterprise for which the would-be-emigrant had borrowed the passage money either from his family or from a local tradesman, and as soon as he was established he would send home a sum to repay the loan or passage money for the next of kin to follow him overseas.

Through tickets from Falmouth across the Atlantic to Michigan were on sale across the counter of village stores and these pioneer travel agents painted an encouraging picture of life overseas; and indeed many Cornish miners flourished in exile.

But to Emily it was clear that they were in need of care and protection—hers. True, many of them were Methodists and deeply religious, but others would undoubtedly be in need of the ministrations of good Episcopalians. Abroad, as at home, Cornishmen—or some of them at least—were known to be heavy drinkers and gamblers. But all were susceptible to the charms of the West Country music with which Emily was familiar. And there was nothing like a whiff of homesickness for reforming a man.

Emily arranged her journey overseas through Archbishop

Benson, whose Archdeacon wrote on Emily's behalf to the Bishop of the Diocese of Minnesota and, from the latter's flock an appeal to come over into Minnesota and help, eventually reached Miss Hobhouse.

'In the wonderful Providence of God,' Archdeacon Appleby said in his report to the 38th Council of the Diocese of Minnesota, 'a daughter of the late Archdeacon Hobhouse of England, a lady of means, has just offered her services to the Bishop for missionary work among miners. I have written her particulars in regard to the Mesaba Iron range, and we hope that Miss Hobhouse will come to us, and she speaks of associating one or more assistants with her in the work.'

Elsewhere in the same report the Archdeacon mentioned that he hoped personally to supervise the work of building a substantial church in the newly established mining centre of Virginia in which the Bishop had said he might spend a month. 'At Virginia, too, I hope, in order to help counteract the baneful influence of forty-two saloons there, to be enabled to establish a men's club, coffee and reading room, similar to one established in my north western mission some years ago, which was the means in the hands of God of untold and widespread good.'

The Archdeacon added that there were twelve mines in the immediate neighbourhood of Virginia, several of which were expanding and that there were four other towns with mines close to Virginia 'so that Virginia must of necessity prove a good centre for missionary operations. In these mines there are several hundred Finns and Cornishmen among whom our church work will be hailed with delight.'

True, there were other features about Virginia which were not so promising. In the first place the average temperature there taking the year as a whole was only 38 degrees Fahrenheit (3°C) not very much above freezing. The average rainfall— $26\frac{1}{2}$ inches— was comparable with that of Britain, but in winter, the snowfall averaged 6 feet (since those days the city has become the centre of a winter sports playground), and in January the mean daily maximum temperature is $18\frac{1}{2}$ degrees Fahrenheit ($7\frac{1}{2}$ degrees Centigrade below freezing). In other words the winter was practically arctic. Summers could be stiflingly hot but in August when Emily arrived the temperature would have been about the same as an English summer's, but the season was a short one with only 100 days between the last killing frosts of spring and the first freeze-up of the following autumn. The mosquitoes nevertheless made full use of it.

These were however no obstacles to mining prospectors, and five years before Emily left Britain, they had discovered iron ore and set up their camp on the Mesabi range. The site lay in virgin territory and was surrounded by virgin timber, for which reason it was decided to christen it Virginia. At first no road led to Virginia, and pilgrims plodded towards their goal along George Stuntz's Old Vermilion Trail which wound through 60 miles of mud, swamp, timber and brush, rock and sand and across rivers and streams. Stage coaches avoided Virginia because of its mud in which teams of six or even eight horses would flounder belly-deep, unable to stir. The settlers themselves brought what they needed on their own shoulders. Log cabins and tents were their shelters and up till almost the end of 1892 visitors had to walk five miles through the woods to reach Virginia from the nearest railway station. In December of that year the settlement was incorporated as a village and John Owens elected as President. The railway reached Virginia by New Year 1893 and big orders for pine lumber soon followed.

The mines, too, prospered largely because soft hematite iron ore could be extracted on the open-cast system with giant steam shovels. By June 1893 Virginia had 12 mines, a huge sawmill, its own business section, a newspaper, a Water and Light Company and a population of about 5,000. But on the 18th of that month, a hot dry windy Sunday, a brush fire swept in from the south west and within forty minutes the town of Virginia had been burnt to the ground. Log cabins, saloons, hotels, stores all had vanished. Many people took the first train and sought shelter in Iron Junction.

Before long, however, the pioneer spirit triumphed again. New buildings were put up, and, on an evening in May 1894, townsmen stood in the streets to watch the electricity turned on to light the electric bulbs and the street lamp suspended over each of the four crossroads. By February 1895 the population had bounced back to 3,055, enough for the town to be officially incorporated as a city.

But only the main streets were 'paved' with logs; the side streets were quagmires impassable on foot, the 'pavements' raised high above the pools and swamps of the street were board walks. An occasional plank took pedestrians from one side to the other. Thus the city was a merger between the Wild West and the Far North.

Emily's journey to Virginia should have served to prepare her for roughing it, as we learn from the *Minnesota Missionary and Church Record*. The report in the September issue ran:

'Miss Hobhouse, daughter of the late Archdeacon Hobhouse of Truro, England, referred to in the Archdeacon's report published last month, arrived in St Paul on Saturday morning the 10th ult., where she remained the guest of Archdeacon and Mrs Appleby till Tuesday night, when, accompanied by Miss Carter, she started by the St Paul and Duluth Railway for Duluth en route for Virginia. At 7.45 a.m. they left for Virginia over the Missabe & Northern Railway, but were detained for about two hours and a half by the sinking of the roadbed about 40 miles from Duluth, caused by muskag, (a Canadian-type bog, more commonly known as "Muskag"; they had therefore to be met on the other side of the muskag by a train from Virginia, and having transshipped their baggage, arrived at their destination at 2 p.m. After dinner they proceeded to hunt up a small house which was rented by Miss Hobhouse, three months in advance, in which she will begin her noble and self-denying work among the miners of Virgina. At 8 p.m. a hearty service was held among the Presbyterian Church and the Archdeacon in a brief address introduced Miss Carter who gave one of her heart-touching missionary lectures on China and Japan which interested the audience in a remarkable manner.'

(These words draw attention to the weak position of the Anglican Church in Virginia. In contrast the Presbyterians had shown considerable enterprise and their first Minister, the Rev Edward N. Raymond who held his services in a hired room in part of Crockett's Opera House, did not hesitate to visit the gaming room in another part of the building even when poker was being played in order to recruit his congregation. Later, the Presbyterians built their own church and allowed the Anglicans to hold services there while their own building was still under construction.)

Two days after Emily's arrival the *Virginia Enterprise*, a weekly paper published every Saturday but printed in Hurley and transported in a trunk to its distributing office, a small room at the back of a gambling saloon, noted that:

'Miss Hobhouse, the lady missionary from Cornwall, England arrived in the city on Wednesday 14th August and will shortly take up her residence in the Bodock House, on Maple Street. Miss Hobhouse has spent much time in missionary work among the miners of Cornwall and her life here will be devoted to a similar mission.'

Emily had not come to Minnesota unequipped for her new life. Her public was impressed when it became known that she had brought her own blankets and sheets and that she had a Cornish girl, Mary Scourey, with her as maid. But in a small town surrounded by pine forests stretching right up to the Canadian border and beyond she felt isolated and lonely. She stayed at a boarding house, which she found neither well run nor clean, while looking for furniture—two second-hand hospital beds and some wooden chairs. But when she moved in, the cottage turned out to be infested with bugs, so it was back to the boarding house for Emily and her maid, until another larger 'cottage' was got ready for her on Central Avenue.

In one of her earliest letters from Virginia she told her sister Mrs Hebblethwaite how it would have amused her to see the company that she, Emily, was now keeping at meals in the board-ing—house—a Miss Whiteley, a London girl stranded in Minnesota, 'a Mr Jackson who runs the grocery store here' and a land agent. But there was to be an unexpected sequel to these mealtime reunions.

Once installed, Emily threw herself into her work, and made some disagreeable discoveries. The first of these was that there were comparatively few Cornish miners in Virginia—possibly because there was little of the deep mining that required their skills. Secondly the Finns and Scandinavians drank more than the Cornishmen and stood in greater need of salvation. Further-more Emily did not like the arrangements that tied her to the Episcopalian Church when she preferred to work for the benefit of sinners of any (or even no) religious denomination.

She called at the public hospital, a clapboard building approached up a wooden staircase, and as no one answered the front door, walked in through the back. She found no doctor or nurse there—only a Swedish janitor sleeping off a hangover on a bed in the lower ward, a crippled patient whose legs had been crushed between two waggons and whose bed had not been made for a month, and six typhoid patients upstairs, all of different nationalities, with no one to take their temperatures. To them Emily sang songs—in as many different tongues as possible, ending with a German song of Mendelssohn's which delighted the German Swiss.

She found herself in a city that was given over to drink and whose revenue came mainly from liquor licences. The city's first barbershop was Ed Burley's establishment consisting of one chair behind the front door of Billy Hayes' saloon. The city's most famous beer garden (for men only) had been thoughtfully placed within thirty feet of the main drinking fountain for horses. There were four houses of ill fame, one of which provided twenty females and a non-stop crap game. As in many other mining communities the prostitute occupied a respected position in the social hierarchy.

The Ministers of the various churches were afraid to speak out against the evils of drink for fear of offending their supporters and losing their revenues. The police, Emily found, publicly flouted the law, the Mayor and Town Council bought their votes with liquor and embezzled the public funds. Theft, forgery, false pretences and violence of all kinds flourished unchecked.

Indeed Emily felt that it would be the best thing for the city if the Mayor and Town Council were thrown into the State Prison, a fate which they had narrowly escaped on one occasion.

Emily started her temperance campaign by holding meetings in her own house to which she summoned the Ministers, and when she found their support fell short of her exacting specifications, she launched her own campaign to establish the Virginia Temperance Union. Despite the opposition of saloon keepers and the studied indifference of the police Emily had no hesitation in appearing in the main street of the city carrying a pad of temperance pledge cards and a pencil at the ready for signing up repentant drunkards. By the Autumn of 1895 she had progressed so far that Mayor Robert McGruer himself attended one of her meetings.

A typical announcement bearing the hall-marks of Emily's style appeared in the Virginia *Enterprise* of December 6th 1895 :

'On Tuesday evening next at 8 p.m. a temperance meeting will be held in the Finlander's Temperance Hall. The chair will be taken by Miss Hobhouse, and two ladies from Duluth, Mrs Merritt and Mrs Scobell, have promised to come and speak on this occasion. The need of some temperance organization on a broad basis has been long felt by the most earnest spirits in Virginia and it is sincerely hoped that all will work together for the furtherance of this great cause the need of which is so apparent.

Let all lovers of temperance and haters of intemperance come boldly forward and show your colours, joining hands together against the mighty curse which is deadening the consciences and ruining the lives of so many of our fellow citizens.

Will not all those who join this temperance organization remember that they bind themselves that others may be free.'

Meetings were held at the Finnish Hall on other Tuesdays, and Emily received warm support from the Finnish Temperance Band, especially after she had addressed the Finnish Brotherhood of Temperance at their National Convention held in Virginia.

As in Cornwall Emily did not confine her work to the hub of the parish. With her maid she walked out along the trails across bogs and creeks deep into the forest to visit Finnish workers in a lumber camp where they would be snowed up for the winter (and was given raw tea drunk out of a tin, and hot cakes). In arctic cold she went out to preach to them across frozen lakes on a sleigh which was taking hay to the horses.

In time Emily learnt the secrets of the forest—she could distinguish the trails left by moose, deer, rabbits, squirrels and others in the snow.

Socially she spent many days with Judge Eaton, a prominent Episcopalian and his son (later a mayor) who operated a horse-drawn dray line. From time to time, she paid visits to Duluth, a larger city about 60 miles away. In Virginia she became popular, even beloved, as a public character, and wrote home with delight to her aunt about the presents of meat, firewood and vegetables that she would find from time to time left on her doorstep.

Another great enterprise was her reading room. For this she called on the Ministers, summoned them several times to her house and held a meeting in the City. Emily was appointed one of the collectors, the men rightly suspecting that a woman would raise money more freely; and indeed she collected two hundred dollars within a few days and a hundred dollars more from Mr Rockefeller who was owner of one of the mines and brother, Emily said, of the wealthiest man in the States.

She ran into difficulties, curiously enough, from the people she had nominally come out to work for, the Episcopalians. Soon after November 1895 the newly built Virginia Epsicopal Church was dedicated and the parish turned over to the care of the Rev.

James McGonicle; and the Reverend James strongly disapproved of the way in which Emily was going about things and came along to her cottage to tell her so. In his view St Paul would not have approved of Emily holding services in a lumber camp, and it was a mistake to set up a public library rather than one for which the church would get the credit. The Rev. McGonicle favoured Sunday closing for the library while Emily had decided on Sunday opening. He wanted a church temperance movement, she felt that it was impossible to work on those narrow lines in a small closely knit community living in each other's pockets. After an hour of to-and-fro Emily rose to her feet, intimating to the Reverend McGonicle that the interview was at an end.

But she received help from an unexpected quarter. J. C. Jackson, whom Emily had first met in the sleazy boarding house, became Vice-President of the Public Library Association of which Emily was Treasurer.

Since those days he had bettered himself to a considerable degree. From the *Virginian* of April 8th 1897 we learn that he had come to Virginia in the Spring of 1893 and was employed as a clerk for E. C. Burke & Co. until June, and that the following September he was in the mercantile business in partnership with Mr H. H. Green, as Jackson and Co. In October 1895 Mr Green retired from business and Mr Jackson then undertook to continue the business under the same firm name and announced that the firm as in the past 'will endeavour to carry a complete stock of staple and seasonable goods'.

A photograph of the Jackson store shows a solid white weather-boarded building on the corner of Chestnut and Wyoming (now 3rd) Avenue, extending some 50 feet back from the main road. Striped awnings frame its two display windows, and barrels, baskets and crates are piled on the timber board-walk outside. An inscription on the side of the building in letters five foot high proclaimed 'Jackson & Company. General Merchandise and Camp Supplies', but to judge from its advertisements, the store offered a good deal more.

Thus in August, at the time Emily arrived, a ten cent coupon for purchase of silverware was given with every dollar of cash sales at Jackson & Co. and an announcement the same month advertised 'the nobbiest line of ladies and gent's fine shoes'. There were raincoats, mackintoshes, 'German sox', blankets, finest crockery and glassware on display, not to speak of hats, caps, flour, feed, hay and grain.

Soon a branch store was opened at the Fayal Mine near Eveleth, Minnesota, and appeared to be equally successful.

Then came a new development. On January 17, 1896 in the *Virginia Enterprise* the following paragraph appeared: 'Spring politics have begun to boil, and it is understood that (Mayor) Robert McGruer and J. C. Jackson have admitted to each other their views of who should be the next Mayor of Virginia.' Not long afterwards J. C. Jackson's name appears as Chairman of the Republican Caucus which elected delegates to the Republican Party County Convention. On March 20th the *Virginia Enterprise* again referred to Mr Jackson, and to the fact that he was a resident of long standing (since before the Great Fire of 1893), it added that he was 'a competent energetic young man known for honourable dealing and held in respect and esteem'.

On April 3rd, four days before the new Mayor was due to be elected, the *Virginia Enterprise* wrote: 'For Mayor, Mr Jackson appears to be the unanimous choice, no opponent being placed in the field.' Towards the end of March the Citizens' Caucus and Convention nominated J. C. Jackson for Mayor. And on April 10th the *Enterprise* confirmed that Mr Jackson had been elected Mayor in a light vote adding: 'We consider the City Government in the hands of honourable and conscientious people.' It is difficult at this distance to be sure how far these kind words were merited since Jackson had clearly been elected with the consent of the former Mayor McGruer, of whose activities Emily had formed such an unfavourable view.

Little if anything appeared at this time in the papers about the relationship between Mr Jackson and Miss Hobhouse, except that Mr Jackson recited 'The Little Stowaway' during the interval of a play in which Emily appeared. But, here, Ruth Fry, Emily's friend and biographer, usually so discreet, provides a clue by recording, without naming any names that, while overseas, Emily became engaged to be married, and that the engagement lasted for more than two years.

And since, as we shall see later, the engagement was broken off in the spring of 1898, it seems probable that it became a fact before Emily came home for a three-month holiday in the spring of 1896. During this trip she hoped, no doubt, to receive the support and approval of her family for this new attachment. But this was not forthcoming at any time and indeed the whole matter was kept a close secret from the younger member of the Hobhouse family who gained second-hand the impression many years later that Emily's betrothed might have been 'a butcher or something like that—and quite unsuitable'. A photograph still hanging in the Council Chambers of Virginia City shows a lean and handsome man between thirty and forty years old. He is clean-shaven, with fair hair cut short and parted on the left. His suit is well cut, and he wears a 'tie-tack', a watch fob and seal. Not unnaturally, however, no one was ready to offer Emily advice on how to make a living on the far side of the Atlantic.

The day before leaving her pleasant cottage on Central Avenue—as the *Enterprise* described it, she offered publicly to receive at her home from 1 to 3.30 p.m. all who wished to send messages or packages to their friends in England.

She was back in Virginia in July but it was clear that she did not intend to stay for good. In September the Executive Committee of the Free Library Association noted the resignation of Miss Hobhouse and accepted it with regret and a few days later the *Enterprise* noted that Miss Emily Hobhouse had left for Cleveland, Ohio, 'where she expects to remain for some time.'

Even at this time not a word appeared in the paper about Emily's engagement, although it would have been natural to expect that in a small city such as Virginia, such things would have become known. One possible explanation was that the publisher of the *Enterprise* Mr W. E. Hannaford, was a close political associate of Mr Jackson, in which case any request from Jackson for no publicity would probably have been respected.

Certainly there was no hint that Emily was intending to go from Cleveland to Mexico, but Ruth Fry reports that Emily and her fiancé had already decided to make their home in that country. This was not only because Emily had already completed her self-appointed task of establishing the Public Reading Room and the Temperance Society. It was because the opportunities for service and indeed for making a living at all in Virginia were sharply diminishing. There was a general period of financial crisis in the United States while at the same time an industrial dispute between the mine owners and the blast furnace operators in and around Virginia became so protracted that the large mines were eventually compelled to close down. The miners—and the customers for the J. C. Jackson store—moved elsewhere, to Alaska, British Columbia or back to Michigan to find work. Unfortunately J. C. Jackson himself could hardly leave Virginia in the middle of his period as Mayor, and Emily thereupon undertook on their joint behalf to look into the possibilities of life in Mexico. Already Mr H. H. Green, Jackson's former partner, had gone off to prospect in the silver districts adjacent to Zacarecas in Old Mexico, though there is no record of his having got any further than Salt Lake City.

Anyway, the second parting between Emily and Virginia was sweet, and the Finnish Temperance Band assembled at 7.30 in the morning to play her all the way down the street and up the hill to the station, where many other friends gathered to wish her a safe and happy journey and to thank her for all that she had done.

The Mexico which Emily was about to visit was in every way worthy of her attention. Porfirio Diaz, a Mexican of mixed blood and a former guerilla leader, five times President of Mexico between 1876 and 1900 and probably the most able ruler the country has ever possessed, had brought unheard of prosperity to the country. Mexican mining production trebled during the last twenty years of his rule and foreign trade increased fourfold during the last quarter of the 19th century. Cattle raising, timber cutting, tobacco, sugar and coffee plantations were all prospering. New railways were opening up the interior.

Emily was lucky in her first visit to the country. On her way down in the train she became acquainted with a Dr Hamilton, a leading surgeon from Pittsburgh, who was on his way with his wife to a Medical Convention in Mexico City. They 'adopted' her as one of the family, conferred an official medical badge on her, and she was soon being driven in the private carriage of the Vice President of the Convention, pulled by two magnificent cream-coloured horses through the streets of the capital in brilliant moonlight.

The whole affair was rather a contrast to Virginia City—there was a Government reception at the Opera House attended by President Diaz himself, a Presidential Reception at the Mexican White House, a castle built on a rock rising out of the plain and approached down a long avenue of eucalyptus trees. Three thousand guests were received on a piazza paved with marble from which they mounted, past stairways, pillars and balconies wreathed with tropical flowers, to another banqueting terrace.

By the end of the century Mexico City had become a capital of elegance and distinction. Sarah Bernhardt had driven up the magnificent Cinco de Mayo Avenue (so named because it commemorated the defeat of the French on May 5th 1862) to play at the National Theatre, and the great soprano Adelina Patti had sung there. Women in carriages, wearing mantillas, and riders on spirited horses thronged the Paseo de la Reforma, turning it into a magnificent pageant.

Houses built round courtyards in Arabian style still abounded and in their cool shade families whiled away the hours balancing delicately this way and that in their rocking chairs, lulled by the tinkle of fountains.

Here Emily settled down to search for opportunities and a career for herself and John Jackson. On her own responsibility she bought an estate and arranged to build a civilized house on it with glass windows and wood floors. Most of the time she spent in Mexico City learning the language and studying the resources of the country. But, throughout that winter, of Mr Jackson there was no sign.

In the Spring however there was plenty of action. On April 9th, roughly at the end of Jackson's year of office, a somewhat ironical paragraph appeared in the hitherto friendly *Virginia Enterprise.*

C. H. Webster on Saturday purchased the entire stock of Jackson & Co. in this city, taking immediate possession. Mr Jackson who has ever been the genial manager of the affairs of the firm on Monday morning departed for the city of Mexico, where he is said to have been offered a lucrative position. It is also rumoured that he is to stop at Chicago, en route for his new southern home, to accept a commission as power of attorney for Miss E. Hobhouse, formerly of this city, who has been in the southern republic for some months and through whose influence his prospective position is said to have been secured. His departure from Virginia was apparently hasty, our honoured mayor scarce bidding adieu to any but his most intimate friends. It is understood others of our citizens will follow him in the near future to accept positions under him.'

A similar but no more friendly notice had appeared in a rival paper *The Virginia* of April 8th 1897. It said:

'Without a handshake or a parting word, Mayor Jackson stepped on the D & I (Duluth & Iron Range) train last Monday morning and as he watched our city recede from sight he soliloquised: "Virginians, I leave you. The parting gives me pain, but if I tarry at thy threshold, methinks it would not be wise, therefore I go. Adieu."

'His hasty departure has caused much comment, but we are informed this was due to a telegram which he received Saturday night requesting him to be in Chicago Tuesday morning. There, it was said, he was to meet Miss Hobhouse. A ceremony was to have followed which would make them man and wife. They were to leave immediately for Mexico where Mr Jackson has a position awaiting him.'

But this was not all. In the first place Mr C. H. Webster who bought up Jackson's stock was compelled to close the store on April 9th 'pending the settlement of threatened legal complications'. What these were can be gathered from a further notice in the *Enterprise* of April 23rd which reported that 'Judge Ensign on Saturday appointed J. D. Taylor as Receiver for John C. Jackson allegedly insolvent.'

Whether mismanagement or something more serious was involved it is hard to be sure. It could well have been that Mr Jackson simply decided that he could not delay in seizing the opportunity which had presented itself for him to leave a dead and alive neck of the woods for a new career. But there were other signs that the ever genial Mayor Jackson's handling of the city finances had been hardly more successful than his commercial operations.

During his year of office the sources of city revenue remained much as before and no more creditable. Of the modest income of 18,750 dollars, 14,000 was ascribed as being provided by Liquor Licenses, a further 2,000 by fines, and the remainder by a Dog Tax, Pedlar's Tax, a General Tax and an item of 50 dollars marked as election.

In general, the business of the City Council was not arduous and appears to have concerned such matters as approving bills for 'the removal of deceased dogs from the lakes' and making ordinances requiring property owners to construct sidewalks and preventing cyclists from riding thereon. Nevertheless a councilman had apparently been appointed as Acting Mayor and had signed the minutes of the City Council for the last two weeks of Mayor Jackson's term.

We may perhaps link this item with a report published in the *Enterprise* of February 26th of a resolution by ex-Mayor McGruer urging that city expenses be cut, on the grounds that the city debt had now reached about 15,000 dollars (nearly a year's revenue) and that its notes were now being discounted below their face value.

Furthermore Jackson's successor, Mayor Scott, in his inaugural address felt impelled to promise to 'take radical measures for the restriction of public funds' by cutting salaries and other desperate remedies. He also said that better records of the city finance would have to be kept in future.

It seems difficult to believe that Emily was aware of these developments and indeed Mr Jackson himself did not seem greatly concerned by them. Thus the *Enterprise* reported on April 23rd that Mr P. P. Field had received a letter from J. C. Jackson announcing the latter's safe arrival in Mexico city and adding that he was highly pleased with the climate and 'the apparent prosperity of the country'. He sent his regards to his many Virginia friends.

It also seems clear that Mr Jackson had not, following Emily's absence, hesitated to tell friends about his plans to leave eventually for Mexico and to take a position arranged for him there by Miss Hobhouse. Presumably, from the fact that he was able to offer positions to his friends, he would have been manager of her ranch. On May 6th the *Enterprise* published a report that a Mr Frank Myars would leave Virginia in about a fortnight for the City of Mexico where he would accept a position under ex-mayor Jackson. The same issue mentioned that 1897 would be a year of 'acute retrenchment in municipal affairs'.

As for Emily, we know that she did, indeed, visit Chicago to meet her fiancé, that she did not marry him there as she had hoped, and that while in Mexico she had been persuaded into putting money into a speculative concession in the hope of getting a settled income. Whether it was necessary under Mexican law for her to sign a power of attorney in order to operate the concession or to complete the house she was having built is not so clear. At any rate she subsequently lost her investment. And it was clear to her that marriage was still nowhere in sight.

For part of 1897 she returned to England where, no doubt, she continued to receive copious amounts of unacceptable good advice from her family and friends. Her resolve nevertheless remained unchanged. On February 10th 1898 she sailed from Liverpool in the tiny 2,168 ton vessel, the *William Cliff*, belonging to the West India and Pacific Steamship Company, a passenger-tramp which called at various ports on the Caribbean. There were 13 passengers—not too good an omen—five for

Kingston and eight, of whom Emily was one, for Vera Cruz. Her wedding dress was packed in her luggage.

With her was a cousin, Annie Batchelor. Annie was a daughter of the Rev. Frederick Thomas Batchelor, Rector of Calstock, Cornwall, who had married Emily's mother's sister. His family was large and not well provided for, and much of Annie's education had been received in the Hobhouse rectory at St Ive. She was fond of painting and in other respects too, an ideal companion for such a trip.

They sailed via St Thomas, Colon, Kingston, Tampico and Florida to Vera Cruz through deep blue seas, visiting seaports set against a background of coconut palms, and wandering through dilapidated picturesque villages of one-storey houses with green verandahs and faded sunblinds. At Colon they found an English church with a black population and heard the ominous news that Mexico might be involved in a war against the United States over Cuba.

On March 11th they passed into the harbour of Vera Cruz between a low coral reef and the prison of San Juan de Ulloa and saw for the first time the snow-capped peak of Orizaba.

The approach to Mexico City from Vera Cruz is far more dramatic than from any other direction and, at the time Emily travelled over it, the steep gradients imposed such a strain on the engines that passengers, as if already in an aircraft, were limited to 33 lb of luggage. Their route lay at first through coffee and banana plantations to the foot of mountains whose summits were hidden in clouds. From there the line snaked up the mountainside past torrents, across ravines, through tunnels, climbing a barrier so fantastic that looking up one can scarcely believe it possible for the train to get up to the next station.

Once again in Mexico City, Emily drank in the blinding sunlight of the country, the gay costumes, crumbling churches, savoured the scent of jasmine, and the sound of guitars, revelled in the punctilious courtesy of the Mexicans and sighed perhaps occasionally at the poverty of the Indians.

But of marriage there seemed no likelihood and Mr J. C. Jackson remained as remote from Miss Hobhouse as from those of his friends who had stayed behind in Virginia. Several explanations are possible as to why the marriage never took place, although the true one may not have been vouchsafed even in Emily's own explanations to her family. Perhaps Mr Jackson had never intended to marry Emily but had been merely using her money as a passport to escape from Virginia. Or he may have intended to marry her when in Virginia but could afterwards have discovered among the Mexican señoritas (who, to Emily, all looked rather the same), one who was in fact different. Or he may have come to consider that the life planned for him by Emily was not the one after all that he wanted. Or he may have found Emily incompatible. Or the scales may have fallen from Emily's own eyes.

Looking back it is hard to be sure why Emily never married either before or after she met J. C. Jackson. Ruth Fry reported that while Emily still lived at home 'lovers' (she obviously meant 'admirers') broke the monotony of her life fairly often but added that none of the affairs matured. This may have been due to Emily's character or to that of her father. A photograph of her taken at the age of 35 when she first became fully independent shows a woman who could still have been highly presentable. There were no extremes. The face was neither narrow nor wide —oval rather than heart-shaped. The mouth was neither full nor tight-lipped but firm. The eyes were wide apart, and pale, the nose regular and neither petite nor prominent; the hair was fine, almost golden, with a delicate wave. The general appearance was one of elegance. It was a face as clear as a mountain pool, an open countenance though without perhaps that hint of mystery, reticence or guile that sometimes sparks the fires of romance.

She had an infectious smile and the natural sense of sympathy which allows one person to enter the mind of another and to convey quite unconsciously to him that, for that moment, he is the only person of real importance in the world. She had a heart of gold.

She was responsive—that was part of her charm—but possibly in a personal sense over-responsive; and as events afterwards showed, the determination which helped her to succeed in apparently unpractical schemes exasperated as many people as it delighted. She was impulsive, highly strung, nervous, and easily upset by injustice; she took strong likes and dislikes to people, which were reciprocated; she did not mince her words in an argument and was impatient and sometimes caustic towards those who disagreed with her.

One could admire her contempt for danger and her indifference, in a good cause, to the opinions of conventional society, but she was obstinate, and, like her father, found it difficult to change her mind when once she had made it up.

She was also possessive; yet treasured her own independence. She was restless. Her husband would have needed time, money and patience in large quantities. He could never have settled anywhere for long, nor could he have laid down the burden of solving some at least of the problems of the human race.

For years Emily had been conditioned from the example of her father to believe that the Church of England, and 'people like us' who were its supporters, should be inspired by selfless idealism to cajole or encourage the less fortunate into a similar state of grace. Her faith in the perfectibility of human nature extended even to Members of Parliament and politicians who, in fact were no more public spirited in Emily's days than they are today.

She demanded much from her fellow creatures and resented it when they failed her. She trusted her fellow beings and expected to be trusted by them; and the discovery that sincerity and unselfishness are qualities more rarely to be found than meannness and dishonesty, came too late to save her from deep disappointments. One doubts whether she could ever have submitted to the compromise and self-deception which too often are needed to make married life today a tolerable if not ecstatic form of existence.

Also, I think it must be accepted that Emily was attracted by and tended to attract men who in one way or another were qualified by their own inadequacy to receive her sympathy, but who for this very reason failed her socially, morally and perhaps intellectually.

Thus it was not surprising that she left Mexico disillusioned about 'men' and distrustful of her own powers of judgement. In two years she had burnt through a lifetime of romance.

3

Before Emily's Time

When Emily returned to England, it was not to the seclusion of Cornwall, nor to the world of Deacons and Archdeacons.

She found London in a ferment with people already sitting up for the dawn of the twentieth century. The human landmarks were vanishing. The Queen Empress had bowed her way through the Diamond Jubilee commemorating the sixtieth year of her reign, and had retired from public life. Tennyson, Browning, Turner, Carlyle, Darwin and others who had brought distinction to Britain during the nineteenth century were dead. The bicycle was new enough to provide jokes for *Punch,* and the plan for a Great Western Railway line from Henley to Marlow was said to be unsettling the Leander Club rowing eights.

New actors, theatrical as well as political, were waiting in the wings, ready to take a cue if not an encore. James Barrie had just produced his first play *The Little Minister.* Shaw, after his grave illness of 1898, had turned serious and become a member of the St Pancras Vestry (afterwards the Borough Council); he was spending his afternoons grappling with local government problems such as drainage, refuse collection, street lighting, paving, and the like. Einstein was 20; Maugham 25.

Politics had never been so bewildering as the old distinctions between the various parties began to disappear. The Liberal Party, as so often in its history, was in two minds. Gladstone had split the party in the eighties over his attempt to give Ireland Home Rule and a separate Parliament of its own. Ninety-three Liberals had walked out; they later joined the Conservatives to form the Unionist Party. This was a source of much distress to Emily, and she urged the Liberals not to give up looking for a leader to replace Gladstone, adding that unless they did so, they would be led down the path of Imperialism by Sir Edward Grey

44

and that, if only she were a man, she would stir Heaven and Earth to prevent this happening. But there was little hope of her making the slightest impression for, as she pointed out, the Liberals were such bad Liberals that they did not invite any women to their meetings.

Then there was the curious case of George Cadbury, the cocoa magnate, who was in close touch with the founders of the Independent Labour Party, which consisted of left-wingers for whom the Liberal Party was too tame.

There was the Prince of Wales taking the chair at times when various Commissions met on questions of housing and sweated trades. And there was the Fabian Society, which, without any Parliamentary representation, had become the Brains Trust for step-by-step pragmatic socialism in such fields as pensions and poor law reform.

Over this wide political spectrum, Emily's friends and relations were scattered fairly evenly across the centre and the left.

There was, of course, Henry Hobhouse V who sat first as an orthodox Liberal MP for East Somerset but could not abide Mr Gladstone's policy on Home Rule and so joined the Unionists. He was married to Margaret, one of the eight daughters of Richard Potter, one-time Director of the Great Western Railway, the youngest of whom, Beatrice, later achieved fame as Mrs Sidney Webb. Beatrice's conscience did not allow her to approve either of her sister or her brother-in-law. 'Maggie,' she said, was 'a high-spirited and rather vulgar sharp-tongued woman who had reduced her standards to suit her husband's intellectual limitations without raising them to conform with her husband's moral standards.' But Henry, too, in Beatrice Webb's eyes, suffered from 'his lack of intellectual initiative and moral experience' though he endeavoured to make up for this by being 'respectful and friendly' towards Sidney, Beatrice's husband. The Webbs habitually entertained the Shaws and less presentable agitators such as John Burns, 'the man with the Red Flag', who was sentenced to six weeks imprisonment for breaking through the police cordon in Trafalgar Square and later became a Cabinet Minister.

And as though this was not enough left-wing leavening, Theresa, another Potter sister, had married Alfred Cripps, father of Stafford Cripps, and Catherine (Kate), the eldest sister but one, was the wife of Leonard Courtney who gave up his seat as Liberal Member for Liskeard rather than become a Unionist. The Courtneys were Emily's special friends through thick and thin.

With her cousin Charles Hobhouse, Liberal MP for East Bristol, her relations were more distant.

Closer blood relatives included her brother Leonard, an admirer of the ways of Oliver Cromwell and author of such works as *The Labour Movement* dealing with trade unions, co-operatives and the control of industry, *The Theory of Knowledge* (1896), *Mind and Evolution* (1901) and many others of like calibre. To the consternation of his father, the Archdeacon, he began while still at college to recruit suitable socialist undergraduates as disciples for the Webbs. Later he rose to be a director of the *Manchester Guardian*.

Finally there was Emily's uncle Arthur who, it was said, could read when he was two, learnt Latin at four, went to school at six, and in due course took a First in Classics at Oxford. When indifferent health forced him to give up his career as a Queen's Council he joined the Board of the Charity Commission and in 1872 was appointed to the post of Legal Adviser on the Governor General's Council in India. There he supported the system by which native judges would in certain cases try white men. He made friends with leading Indians and deeply regretted the social gap which existed between the British members of the Indian Civil Service and the subjects whom they ruled. And no doubt this helped to give weight in India to the decisions of the Judicial Committee of the Privy Council—the final legal court of Appeal for overseas territories of the British Empire, of which he became a member.

Before leaving India, while still a Civil Servant, he found himself strongly disagreeing with Disraeli's plan to send a British Mission to Afghanistan and deplored the Afghan War which followed the Ameer's refusal to receive the British Resident. After leaving India Arthur Hobhouse declared, in the *Fortnightly Review,* that it was immoral for Britain to seize territory in order to improve her position. He signed a memorial protesting against the Second Afghan War and the execution of Afghan patriots who had fought in it, and he went so far as to ask his nephew Leonard Hobhouse to collect examples from history to show that a nation which throws itself into the business of conquest loses its own liberties and with them its power of initiative and judgement.

'It is obvious,' he wrote in a letter to his kinsman Sir Charles Hobhouse, 'that the military habit necessary for a conquering nation must crush individual freedom. And where is the instance of a people who set themselves to subjugate their neighbours and have remained free themselves. . . . ? We have thrown away the immunity from great armies which our insular position has given.'

Disapproval of militaristic imperialism was not of course confined to Britain. In the summer of 1899 Tsar Nicholas II of Russia called an international conference which met at the Hague to consider disarmament and the settlement of international disputes by peaceful means. Twenty-six states attended the meeting, with the United States and Mexico among them. No great success was recorded in the field of disarmament, but a convention revising the laws of war and outlawing poison gas, expanding bullets and the discharge of projectiles from balloons was agreed—at least by some states.

Under what was known as the Hague Convention, a Permanent Court of Arbitration was set up—the first case to be tried before it being a dispute in which the United States, acting on behalf of the Roman Catholic Church of California, claimed from the Mexican Government half a charitable bequest. Mexico lost the case.

It was in this atmosphere that the world, more especially the one in which Emily moved, watched the growing antipathy between the British Government and the Kruger regime in South Africa. It followed the errors and evasions of three centuries of British rule and led, in the closing years of Queen Victoria's reign, to a crisis in the conflict between British Liberals and Imperialists.

Over the centuries many a British philanthropist has discovered in South Africa, six thousand miles away, the cause dearest to his heart and most worthy of his benevolence, and Emily, in her struggle to maintain human rights, was to find herself among the latest of a long line of more or less genteel agitators who, with assumed infallibility, recommended to HM's Ministers where their moral duty lay towards the peoples South of Capricorn.

Emily was neither a missionary nor a politician, yet both missionaries and politicians set the stage for her work, and to understand why she found herself in the midst of a conflict, in which Parliament and even individual families were split in two over the rights and wrongs of the South African war, we must go back a little.

In the early years of the nineteenth century the missionaries were, perhaps, the most active of Britain's moralizers. They it was who interfered most assiduously with the Hottentots, the

Basutos and other Bantu tribes, converting them first to Christianity, and then implanting in them the conviction that those who remained in good standing with the missionaries had little or nothing to fear from any other white man. This might in earlier times have been Emily's attitude. The missionaries had, of course, garnered most of the credit among the natives for the abolition of slavery which came to pass in South Africa and elsewhere in the British Empire in 1833, the year after a Government composed of Whigs and Radicals (labelled with the newly minted political description 'Liberal') had come to power.

It was, however, beyond the powers even of the Liberals and missionaries together to devise an undeviating policy towards South Africa and from time to time the two sides fell out. One reason for this was that, during the greater part of the nineteenth century, the missionaries themselves were the real imperialists of Africa; for they planned to convert not only those natives living in South Africa, but also those in southern and central Africa, further and further away from the Cape. Not only were the missionaries imperialists; they prevented successive British Governments from rejecting imperialism, urging that to withdraw British troops from South Africa would be to abandon the natives.

A second source of discord between the Liberals and missionaries was the latter's claim to possess a special understanding of the psychology and mental processes of the native chiefs not apparently revealed to lay administrators.

Neither of these propositions was acceptable in the long run to His (or Her) Majesty's servants in Whitehall. For the extension of the British frontier northwards and ever northwards meant extra expense, for which, in the first half of the nineteenth century at least, it was clear to the British electorate that no visible return would be forthcoming; while the claims of the missionaries to know more about native affairs than the Mandarins of the Colonial Office or the War Office could not for one moment be entertained. Nor were successive Governments, even Liberal ones, prepared to enter into a partnership agreement with the missionaries which would make them jointly responsible for the welfare of the natives throughout the whole of Africa. Liberals, like Conservatives, had to work with the Administrators of South Africa and the Administrators complained that the missionaries encouraged the natives to believe themselves equal before God with the white man and therefore under no obligation to work for any white boss.

Furthermore, the administrators had white subjects to look after as well as black—in particular farmers whose welfare depended on a stable frontier and the absence of border disputes —and for whom it was necessary to battle at times against the Bantu and even to kill them.

Thus the British pro-consuls and military commanders in South Africa had a vested interest in combating well-meaning meddlers who raised obstacles to the maintenance of law and order and ignored the facts of African life. It was the native spears and guns that worried Britain rather than the natives' souls. And in the end, in a world where the natives had come to live inside rather than beyond the white man's borders, missions played a less and less important role.

The main difficulty faced by all British administrations was, as we have noticed, that while South Africa had the natural boundary of the ocean on three sides, there was, until comparatively late in the nineteenth century, no clearly defined frontier in the north. The tribes fought there against the whites and also against each other, making a permanent peace far more difficult then than now. One of the earlier Governors at the Cape, Lord Charles Somerset, planned to establish a firm northern frontier studded with defence posts manned by redcoats, each post being set up within easy reach of the next. (It was not so different from the scheme ultimately adopted by Kitchener in the South African war.)

But in Somerset's case the idea had to be abandoned when the British Treasury, its funds exhausted by the Napoleonic wars, stopped paying the bills. In 1819 therefore a second plan was tried. It was decided to set up an uninhabited neutral zone between the colonists and their Bantu neighbours to the north and east, and to patrol this area to make sure that no-man's land stayed no-man's land.

But neither side respected this arrangement. The Afrikaner farmers continued to send their cattle beyond the border, and the Bantu refused to leave the neutral zone, complaining that their former places had since been taken over by others. Later, a third plan was tried. It aimed at fixing the northern frontier and preventing incidents on either side of it by concluding a series of treaties between the Cape Government and the leading or Paramount tribal chiefs. In these treaties the British recognized the authority of the Chiefs over certain defined territories and, in return, the chiefs were responsible for keeping order and for preventing cattle raids. This plan, strongly favoured by Liberals and missionaries alike, had in its turn to be dropped when it became clear that the Afrikaners had trekked north round the side of the tribal barrier, crossing first the Orange River and later the Vaal, and so had reached the coast beyond it in Natal, leaving the British behind and on the wrong side of the native barrier. The British, in order to re-establish control over the Afrikaners, replied by annexing, over the years, most of the intervening tribal territory.

During the annexation a zig-zag course was pursued, each successive British Government punctiliously reversing the course previously followed by its opponents, economizing where its predecessors had spent, pressing forward against the Bantu, and supporting the local commanders where the previous administration had humbled and disconcerted them. No Government succeeded in striking a balance between the expense of protecting an expanded Empire in South Africa and the cost of failing to do so.

Meanwhile a new issue, connected with neither missionaries nor natives, had arisen to sow discord between the British Conservatives and Liberals—the problem of independence for the Afrikaner—the 'good' Liberals including Emily's nearest and dearest being on the whole in favour, the Conservatives against.

The Afrikaners, though they had had a comparatively short start on the British in their Great Trek, had reached and occupied territory more than a thousand miles from the Cape and the more penny-pinching advisers among the British began to ask themselves whether there could be any sense in trying to subdue these self-willed unyielding 'Dutch' who, if once allowed to govern themselves, might prove to be the best of all possible barriers against the Bantu raiders. And so, in the hope of solving two problems in one, the Sand River Convention was signed in 1852 giving independence to South Africa's most northerly territory, the Transvaal, which thereupon styled itself the South African Republic. Two years later the same privilege was extended to form a second Republic, the Orange Free State, lying between the Transvaal and the Cape Colony.

This solution suited Whitehall, anxious as ever to save money, and at the time met with general approval both in Britain and South Africa.

In the following decades, however, three events occurred which radically changed the history of South Africa and the attitude towards it of the political parties in Britain. First, while

Emily was still a schoolgirl, diamonds were discovered on territory which was generally believed to lie in the Orange Free State; next the great European powers—especially Germany—became interested in the scramble for African colonies; and, in 1884, at about the same time, prospectors struck gold in a reef which was to become the world's richest goldfield.

These three events served wonderfully to concentrate the minds of Britain's Empire-builders among the Conservatives and to convince them that giving away those two northern provinces in South Africa had been not only an error of political and economic judgement, but a blunder of the first magnitude in foreign policy, since the two pocket republics, though not fully independent in their foreign affairs, were not precluded from giving concessions to alien firms or even foreign governments. And so, from 1870 onwards, a tremendous campaign was launched in Britain to recover what had been lost.

The earliest phase of the recovery programme began over the diamond fields. The first diamond had been found in 1866 by a small boy Erasmus Stephanus Jacobs on the de Kalk farm near Hopetown and there was no dispute over the fact that Hopetown was situated in Cape Colony and therefore under full control of the Crown.

But other diamonds were discovered at two places, Klipdrift and Hebron, on the north bank of the Vaal river—which was clearly outside Cape Territory—and in 1870, even richer finds were made in the 'dry' diggings at Kimberley, which, though not north of the Vaal, was beyond the Orange River which formed the political boundary between the Cape Colony and the Orange Free State.

Until that time the western area of the colony, as of the two pocket republics, had been relatively neglected, having a rainfall of little more than five inches a year. From then on none received greater attention.

The Transvaal laid claim to the more northerly diamond fields under the Sand River Convention, which had recognized the independence of Afrikaners north of the Vaal river. The Orange Free State equally claimed those mines south of the Vaal river but north of the Orange River, since this territory had been allotted to the Free State under the Bloemfontein convention. President Brand of the Orange Free State also claimed certain land north of the Vaal River which, he said, had been purchased by the Free State from coloured tribes in 1861.

But strange to relate, neither the Free State nor the Transvaal received, in the end, a single acre of carat-bearing land.

First, Nicolaas Waterboer, a local chief, claimed that the tribes which had sold land to the Free State were his subjects and therefore without the power to sell. Then Sir Henry Barkly, Governor at the Cape, persuaded the Transvaal's President, M. W. Pretorius, to agree to an arbitration, in which Robert Keate, Governor of Natal, would have the casting vote between his claims and those of Waterboer and other similarly placed tribes. The arbitration, despite the Transvaal's apparently unassailable case, went against Pretorius. Thereupon Waterboer declared himself and was accepted as a British subject, and Governor Barkly, in defiance of the Sand River and Bloemfontein Conventions, annexed the diamond fields.

President Brand refused to accept British arbitration on his dispute and was eventually proved right on legal grounds, but by then so many thousands of Britons had flocked into the territory that it would have been politically impossible to place them under his authority. So he accepted compensation of £90,000, in full settlement of the world's richest diamond fields. As part of the deal, the boundary between Waterboer's territory and the Free State was eventually adjusted to place Kimberley on the British side of the line.

During this legal charade British diggers, encouraged by Acting Govenor Charles Hays from the Cape, had set a precedent by establishing their own mini-republic under a British Magistrate at Klipdrift in the disputed territory. The British plan had been to merge the fields with Cape Colony, but the Afrikaners in the Cape Parliament, believing that the area rightly belonged to the Free State, refused to accept their new treasure which, with its gem-mad diggers, had, for the time being, to be administered independently.

Manoeuvres of this kind could hardly have appealed to the Liberals then in power in Britain but at least there was no war or inhumanity. And there was Mr Gladstone in full possession of the Liberal conscience.

The next step towards recovering British authority over the two lost republics came with Disraeli's Ministry, which flourished from 1874 to 1880. This was a scheme for federating the two Republics with Cape Colony; but the coup in the diamond fields had aroused so much distrust among the Cape Dutch, as well as among Afrikaners north of the Orange River, that the plan had no real chance of success, so long as the Transvaal retained its independence.

So the British Empire-builders, partly to forestall rival Europeans, simply annexed the whole of the Transvaal. At first sight it is difficult to see how this could have come about without a world-wide public scandal. Nevertheless, it was accomplished without a drop of bloodshed and with the help of just twenty-five mounted police. Britons were told, and most believed, that the South African Republic was a bankrupt state, in which the Postmaster General was compelled to accept his salary in stamps, and that it was therefore a danger to white supremacy. And indeed it was true that the Transvalers, at loggerheads with their President, had refused to pay taxes needed to defend their country against the Zulus, and to finance the much-needed railways. The Transvalers were accordingly informed that a British Commissioner, Sir Theophilus Shepstone, had been sent (he arrived uninvited) to inquire into the causes of 'recent disturbances' and to prevent their recurrence. When cross-examined by his 'hosts', Shepstone said that he had come to dispose of certain financial complaints.

Some inhabitants of the Transvaal hoped, perhaps, that British investment would raise their own standards of living or that British troops would help them against their most formidable foes, the Zulus. But Shepstone was cautious about stating the benefits that would accrue to the Afrikaners through his presence. It was clear, however, that he hoped that the Transvaal, once captive, would accept a form of federation with Britain's two South African Colonies, Natal and the Cape, and that, in the meantime, the Transvaal would be turned into a 'going concern' (by British standards at least) with a 'proper' system of taxation and administration, in which case a new loan might be forthcoming.

But the Afrikaner farmers had not trekked northwards to join up once more with the Cape, or even to pay regular taxes, and Shepstone got little co-operation either from the Volksraad (the People's Council) nor yet from the Council's Executive Committee. This perhaps was of small import, for, unknown to the good people of the Transvaal, Shepstone carried with him secret instructions from the British Colonial Secretary, the Earl of Carnarvon, empowering him to annex and rule such territories as he should think fit, provisionally and during the Queen's pleasure provided the inhabitants 'or a sufficient number of them' desired to become the Queen's subjects. It was left to Shepstone to decide how many citizens constituted 'a sufficient number' and he had indeed received encouragement from British prospectors and businessmen in the Transvaal, who considered the territory was, as we should put it, 'ripe for development'. This, coupled with the fact that the Transvaal at that time had no leader who was prepared to plunge the country into a full scale war, made it possible to annex this vast territory by simple proclamation. Rider Haggard, author of *King Solomon's Mines*, was one of Shepstone's staff and helped to hoist the Union Jack in Pretoria on April 12th 1877.

However, on the very day before the annexation was proclaimed, the Transvalers decided to send a deputation of two representatives to London, feeling that, once the British Government and public had heard their side of the story, all might yet be well. Their instructions were to bring the facts to the notice of the British Government and if this did not produce the desired result to seek allies where they could.

At their first meeting with Lord Carnarvon in London in July and in three further sessions, they sought to persuade him that a sufficient number of burghers had *not* desired to become the Queen's subjects; and indeed that a majority were positively against the idea. But Carnarvon, fortified by reassurances from Shepstone, declined to be convinced and refused, too, to submit the issue of the annexation to a popular referendum. When the Afrikaner deputation got back empty-handed to Pretoria the burghers organized their own opinion poll which gave 6,591 votes against the annexation and 587 in favour, but this was not quite the same thing.

So, in June 1878, a second deputation set off once more for London. They found that a new Minister, Sir Michael Hicks-Beach, had been appointed but that he had the same opinion as his predecessor, which was that the question of reversing the annexation was not one for discussion. To drive home the point Sir Garnet Wolseley, a soldier of renown, was sent out as Governor and High Commissioner of the Transvaal.

Only one thing now prevented a rising by the disgruntled burghers; this was the hope that the Liberals in Britain would succeed where they had failed.

The fact that the Transvaal had been annexed under a Conservative Government had added strength to the swelling chorus of disapproval from the Liberal Opposition and William Gladstone, the Liberal Leader who was to serve four terms as Prime Minister, had during his Midlothian election campaign of 1880 sharply attacked Disraeli's policy towards the Transvaal and had declared that the annexation was unjustified and immoral. Consequently, when the Liberals won the election in April, the Transvalers concluded that patience might yet win the day for them, and their leaders Joubert and Kruger bestirred themselves and wrote a letter to Gladstone desiring that independence should once more be restored. While they were still in the Cape (they had gone to urge the Afrikaners there not to agree to a merger between the Transvaal, the Orange Free State, Natal and the Cape), they got the bad news. Gladstone's answer was that the Queen would not agree to independence being restored to the Transvaal and that the Afrikaners could have local self-government only if the Transvaal would agree to the hateful merger.

Now it is a temptation for the historian to discover 'watershed decisions' in many events which, but for other accompanying circumstances, would have been of merely passing significance. But it is difficult to overestimate the political effects of Gladstone's breach of faith on the relations between Britain and South Africa. In the first place, many Liberals in Britain, among them Emily's close friends, disapproved of Gladstone's opportunism and began to dissociate themselves from his policy. A split in the Liberal Party can be traced from this point. Secondly, the Afrikaners lost faith in the Liberal Party, which, they saw, was ready to use South Africa as a stick for the British Government's back only so long as they were not in power themselves. Thirdly, Gladstone's somersault brought to power the leader who, in his efforts to mould his people into a nation, defied the majesty of the whole British Empire.

Paul Kruger, as described by Englishmen for Englishmen, was incapable of inspiring hero-worship. It was known for example that he had little education and disdained to speak the language of civilized Britons and they in turn were in nowise attracted when Kruger spat at random or blew his nose through his fingers. He did not trouble to conceal his disapproval of foreign customers, out of keeping, as he saw them, with the teachings of the Bible. His expression was sullen and his manner gruff, his scrubby beard and puffy eyes were a gift to the cartoonists and the way they drew his top hat added incongruity rather than dignity of his image.

Theophilus Shepstone's lawyer Mr Morcom recorded a typically unfavourable impression. According to him Mr Kruger was 'an elderly man, decidedly ugly with a countenance denoting extreme

55

obstinacy and also great cruelty. His conduct at the public luncheon on Tuesday was, as the Belgian Consul described it "gigantically horrible". His dirty wooden pipe was visible for it stuck out of his breast pocket, his scanty hair was in such a state of greasiness that it lay in streaks across his head, the drops of rancid coconut oil gathering at the ends of each streak of hair and thus rendering necessary the use of his pocket comb during lunch. The napkin was turned to strange uses during lunch.'

To fellow Afrikaners he was accessible; but unwelcome callers were told he was at prayer and visitors who were admitted complained that he was apt to bury himself behind a cloud of smoke from his pipe and say almost nothing.

'In ordinary talk,' wrote a British observer, 'he exercises little self-restraint—if any point of controversy arises, he will bring his big fist down upon the table with alarming force.'

According to the British High Commissioner, Sir Bartle Frere (June 1877) Kruger 'is a rough and plain likeness of Mr Edwin Chadwick . . . I am assured by those who know him well that he is a very shrewd fellow, who veils under an assumed clownish manner and affectation of ignorance considerable ability, that he has great natural eloquence and powers of persuasion.'

A more sympathetic explanation of Kruger's thought processes and actions came from the political publicist J. A. Hobson, who wrote; 'In politics, as in religion, Paul Kruger is governed by a few simple deeply rooted notions. The notion that he is a far-sighted foxy politician seeking his own ends seems to me to be quite unwarranted, and arises from the situation which often forces him to give reasons and arguments for actions, which are really based on sentiment, intuitive caution or set prejudices. Mr Kruger has continually been fighting for the independence of his country, as he conceives it, warding off the danger of an overwhelming rush of alien influences. When called upon suddenly for a set defence of his position, he has no ready dialectic, but often blurts out reasons which are not the real activating forces. His evasions and dilatory bargaining are not really a conscious statecraft so much as a rude instinctive fence which has been successful against a 'politician' like Mr Chamberlain because the latter, by a characteristic fallacy, supposes his antagonist to be the same manner of a man as himself. At the same time, able men that know him well tell me that Mr Kruger is a powerful thinker, who drives right down to the bedrock of an issue, has a keen nose for fallacy in an argument and is even willing to admit an error when it is clearly pointed out to him.'

Kruger was a member of the delegations sent to London to protest against the annexation of the Transvaal. And when President Burgers went into retirement soon after annexation day, Kruger took over his duties as Chief Executive. It was he, in fact, who, after the failure of the second mission to London, dissuaded the more impetuous among his fellow countrymen from taking up arms, despite the fact that he had been dismissed by Shepstone from his post on the Executive Council. But once Gladstone's 'treachery' became public there was no turning back. In December 1880 the Boers defied an official veto and held a mass rally at Paardekraal; they established their own Parliament, announced the rebirth of the Republic, and proclaimed Kruger and two others as their three-man Cabinet.

Soon they were fighting in the field. The British, in their first engagement at Bronkhorstpruit on 20th December, lost one hundred and twenty men and a large number of oxen, despite the fact that a Boer carrying a white flag had warned them to advance no further along the road to Pretoria. The British garrison at Potchefstroom was compelled to surrender and other detachments at Pretoria, Rustenburg and Standerton were surrounded.

In January the British reinforcements on their way to the Transvaal from Natal suffered a second defeat at Laings Nek and in February a third on the banks of the Ingogo River, and finally at Majuba on February 27th, the British lost half their force of five hundred and forty men and General Colley, their commander, was killed.

Too late, Gladstone decided that independence was the better part of valour, and that British withdrawal from the Transvaal offered the only possibility of promoting a federation, in which Britain's colonies, the Cape and Natal, could be included. A Royal Commission composed of Sir Hercules Robinson, the Governor of the Cape Colony, Chief Judge Henry de Villiers and Sir Evelyn Wood, Colley's successor, met the Transvaal's Committee of Three to agree on peace terms, which were eventually set out in the Pretoria Convention of August 1881. They restored independence—though not sovereignty—to the Transvaal.

The Pretoria Convention established Krugerland as the Transvaal State, but a state which was not free to conclude pacts or treaties with foreign states or to legislate for the Bantu and a state through which the British Government would have the right to send troops in time of war. Moreover there was no write-off of the Transvaal's outstanding debts.

In 1884, with the Liberals still in power yet another deputation, consisting of Paul Kruger, now President of the Transvaal State, the Rev S. J. du Toit, Superintendent of Education in the Transvaal, and General Nicolaas Smit was sent to Britain. They returned home with a new and improved agreement known as the London Convention. This restored the name 'South African Republic' to the Transvalers; it gave them freedom to make laws affecting the Bantu, relieved them from having to allow British troops to pass through their territory in time of war and permitted them to make treaties with the Orange Free State and with other external states, subject to the approval of the British sovereign.

The new Convention also dropped the preamble to the previous agreement according to which Her Majesty, her heirs and successors, retained full sovereignty over the Transvaal—although London maintained some years later that the 1881 preamble applied to both agreements.

The London agreement also declared that British subjects had the right to live in the Republic, and could own property and carry on business there. They could not be taxed more heavily than the burghers of the Republic, nor could the Republic discriminate against goods from British colonies. In return for this the Transvaal debt was scaled down by rather over £250,000.

But the Conservatives cared for none of these things. They smarted under the disgrace of military defeats. They mourned for the lost territory which was daily becoming more valuable. But most of all they despised the Liberals for abandoning the 'loyalists' in the Transvaal who looked to Britain for protection. And the fall of the Liberal Government in August 1886 when Emily was still in her mid-twenties and living at St Ive was the starting signal for an adventure to end all adventures.

4

The Road to the War

To Emily and other Liberals, Cecil Rhodes, the Empire-builder with the countenance—and shapeless figure—of a Roman Emperor, was Mephisto the arch-imperialist. He it was who inspired Britain's drive to the North, an adventure which in the long run was to cost his country 21,000 lives and much of her prestige.

Before becoming Prime Minister of the Cape, Rhodes had already made a fortune in diamonds and was hoping to do almost as well in the newly discovered goldfields of the Rand. And now, spurred by the landing of Germans sent by Kaiser Wilhelm II in the 1880s to colonize South West Africa, Rhodes pressed northwards with the Union Jack.

He blocked attempts by Kruger to expand the Transvaal frontier westwards because this would have interfered with his trade route to the north, and he persuaded the new British Government to annex Bechuanaland (now Botswana), thus separating the Transvaal from the newly arrived Germans on the west coast of Africa. He ousted President Kruger's representative from Matabeleland to the north of the Transvaal, and established the British South Africa Company which eventually colonized Matabeleland and the territory to the north to form Rhodesia.

At this point, the South African Republic was at last cabined and confined as a land-locked state without access to the sea. For Britain, in addition to occupying Bechuanaland on the west and Rhodesia on the north, had taken St Lucia Bay to the east, which the Transvalers had hoped to develop with German capital as a possible harbour on the Indian Ocean. And in 1895 Kosi Bay, South Africa's last and most northerly harbour, was annexed by Britain too for fear it should be exploited by the Germans.

Kruger was left with two alternatives. Either he could merge the South African Republic in a Federation with the British colonies of Natal and the Cape as Whitehall wanted, or he could make a deal with the Portuguese to run a railway eastwards to the Indian Ocean through the territory of the Portuguese Colony of Mozambique. He chose the Portuguese project and from then on was under even closer surveillance by the British imperialists.

Kruger's choice would doubtless not have troubled London so acutely if the Transvaal had not become one of the most prosperous regions of the British Empire.

In 1886 the total revenue there amounted to barely £200 million. Next year it was three times as much; ten years later the leading companies at that time had combined assets worth £215 million. A Chamber of Mines had been formed in 1889 to represent the capitalists and safeguard the interest of the investors.

The population also grew apace. In 1880 their numbers were listed at 50,000; by 1890 the figure had reached 119,000 and five years later it had soared to a quarter of a million.

But the result was a sharp division between two classes of people within the Republic—original inhabitants and the new immigrants. Johannesburg was a city of financiers, businessmen, traders, engineers, skilled workers, professional men and miners from many different countries. As in the diamond fields, a fair proportion were gamblers and hard drinkers, who were not averse to other worldly forms of entertainment such as prize fights and the can-can. Few were capable or desirous of forming a partnership with the Afrikaner farmers who had hitherto ruled the South African Republic. Certainly they had no desire to waste time learning to speak 'Dutch'. Nor could they understand why the Afrikaners should wish to stand aloof from the wonders of science and the mantle of the British Empire. The Bantu in their view were a source of cheap labour for the mines, regardless of the fact that, once out of the tribal areas, they would probably become rootless and restless; also the mine owners had no hesitation in offering arms to the natives as an inducement to them to leave home to live in the mine compound.

Kruger saw the dangers which the South African Republic, poorly armed and poorly endowed with administrators and diplomats, would face if it became involved in big power politics. But he hoped to keep his country as free economically as she was politically. He was free to encourage local industries, which he did by slapping tariffs on foreign imports, to encourage German and French investment to counterbalance the British influence, and he could promote his railway line through Mozambique to free himself from dependence on the British ports in the Cape and Natal. He could go further and impose duties on goods such as tobacco, maize and brandy, the bulk of which came as it happened from the Cape or Natal, using this as a lever towards getting a reduction on customs and freight charges on goods travelling to the Transvaal. In 1890 Kruger imposed a value tax of five per cent on all imports, and higher rates on tobacco, butter, cheese, coffee, tea, sugar, rice and soap. Two years later he raised the general rate to $7\frac{1}{2}$ per cent.

He also did his best to see that his own railway line from Johannesburg through Mozambique to the coast should get a head start over railway lines passing through British territory. But the construction of the railways was only one of the issues on which Kruger proved stubborn. Next came the question of what freight should be charged on them. The Cape, having invested some £20 million (70 per cent of her State debt) in the railway network, made hay in the two years during which the colony had the monopoly of rail traffic to the Rand. But as soon as the Mozambique line was opened, Kruger decreed that its rates for the 341-mile section of the line running through the Transvaal, should be considerably lower than those charged for the much shorter distances travelled by the other lines across Transvaal territory.

In addition to this handicap, the Cape railways suffered from unaccountable hold-ups on the Transvaal section of their line. In desperation traders began sending their goods to Viljoens Drift and other river crossings in the Free State, just short of the Transvaal border, where the consignments were off-loaded and forwarded to Johannesburg by ox-waggon. Kruger then offered to let the Free State send its goods to Johannesburg at reduced rates if it would ban Cape traffic across the Drifts. Rhodes at once appealed to the home Government; British troops, then en route for India, were ordered to sail to the Cape and war was narrowly averted when Kruger backed down and reopened the drifts. Gun-boat diplomacy worked wonders once again for Britain.

But this did not serve to allay the discontent which existed in the Transvaal, both among the leading British business men and, to some extent, among the less important members of the British community. One reason was that Kruger was not in

61

favour of free enterprise but preferred to grant local monopolies to individual companies to import or produce particular commodities, the company in many cases being owned or managed by Afrikaners, whom he was prepared to trust—especially if they included his close friends or relatives. One such concession was for dynamite, a product essential for the country's defence but also for mining operations. As with most monopolies, the prices charged were excessive and customers complained that the Kruger régime was exploiting them and furthermore, raising obstacles to the growth of the economy. Also, the foreign community, known to Kruger as 'uitlanders', were not long in demanding better standards in Johannesburg than the Afrikaners, including Kruger himself, had ever enjoyed; e.g. schools for English-speaking children, more baths, playing fields, and the like. And more political influence. In the original Constitution of the South African Republic, burghers enjoyed full civic rights, including the vote, provided that they had lived in the Republic for one year. But 1882 saw the qualifying period raised to five years. The result of this was that Johannesburg's first representative in the Volksraad or 'People's Council' was an Afrikaner, Jan Meyer, who knew nothing about mining and could not speak a word of English. His speeches on behalf of his constituents had to be translated to them by the district magistrate.

Kruger was nevertheless daunted by what might happen if the uitlander population were granted the vote. His solution was to create a second Volksraad, which could legislate on mining, roads, posts and telegraphs, public health and allied subjects but whose Bills could be vetoed by the first Volksraad. Foreigners could belong to the second Volksraad, provided that they had lived in the Republic for four years. But only the first Volksraad could elect the President, and the qualifications for belonging to it were stiff. All those who already had a vote before the law came into force in 1890 qualified, as did their sons when reaching the age of sixteen. But foreigners had to remain in the country for two years before receiving naturalization. After a further two years the naturalized subject could be elected to the second Volksraad and after serving there for ten years he could be elected to the first. This meant an 'apprenticeship' of no less than fourteen years. Furthermore only those who had resided in the Transvaal before the 29th May 1876 could automatically qualify as burghers fit to vote in the first Volksraad. All others required the vote of the majority of the burghers in their ward which, even if positive, could be over-ruled by the President and his Executive Council.

A storm of protest followed the passing of the new law. Deputations were sent to Kruger and turned away. Public meetings were held; newspaper campaigns were mounted but an unreasoning fear (quite unjustified as the latest estimates show) that the uitlander population would swamp the Afrikaner completely, possessed the minds of Kruger's supporters. None of them were prepared to risk losing their independence to foreigners. Eventually the uitlanders both great and small formed the Transvaal National Union, which organized a petition signed by 35,000 people calling for equal rights for all white people and a larger say in how the State income, of which they provided nine-tenths, should be spent. (They also refused military service, which was compulsory for the Afrikaner members of the population.)

The next step was an order from London for Sir Henry Loch, Her Majesty's High Commissioner at the Cape, to go to Pretoria for negotiations on behalf of the uitlanders. This served only to inflame the fears of the Afrikaners that Britain and the uitlanders together were planning another Shepstone-style annexation. Already Lionel Phillips, the Leader of the Transvaal National Union, expressed fears to Loch that the uitlanders might revolt if their grievances remained without redress. But President Kruger told Sir Henry not to interfere in the internal affairs of the Republic and passed a law banning demonstrations. The uitlanders replied on Boxing Day 1895 with a Manifesto setting out their grievances and calling for a new Constitution with a 'just' electoral system, full rights for the English language in the Courts and in Parliament and free trade for South African products, plus a Budget controlled by Parliament.

Earlier that year leaders of the uitlander movement began to hatch a plot to rise and seize power with the tacit encouragement of Cecil Rhodes. As Prime Minister of the Cape, Rhodes could not very well act himself but he could rely on others to help the uitlanders of Johannesburg. Joseph Chamberlain, the man with the monocle and a weakness for orchids, a dedicated Empire-builder, had become Colonial Secretary in June 1895, an appointment which proved a great source of encouragement to Rhodes, and a further warning to the Liberals in Britain. Rhodes' first move in the game was to ask the Government to grant his British South Africa Company the right to administer the Bechuana Protectorate, which lay along part of the western border of the Transvaal. Whitehall, however, thought that this would put too much power into the hands of one man and Rhodes drew back and petitioned instead for control of certain sections of land near the Transvaal border, which, he said, he needed to protect the railway that he was preparing to build to the north. (He might not have got even this much but for Kruger's blunder over the drifts.)

Soon after, Rhodes' agent, Dr Rutherfoord Harris, confirmed to Chamberlain what Sir Henry Loch had already told Chamberlain's predecessor, the Marquis of Ripon, that there appeared to be trouble brewing in Johannesburg. Rhodes gave a similar unofficial warning to Sir Hercules Robinson. Dr Jameson, a trusted friend of Rhodes, who had been appointed Administrator of Rhodesia, now recruited a mixed force of mounted troops and brought them down to Pitsani near the Transvaal border, nominally to look after Rhodes' railway interests. Arms were smuggled into Johannesburg for use in the proposed rising and hidden in the disused shafts of goldmines.

Dr Jameson, moreover, did not neglect to get a letter signed by five of the uitlander leaders, appealing to him to come to their assistance 'if a disturbance should arise here'. The date of the appeal was left blank, presumably so that it could be filled in and published not too far in advance of the expected 'disturbance'.

No-one knew quite when the uitlanders planned to rise but most Johannesburgers took advance precautions. A brigade of cyclists was formed to protect those wives and families who had not already sought refuge in one of the English clubs in Johannesburg and even President Kruger in Pretoria was believed to have slept fully clothed with a rifle beside him and his horse saddled.

Chamberlain, of course, was well aware of what was afoot and on December 18th 1895 told Sir Robert Meade, Permanent Secretary at the Colonial Office, that there would be less risk of foreign interference if the crisis occurred right away. Eight days later he told Lord Salisbury that a rising, which he had done nothing to provoke, was imminent and that he had already told the High Commissioner how to deal with it.

But, in the event, the whole scheme miscarried. Jameson was over-anxious for the rising not to be delayed. He rejected the pleas of the uitlanders that they were not all of one mind; he disregarded Rhodes' cables warning him to hold off, and he set off on a ride of nearly 200 miles to Johannesburg without sufficient regard to the difficulties of the journey. The Afrikaners met him and edged him off on to a dead-end trail where he was compelled to surrender. The uitlanders never risked leaving Johannesburg to help him. The sequel was disastrous for Britain. Rhodes suffered a heart attack and had to resign his office as Prime Minister of the Cape; the leading uitlanders were tried and given death sentences (commuted later for some whacking fines and a promise of political neutrality for the next fifteen years) and Chamberlain barely escaped with exposure in the official enquiry that followed.

The Liberals in Britain, of course, became more and more vociferous. They had witnessed two abortive attempts by the Conservatives to gain control of the Transvaal, the first through Shepstone's take-over, the second by means of the Jameson raid. They were prepared to go to considerable lengths to prevent a third adventure. Yet in fact this was exactly what the Conservatives were contemplating under Lord Salisbury's administration about the time that Emily Hobhouse returned to England from Mexico. The Conservatives had suffered two public defeats over the Transvaal; one when Gladstone had stopped the fighting after Majuba, the other when Kruger had triumphed over Dr Jameson. But surely the Empire, on which Britain's prosperity depended, must still be an ideal worth preserving and even extending.

In 1897 Chamberlain sent out a top administrator, Alfred Milner, to the Cape. His task was to protect Britain's interests in South Africa, and especially in the Transvaal. He was a Treasury man, a somewhat gaunt figure with a reserved manner, respected rather than loved, of great ability and powers of reasoning, effective in argument and negotiation, and a dedicated believer in a British Empire made up of territories such as Australia, New Zealand and Canada and peopled as far as possible with British emigrants, bound by ties of affection and gratitude to the motherland.

In South Africa on the other hand he faced two potentially hostile 'Dutch' Republics in the Transvaal and the Orange Free State and the possibility of a rising by the 'Dutch' in the Cape.

Probably the best that could be hoped for was an agreement safeguarding the interests of the uitlanders in the Transvaal, after which it might be expected that more and more Britons would want to emigrate there. But Kruger, now thoroughly alarmed by the disclosures of the enquiry into the Jameson raid, was not prepared to discuss the uitlander grievances unless his own were settled—and they included a claim to Swaziland and the concession of a free port on the Indian Ocean.

Britain hit back by setting up a customs union between the Cape and Natal, and granted a loan to Portugal, on condition that the Portuguese would grant no free port to the South African Republic. But Chamberlain still hoped, late in the autumn of 1898, that the uitlanders and Kruger could settle their differences by direct negotiations.

Kruger, however, went on to curb the pro-British press in Johannesburg. He restricted the right to present petitions, and introduced an Aliens Imigration Law, which was withdrawn only after Chamberlain had sent British troops once more to the Cape and the Royal Navy to Delagoa Bay.

In May 1899 Milner told Chamberlain that the case for intervention in the Transvaal was overwhelming, since the alternative policy of hoping that things would right themselves had let matters go from bad to worse. The failure of the Jameson raid 'had given the policy of leaving things alone a new lease of life with the old consequences', Milner wrote, and he added that the spectacle of British subjects being kept in servitude in the Transvaal 'like helots' was undermining the influence and reputation of Great Britain and the British Government within its own Dominions—i.e. in the Cape.

One more attempt to settle the dispute round the conference table was made at the suggestion of President Steyn of the Orange Free State and of W. P. Schreiner, who had succeeded Rhodes as Prime Minister at the Cape. The negotiations, held at Bloemfontein, lasted six days and turned on the question of whether the uitlanders should be entitled to full voting rights after five years' residence starting in 1894, or whether the period should be seven years, in which case none of them would qualify until 1901.

When the talks broke down Chamberlain declared that a new situation had arisen in South Africa. A last-minute offer was made by the Afrikaners who hoped that by playing for time they could gain support on the Continent of Europe and perhaps expect a return of a Liberal Government in Britain. They proposed that Milner's five-year period should be accepted (this was expected to give the uitlanders ten out of thirty-six seats in the First Volksraad and a voice in electing the President) in return for which it was 'assumed' that Britain would drop her claim to suzerainty over the Republic, would not interfere in future legislation, and would submit other questions to an

Arbitration Court. But this, too, was considered unacceptable on the grounds that it did not sufficiently safeguard the future position of the uitlanders.

From then on, war became unavoidable, at any rate in the Conservative view, and, if Emily had had any natural interest in politics, this would have been the moment when she would have volunteered to serve the Liberal cause.

Instead she went on a care-free winter-sporting holiday to Switzerland with her brother and a party of friends. In the summer there were once again family gatherings at Charlton with her uncle and aunt.

She was still uncommitted in every way. She was short of money—at times very short—as the result of her unsuccessful adventures in Mexico, but she might, if she had been more dependent a personality, have settled quietly into the role of Cousin Emily, a lively, intelligent, well-informed, witty, good-humoured but dependent relative, with a zest for life and the ability to entertain; Cousin Emily, whose appearances on the rounds of visits so fashionable in those days when extra guests meant no trouble (except for the servants) would always have been welcome, particularly in houseparties where a little self-help and organization of round games, songs round the piano, and other harmless diversions would not come amiss.

But she was very far from being dependent by nature. She decided to work for the Women's Industrial Council and moved into a flat in Rosetti Mansions, some way from the Kings Road, but close to her friends the Courtneys, who lived at No. 15 Cheyne Walk. Throughout her life Emily liked to speak with authority and for this reason she attended (like Lenin) the Reading Room of the British Museum in order to study Industrial Law and the provisions of the Factory Acts.

But soon a far more dramatic event supervened. In Emily's eyes the affairs of the Women's Industrial Council paled into insignificance. The Boer War (or the Second War of Independence as Afrikaner historians prefer to call it) lasted from October 1899 to June 1902, and was like no other. It was the first in which radio was used, the first to be recorded on movie-film and the first in which a leading military power was tied down and almost worn out by guerilla freedom fighters, who, apart from propaganda, received almost no foreign aid. And it was close to being a civil war, in which brother fought brother, for many English-speaking South Africans had married 'Dutch' girls in the Transvaal, and produced families with mixed allegiances. It was a conflict of surprise since the Boers were the first to declare war. They did so because the green grass of the South African spring was finally sprouting and because, the longer they waited, the more reinforcements the British would be able to land. The Boer strategy was simple. They would lay siege to a number of key cities: Kimberley with its fabulous diamond mines, Mafeking, because it controlled the road to the North, and Ladysmith, in Natal, because these moves would serve to draw British troops away from the Cape Colony, in which it was hoped to foster a rising.

Many distinguished war correspondents flocked from Britain and elsewhere to report the scene, including the brilliant descriptive writer and artist Henry Nevinson, thriller-writer Edgar Wallace, Rudyard Kipling and of course Winston Churchill. But one of the most professional, G. W. Steevens of the *Daily Mail,* had the knack of recording those details that carried the sound and scent of the campaign over a six thousand mile journey home.

In a few sentences he sums up the atmosphere in the early days of the war in a little dorp or hamlet in the Cape not far south of the Orange River:

'Burghersdorp (Cape Colony) Oct. 14

'The village lies compact and clean-cut, a dot in the wilderness. No fields or orchards break the transition from man to nature; step out of the street and you are at once on rock-ribbed kepje or raw veldt. As you stand on one of the bare lines of hill that squeeze it into a narrow valley, Burghersdorp is a chequer-board of white house, green tree and grey iron roof; beyond its edges everything is the changeless yellow brown of South African landscape.

'Go down into the streets, and Burghersdorp is an ideal of Arcady. The broad, dusty unmetalled roads are steeped in sunshine. The houses are all one-storeyed, some brick, some mud, some the eternal corrugated iron, most faced with whitewash, many fronted with shady verandahs. As blinds against the sun they have lattices of trees down every street, white blossoming laburnum, poplars, sycamores.

'Despite the verandahs and trees, the sunshine soaks down into every corner—genially, languorously warm. All Burghersdorp basks. You see half-a-dozen yoke of bullocks with a waggon, standing placidly in the street, too lazy even to swish their tails against the flies; pass by an hour later, and they are

68

still there, and the black man lounging by the leaders has hardly shifted one leg; pass by at evening and they have moved three hundred yards and are resting again. In the daytime hens peck and cackle in every street; at nightfall the bordering veldt hums with crickets and bullfrogs. At morn come a flight of locusts—first yellow-white scouts whirring down every street, then a pelting snowstorm of them high up over the houses spangling the blue heaven. But Burghersdorp cared nothing; "the frost killed everything last week."

'British and Dutch salute and exchange the news with mutual tolerance. The British are storekeepers and men of business; the Boers ride in from their farms. They are big, bearded men, loose of limb, shabbily dressed in broad-brimmed hats, corduroy trousers and brown shoes; they sit their ponies at a rocking-chair canter erect and easy; unkempt, rough, half-savage, their tanned faces and blue eyes express lazy good-nature, sluggish stubbornness, a dormant fierceness. They ask the news in soft lisping Dutch that might be a woman's; but the lazy imperiousness of their bearing stamps them as free men. A people hard to rouse, you say—and as hard, when roused, to subdue.

'A loitering Arcady—and then you hear with astonishment that Burghersdorp is famous throughout South Africa as a stronghold of bitter Dutch partisanship. "Rebel Burghersdorp" they call it in the British centres, and Cape Town turns anxious ears towards it for the first muttering of insurrection. What history its stagnant annals record is purely anti-British. Its two principal monuments, after the Jubilee fountain, are the tombstone of the founder of the Dopper Church—the Ironsides of South Africa—and a statue with inscribed pedestal complete, put up to commemorate the introduction of the Dutch tongue into the Cape Parliament. Malicious comments add that Afrikaner patriotism swindled the stonemason out of £30, and it is certain that one of the gentlemen whose names appear thereon most prominently, now languishes in jail for fraud. Leaving that point for thought, I find that the rest of Burghersdorp's history consists in the fact that the Afrikaner Bond (the Dutch political Party) was founded here in 1881. And at this moment Burghersdorp is out-Bonding the Bond: the reverend gentleman who edits its Dutch paper, and dictates its Dutch policy, sluices out weekly vials of wrath upon Hofmeyr and Schreiner (Dutch leaders in the Cape) for machinating to keep patriot Afrikaners off the oppressing Britain's throat.

'I went to see this reverend pastor, who is a professor of a school of Dopper theology. He was short, but thick-set, with a short, shaggy grey beard; in deference to his calling, he wore a collar over his grey flannel shirt, but no tie. Nevertheless, he turned out a very charming, courteous old gentleman, well-informed, and his political bias was mellowed with an irresistable sense of humour. He took his own side strongly, and allowed that it was most proper for a Briton to be equally strong on his own. And this is more or less what he said:

' "Information? No, I shall not give you any; you are the enemy, you see. Ha, ha! They call me rebel. But I ask you, my friend, is it natural that I—I, Hollander born, Dutch Afrikaner since '60—should be as loyal to the British Government as a Britisher should be? No, I say; one can be loyal only to one's own country. I am a law-abiding subject of the Queen and that is all that they can ask of me.

' "How will the war go? That is impossible, quite impossible, to say. The Boer might run away at the first shot and he might fight to the death. All troops are liable to panic; even regular troops, much more than irregular. But I have been on commando many times with Boer, and I cannot think of him other than brave man. Fighting is not his business; he wishes always to be back on his farm with his people; but he is a brave man . . .

' "Well, well; it is the law of South Africa that the Boer drive the native north and the English drive the Boer north. But now the Boer can go north no more; two things stop him; the tsetse fly and the fever. So if he must perish, it is his duty—yes, I, Minister, say it is his duty to perish fighting." '

At first the war was fought with chivalry on both sides, and Steevens, among others, reported that after a British surrender at Nicholson's Trek it was decided that the British wounded could be sent to Ladysmith, where they would be under British care, rather than as captives to Pretoria, which was further away.

'They gave the white men water out of their own bottles; they gave the wounded the blankets off their own saddles, and slept themselves on the naked veldt. They were short of transport and they were mostly armed with Martinis; yet they gave captured mules for the hospital panniers and captured Lee-

Metfords for splints. A man was rubbing a hot sore on his head with a half crown; nobody offered to take it from him. Some of them asked soldiers for their embroidered waist-belts as mementoes of the day. "It's got my money in it," replied Tommy—a little surly, small wonder—and the captor said no more.

'Then they set to singing doleful hymns of praise under the trees.'

The Boer leaders were as unpretentious as the men they led. There was Piet Joubert who favoured a blue frock-coat topped with a brown slouch hat with a crepe band, his white beard contrasting with his sunburnt complexion. His manner was un-affected and his intelligence was said to be shrewd, though it must be confessed that his last victory over the British had been won eighteen years earlier.

Then there was General Schalk Burger, who had once run for the Presidency in opposition to Kruger and was now representing him in the field. He reminded one of the French volunteers who fought alongside the Boers or of a 'journeyman carpenter and one instinctively looked to see if the leg of a compass were not appearing from his trouser pocket'.

General Beyers, later one of the rebels who refused to fight for Britain against Germany in the First World War, struck one observer as being relatively polished, possibly because of his Huguenot ancestry, but General Cronje, who had compelled Jameson to surrender, restored the average with his loose trousers and nut-brown overcoat green with age, and his large grey hat. The General was happy to eat his lunch, a meal of steamed pork, sitting on a packing case, with water from a pail standing on the ground nearby to wash it down.

Mrs Cronje, like the wives of many other Generals, accom-panied her husband and cooked for him on his campaigns. Her company—rather than her cooking—was one of the reasons why he was compelled to surrender at Paardeberg with the loss of 4,000 men.

President Steyn of the Orange Free State became a guerilla at the age of forty-two, when his mini-republic joined in the battle against the British. An American correspondent described him as a typical Afrikaner, six foot high, with a powerful frame, large head, large eyes beneath arched eyebrows, flat nose and a full dark beard. 'Never again,' said Steyn, 'shall I be a party to nor shall I sign any Convention with the English.' He kept his word. His wife, Tibbie Fraser, a Scottish lassie, was one of Emily's most regular correspondents. Steyn used to drive round the battle lines in a blue farmer's cart, without a hood, and was once seen waiting politely outside a primitive hotel at Jacobsdal until his men had finished their breakfast before going in for his own.

But if the Boers were over-modest, the British were over-confident and unimaginative in their approach to war. Set battles in which the infantry advanced in close order and fired only when ordered to do so and set cavalry charges by heavily encumbered troops which, it was believed, the Boers could never face, were to be the recipe for success. They proved to be the way to disaster.

Ten or fifteen miles a day was the most a British force could advance because of the huge column or convoy that went with it—literally at the pace of the oxen that had to be outspanned for a consideable time every midday for grazing.

In contrast the Boers fought in extended order and seldom offered the kind of target the British could hit. They knew the country and how to conceal themselves in it far better than the British. They were excellent marksmen and the new smokeless powder made detection even more difficult. In addition, slipshod ineffective reconnaissance and faulty communications added to the handicaps under which the British soldier fought and a number of ignominious surrenders followed.

In the 'Black Week' of December 1899, the British lost 600 men taken prisoner at Kissieberg because Sir William Gatacre had neglected to give them the order to retire. A thousand more were killed in two days at Magersfontein Ridge, because the Boers had adopted the unorthodox tactic of digging their defence trenches at the bottom of the slope; and at Colenso, four hundred men were mown down in a loop of the river into which a 'guide' had conveniently led them. Boer commandos from the Orange Free State were able to take over many districts in the northern part of Cape Colony including Colesberg, Albert, Aliwal North, Wodehouse and Barkly East.

On January 16th 1900—A gentleman 'lately resident' in Vryburgh who had been sent to Cape Town by Mr Wessels, Bond member for that district, reported to Milner: 'All the farmers in the Vryburg, Kuruman and Taungs districts have joined the Boers and I do not believe that you will find ten loyal British subjects among the Dutch community in the whole of Bechuanaland. Field cornets and Justices of the Peace on the Dutch side have all joined.' He adds: 'the conduct of the rebels has been unbearable.'

When Commandant Olivier moved across the Orange River and occupied Aliwal North (which he re-christened Olivier-fontein), the Magistrate was made to stand on the bridge during the crossing of the 450-strong commando force as there were rumours that it had been mined.

Milner quoted reports of loyalists fleeing from Barkly East through native areas—an unedifying spectacle for the natives—and carrying with them such scanty property as they could save from the invaders.

Along the roads to Queenstown, to Herschel, to Basuto-land, to East Griqualand and the Transkei were to be seen the families of British farmers, fortunate that they still had a waggon to convey them from their empty farms. The last stage of anarchy was reached in Barkly East with the throwing open of the gaol: 'On Thursday last the keys of the gaol were demanded from the gaol keeper, the prison doors opened and the prisoners asked if they would like to be set at liberty. There were long-sentence prisoners and one or two convicted on serious charges but the answer was in all cases, "Ja, baas." They were all released.' One magistrate spoke of British 'being hunted out of town after town like sheep'.

The defeat that followed in the New Year at Spion Kop was so calamitous that the resulting debate in the House of Commons lasted for six days. For it looked as though Britain might be facing not only a rising in the Cape and the loss of the whole of her South African possessions but the collapse of her empire as a whole. After Colenso many theatres in London had closed for want of an audience.

The reactions of Emily's family and friends to these disasters varied. Margaret Hobhouse wrote in December 1899 to her sister Mary Playne: 'What a blessing it is that our Government is taking these dreadful reverses with courage and decision. I wish I had a son who could go out and fight and help to regain our lost position. It seems that the whole credit of England and her colonies is at stake.' And to another sister, Georgina: 'The war has been sickening but I hope for better things. We are very enthusiastic here about sending out troopers. I most ardently desire completely to smash up the Boer Power—they and their works are odious. It will be a bad day for England if we can't do it—and goodbye to our greatness.'

Beatrice Webb on the other hand wrote from Torquay: 'The

Boers are man for man our superiors in dignity, devotion, capacity. Yes in capacity. That, to a ruling race, is the hardest hit of all.' She added that we appeared to be incapable of statesmanship or generalship and that 'if we win we shall soon forget the lessons of the war and go Empire-building again.'

In time, sheer weight of numbers allowed the British to capture the main cities of the rebellious Republics. The siege of Kimberley—with Rhodes inside it—was raised on February 15th 1900; Ladysmith twelve days later. Bloemfontein, capital of the Orange Free State, was taken in March, Mafeking was relieved in May, a week before the Orange Free State was annexed by Britain. British troops marched into Johannesburg on May 31st and into Pretoria the following month.

There, the United States had accepted the responsibility of caring for British interests and United States correspondents had made up for the absence of British war reporters. One of the Americans, R. H. Davis wrote as follows in *Scribner's Magazine* of the 'Last Days of Pretoria':

'I left Pretoria with every reason for regret. I had come to it a stranger and had found friends among men whom I had learned to like for themselves and for their cause. I had come prejudiced against them, believing them to be all the English press and my English friends had painted them: semi-barbarous, uncouth, money-loving and treacherous in warfare. I found them simple to the limit of their own disadvantage, magnanimous to their enemies, independent and kindly. I had heard much of the corruption of their officials; and I saw daily their chief Minister of State, at a time when every foreigner was driving through Pretoria in a carriage, passing to and from the government buildings in a tram car, their President living in a white-washed cottage, their generals serving for months at the front without pay and without hope of medals or titles. . . .

'Still, in spite of his cause, the Boer is losing, and in time his end may come and he may fall. But when he falls he will not fall alone; with him will end a great principle, the principle for which our forefathers fought—the right of self-government, the principle of independence.'

For Britain even victory was beginning to look a little tarnished. But Joseph Chamberlain, the man behind the Government, decided nevertheless that this would be the year to hold a General Election. The split in the Liberal Party had gone deeper than ever. Lord Rosebery, who had become Liberal Prime Minister on the retirement of Mr Gladstone in 1894, repudiated the Liberal Party in 1896 and decided to 'plough his own furrow'. It was not until 1899 that the party had an acknowledged leader in the House of Commons—Sir Henry Campbell-Bannerman; and even then his followers were not of one mind about the war.

Asquith, future Prime Minister, Haldane and Sir Edward Grey took the view that the war in South Africa had been inevitable and that independence for the Boers was out of the question.

Sir Henry Campbell-Bannerman adopted an intermediate fence-sitting position and argued that it was too late to abandon the conflict but that the policy that led to it was wrong and also the objects and methods of the campaign.

Further to the left in the Fabian Society, Mr James Ramsay MacDonald, future Prime Minister of Britain, resigned with fourteen other Members, including his wife, in order to be free to support the Boer cause, and H. W. Massingham, Editor of the *Daily Chronicle* was dismissed from his post in December 1899 for favouring the 'Dutch' cause.

In the so-called 'khaki election' of 1900 Emily's relatives met with varying fortunes. Henry Hobhouse was returned unopposed as Unionist member for Somerset East. His cousin Charles Hobhouse, an orthodox Liberal, entrenched himself firmly at Bristol East, which he was to represent for nearly twenty years.

Leonard Courtney, Henry's brother-in-law by marriage, was not so fortunate. Courtney had acquired a high-sounding but unpopular reputation as the 'conscience of the House of Commons'. He had urged Gladstone to restore independence to the Transvaal without waiting for a rebellion. He had attacked Rhodes and objected to his remaining a member of the Privy Council after the Jameson raid. He had tried—unsuccessfully —to compel Mr Hawksley, Solicitor to the British South Africa Chartered Company, to produce telegrams which, it was believed, would connect Rhodes and perhaps the Government with the Jameson conspiracy.

Speaking at Liskeard shortly after the outbreak of the Boer War, he said that he regretted the Boer ultimatum. 'It would have been finer, nobler, greater, if they had stood waiting for our assault, but that was almost too much for human nature. At last they said, "Must we die like rats in a hole? We must fight for it." ' But when he reminded the audience of the Hague Convention which provided for the settlement of disputes by peaceful means, he was hissed. An amendment was passed changing the motion that he had proposed, so that it pledged full support for the Government to get 'justice for British subjects'. Courtney's popularity was not increased by the fact that General Symons, who fell in the early days of the war, was a Cornishman. 'What a pity a soft-nosed bullet cannot be lodged in the place where your brains are supposed to be,' wrote one strongly-moved citizen. 'To the Little Englander Mr Leonard Courtney, Knight of the White Feather, House of Commons,' wrote another correspondent, 'The Constable of the Tower will make room for you. A rope and short shrift for traitors.' His party association made it clear that they did not wish him to stand as their candidate for East Cornwall in the forthcoming election.

Nevertheless the Government's boast, on which the election had been won, proved empty. For the war was not over. It would have been if Britain had been fighting a conventional foe in a country that depended on large cities and their 'civilization' for its existence. But things were very different in South Africa.

A few, but not many, had foreseen what was going to happen. One of them was Professor A. Kuyper, then President of the Dutch Press Association and later Prime Minister of the Netherlands, who wrote in the *Revue des Deux Mondes*:

'Suppose that General Lord Roberts succeeds in forcing the passes of the Drakensberg or of Spytfontein; that Bloemfontein is occupied, and that siege is laid to Pretoria, it is then, surely, that the difficulties of the English, far from being ended, would only be commencing. They would require an army of 50,000 men at least to secure the communications with their base of operations at Capetown, Port Elizabeth and Durban. Their camp would be constantly harrassed and their army of investment would be subjected to alarm day and night by the Boers, buzzing in swarms about their camp. Even the boldest tacticians avow that there are distances and elementary forces which defy all human strength.'

And so it was. As Captain L. March Phillipps, who was with Rimington's Scouts, put it:

'So far we only really hold the ground on which our armies stand. If I were to walk out from this tent a mile or two over the hills yonder, I should probably be shot. Kronstadt has been ours for four months. The country all round is being repeatedly crossed by our troops. Yet an Englishman would not be safe for a minute out of range of those guns.'

Towards the end of November 1900, five months after the fall of Pretoria, M. Phillipps was writing:

'Frankfort is one of our small garrison towns. It exists in a perpetual stage of siege, like Heilbron, Lindley, Winberg, Bethlehem and a dozen others in the neighbourhood; in fact like all towns held by us not on the railway. . . . This vagrant form of war is more formidable than it sounds. These wandering bands can unite with great rapidity and deal, when least expected, a rapid blow. As we cannot catch them we must be prepared to receive them at all points. The Veldt is a void to us, all darkness, and it hides a threat which, as it may fall anywhere, must be guarded against everywhere. This, what with all our garrisons and enormous lines of communication, means that the far greater part of our army has to act on the defensive, to sit still waiting for an enemy who may be a hundred miles off or behind the next hill. As for our wandering columns, they have about as much chance of catching Boers on the veldt as a Lord Mayor's procession would have of catching a highwayman on Hounslow Heath. The enemy are watching us now from a rise a few miles away, waiting for our next move, and probably discussing some evil or other they are up to. The line of our march is blotted out already. Where we camp one day they camp the next. They are all round and about us like water round a ship, parting before our bows and reuniting round our stern. Our passage makes no impression and leaves no visible trace.'

The Boers were so successful in cutting supplies that some of the British troops were reduced to wearing prison clothes with O.V.S. (Orange Free State) stamped on them—taken from the Frankfort Prison.

'Our maps are worse than useless,' Lt General Hunter wrote in his report to Lord Roberts. 'They are a positive danger and delusion. The constant cutting of our telegraph wires upsets communications with distant Generals.'

The Boers, too, suffered, though perhaps they were more accustomed to hard living. They subsisted largely on Boer Biscuits made from flour and fermented raisins (instead of yeast), doubly baked, and of course on Biltong—strips of meat sprinkled liberally with salt to preserve it and with pepper to taste, and dried. (The meat was handed out by the commando butcher with his back turned towards the recipient so that there should be no favouritism.)

They fought with tremendous skill, attacking from behind cover and then disappearing into smoke screens created by setting fire to the veld. These tactics often prevented the British summoning help by signalling with heliographs. The Boers also seemed to be able to see almost as well at night as by day.

Good leadership helped to maintain the Boer resistance. Kruger, a liability in the field because of his age, had been given leave of absence in September 1900 to scour Europe for help. But Louis Botha in the north and General De la Rey, Lion of the Western Transvaal, had the knack of uniting and inspiring their men. The most famous of them all was General Christian De Wet. Thomas F. Millard, another contributor to *Scribner's* relates how, when in search of De Wet during the Boer retreat after the disaster of Paardeberg, he asked the way to the General's Headquarters. He was directed to the General's tent by De Wet himself, who was too modest, or cautious, or busy, to say who he was. Millard notes that he was of middling height, stocky, well-set, and that he gave an impression of physical strength. His face was weather-beaten. He wore a slouch hat, cow-hide boots, into which he tucked his trousers. He made no attempt at a uniform. A dingy dark blue sweater concealed his shirt, if there was one. His trousers were an ordinary pair of dark brown overalls. He had no coat. He had no indication of rank but was identifiable by a bedraggled cockade of black ostrich feathers stuck in his hat band, and it was said that his dilapidated appearance was the result of exchanging clothing with his men.

De Wet was always approachable by any of his men without the formality of a salute, and the least privileged man in his camp could speak to him on any subject with the certainty of receiving his personal attention. His manner was courteous and he seldom spoke to one of his men without first clasping him by the hand. His three sons with him on Commando were probably the only ones not on nickname terms with him. In action he was ruthless with his own men as he was with the enemy. He regarded 1500 men with five hundred horses in reserve, and 150 rounds of ammunition per man, as the ideal size for a guerilla force. Supplies for his men were carried on six trolleys, each drawn by ten or twelve mules. A few tents were carried but rarely pitched. Two light field guns, a machine gun and a

Cape cart carrying the doctor, just about completed the outfit. No wonder he was hard to catch.

At home, the critics of the Government became more persistent in their inquiries as to why Boer resistance had not ended; those who had opposed the war from the start became increasingly vocal. The strongest arguments came from people who declared that the war should never have been started. They recalled the speeches in which Chamberlain had himself rejected the idea of going to war with Kruger. In 1881 at the time when Gladstone was about to commit British troops to the disastrous campaign of Majuba, Chamberlain had said of the Boers:

'They are a homely industrious nation of farmers living on the produce of the soil. They are animated by a deep and somewhat stern religious sentiment and they inherit from their ancestors—the men who won independence from the oppressive rule of Philip II of Spain—their unconquerable love of freedom and liberty. Are not these the qualities which commend themselves to men of English race? Are they not the virtues which we are proud to believe form the best characteristics of the English people? Is it upon such a nation that we are to be called upon to exercise the dread arbitrament of arms?'

Fifteen years later, he was still of the same mind about keeping out of the Transvaal. On February 13th 1896 he said, 'We are entitled to give him (Mr Kruger) friendly counsel, but if this friendly counsel is not well received, there is not the slightest intention on the part of Her Majesty's Government to press it.' On May 8th 1896 Mr Chamberlain repeated his argument: 'We do not claim and have never claimed,' he protested, 'to have the right to interfere in the internal affairs of the Transvaal. The rights of our action under the Convention are limited to the offering of friendly counsel, in the rejection of which, if it is not accepted, we must be quite willing to acquiesce.'

In August 1896 his sentiments were even more strongly expressed. 'A war in South Africa,' he said, 'would be one of the most serious wars which could possibly be waged. It would be in the nature of a civil war. It would be a long war, a bitter war and a costly war. It would leave the embers of strife which I believe generations would hardly be long enough to extinguish. To go to war with President Kruger, to force upon him reforms in the internal affairs of his State, standing in this place, having

79

repudiated all right of interference—that would be a course of action as immoral as it would have been unwise.'

And the grievances which the 'uitlanders' alleged could not be remedied save by interference—how real were they? How many of the miners, many of them unmarried, or with families in Britain, would have been prepared to renounce their British citizenship to get Burgher rights to live and vote in the Transvaal? Could the English press in South Africa, with its malicious caricatures of Kruger and its magnification of the defects of Afrikaner rule, be doing a service to Britain? Or was it a danger to peace? Were many Britons in fact ill-treated? Was there really a conspiracy among the Afrikaners to overpower the British in South Africa or was Britain making an attempt to turn the Afrikaners in the Cape into what they could never be—Englishmen? Were the British really fighting to right the wrongs of British citizens or was it to take away the independence of the Afrikaners who occupied Naboth's vineyard?

Opponents of the war argued that the real quarrel lay between the Rand capitalists, who wanted a Government in the Transvaal that would assure them cheap native labour in the mines, and the Afrikaner Government which preferred cheap agricultural labour; the capitalists, it was alleged, had no more intention than Kruger had of benefiting the British immigrants as a class. Indeed the *Mining World and Engineering Record* of December 1899 said:

'White wages have not been reduced in the past because the uitlanders desired to work together for political salvation and any attack upon the White Labourers' pay would have caused a split in the ranks. However, when new conditions prevail, white wages must come down.'

And some left-wingers went so far as to say that this was not a race war against the Afrikaners but a war to conquer Labour.

The idea that the Transvaal might eventually be peopled, and the Dutch outnumbered by British farmers was, they said, equally fantastic. Most of the best land had already been taken, and that which remained would require heavy investment. Furthermore, the style of farming, the isolated living conditions, were not suited to British farmers, who, even if they knew how to run a farm at home, would be quite unable to cope with the kind of emergencies to be found on the veld. The idea that Dutch majorities in the Cape, the Orange Free State and the Transvaal could be held down indefinitely was untenable;

they would have in the end to be allowed to govern themselves and in the meantime war would preclude a reconciliation between the Dutch majority and the British minority.

Such were the criticisms being voiced by the opponents of the Government at home. Nor was Britain getting a good press in the world at large. In the United States a formal petition asking President McKinley to offer his friendly services in the hope of putting an end to the conflict was presented by 104 senators, and Chamberlain felt impelled to write a letter of thanks to J. N. Ford, the London Correspondent of the *New York Tribune*, in praise of U.S. sympathy for Britain, which he equated with Britain's support of the U.S. for American action in Cuba.

Predictably, the German *Kolonial Zeitung* said that 'any further increase in British power is fraught with the gravest danger to the peace of the world.' The *République Française* said that 'Anglo-Saxon Pharisaism has never been affirmed with more hypocrisy and impudence,' and *Le Temps* complained that Swinburne and Kipling (both supporters of the war) had descended to the music hall.

Yet tragedy rather than comedy was to be played on the world stage by British politicians and generals in the months to come.

5

How the Veld was Scorched

To Emily Hobhouse, the South Africa war was inhuman from the moment that it broke out. But to many onlookers, its brutalization first became apparent in the proclamations numbering some forty—issued from March 1900 onwards by Lord Roberts, the Commander-in-Chief, during his progress through the country. As we shall see, these demonstrated a mounting ferocity.

In the earliest of them Roberts offered peace and security to all burghers of the two Republics, who, even though they might previously have fought, were now prepared not to help 'the enemy' with supplies or information. (The Queen's subjects in Cape Colony were of course liable to be treated as rebels if they joined the enemy.) Burghers who were not prepared to renounce the enemy and his works would be dealt with 'according to the customs of war', Roberts said. Nor was it enough for them to remain neutral. They were to supply the British with food, fuel and shelter and with forage for the horses, which if provided without demur, would be paid for on the spot. 'Orders have been given by me,' the proclamation ran, 'prohibiting soldiers from entering private houses and molesting the civil populations on any pretext whatever...' But of course the whole proclamation was effective only in so far as the British were able to prevent 'the enemy' from descending likewise on their own farms and asking for that very food and information that the farmer's wife had been forbidden to give.

Roberts' second proclamation in March 1900 spread the net wider. It said that those who had left their homes could return and would not be regarded as prisoners, provided that they took an oath pledging themselves to non-resistance. 'Persons living near the line of march must respect and maintain their neutrality and the residents of any locality will be held respon-

82

sible both in their persons and their property if any damage is done to the railway or telegraph or any violence is done to any member of the British Forces in the vicinity of their homes.' Thus 'neutrality' meant that the Boers living near the railway must guard it and the telegraph wires against sabotage.

The new proclamation was however no more effective than the first because on the one hand President Steyn threatened to shoot those who took the oath, while on the other hand, if the British forces could not prevent telegraph wires from being damaged, neither could civilians living on farms nearby.

By the summer of 1900 the British lifeline had stretched northward into the Transvaal and had thereby become more vulnerable. Stronger measures were needed. Accordingly Roberts' proclamation of June introduced the principle that people living in an area where railways, telegraph lines or public buildings were damaged, would be held severally and jointly responsible. In addition they would be subject to a levy of 2/6 per *morgen* (nearly an acre) upwards and to the cancellation of any receipts previously given for goods supplied to the British Government. Houses near the scene of an incident 'will be destroyed and the inhabitants dealt with under martial law'— which could mean the death sentence for a good deal less than murder—the proclamation said. Furthermore, as a deterrent to train-wrecking the principal residents of each area would be required to travel as hostages on the military trains passing through their districts.

A typical notice, addressed to Mr A. Fichardt of Bloemfontein, read as follows:

'With reference to my communication of 29th June appointing you a "Principal Resident" you are hereby ordered to report yourself to the railway officer at the railway station Bloemfontein at 6 p.m. on 1st July 1900. You will have with you food for four days and the necessary rugs. Failure to comply with this order will entail severe penalties.
By Order—B. Burnett-Hitchcock, Captain
Assistant Provost Marshal
Orange River Colony   30th June 1900'

In August Roberts cancelled arrangements by which those prepared to swear the oath of neutrality could return to their farms. He argued that the burghers had in many cases not respected the oath and could not, since they wore no uniform, be distinguished from enemy combatants. Accordingly all burghers who had not already taken the oath would be regarded as potential prisoners of war. In addition 'all buildings on which scouts or other forces of the enemy are harboured will be liable to be razed to the ground.'

The proclamation went on to demand that the Transvalers should in future help more actively in the prosecution of the war. 'Persons must acquaint Her Majesty's Forces with the presence of enemies on their farms, and failing to do so, they will be regarded as aiding and abetting the enemy,' it said, thus requiring that a mother, whose son came home on leave for a night, fulfil the duty of denouncing him to the authorities.

In the Orange Free State, burghers were told that, if found with arms, they were liable to the death penalty unless they could prove that they had not taken them up since May 1900, when the Orange Free State was annexed. Their farms, too, were liable to be razed.

Towards the end of September the burghers of the Transvaal and Orange River Colony (which the Free State had now become) were confronted with a Proclamation which made clear that 'razing' was being adopted as a general policy. Leaders, oath-breakers and those who did not surrender voluntarily might be transported from South Africa; the houses of leaders and houses used by snipers would be burnt. Oath-breakers, those on commando and those whose houses were used for sniping, would forfeit their livestock. Farms within a radius of ten miles of any place where an attempt had been made to sabotage a railway line or train would be cleared of their stock, supplies etc. If it became necessary to burn other farms, a list of those selected, together with the reasons, would be issued. It was a policy that commended itself to generals and troops alike. H. S. Gaskell, wrote, in *With Lord Methuen in South Africa* :

'We are at last beginning to realize (Sunday October 7th 1900) that the only way to stop this war is to burn, and many farms we come to where the man is in commando are burnt. There are three blackened ruins in this camp.

'The day before yesterday (Sunday November 4th 1900) General Methuen said in his usual post-church parade address, that we were now doing more good than we ever had done before in the present campaign. He said that he had always urged that the best way to deal with the Boers was not to rush about the country after them but to demolish all the farms, crops and land around, in fact, as he said "thoroughly denude the country".'

The correspondent of the *Times* wrote on April 27th 1900 that General Pole-Carew's column

'was moving out of Bloemfontein with definite instructions to render untenable the farms of men who, having surrendered, were found to be still in league with the enemy or were making use of British magnanimity as a means to save their property, while they still actively favoured the enemy.'

How far the British were entitled to adopt and pursue these tactics is a matter for legal dispute. The Hague Convention of July 1899 on the Laws and Customs of War provides safeguards for combatants, non-combatants and civilians which should be respected during an armed struggle. But it makes a distinction between belligerents, who observed certain rules and received in return certain privileges, and other fighters who did not. And the key question was 'Were the Boers and their families belligerents or not?' Belligerents included not merely regular armed forces but militia and volunteer forces, provided that they were:

1. Responsibly led, i.e. obeying a chain of command
2. Identifiable at a distance by fixed or distinctive uniforms or emblems
3. Carrying arms openly
4. Observing the laws and customs of war

A people rising spontaneously to resist an invader might also qualify for belligerent rights—even if they were not individually identifiable at a distance, provided:

1. That there had been no opportunity to organize regular forces
2. That the combatants carried arms openly and respected the laws and customs of war and
3. That they were operating on territory as yet unoccupied. Non-combatants who were taking part in the war might also be included

All these categories were to be given the privileges of belligerents, which included in the case of combatants the right to kill without being held guilty of murder, the right to save their own lives by surrender and the right, when captured, to be treated as prisoners-of-war and not as common criminals.

Non-belligerents on the other hand had no belligerent rights. They could be treated as ordinary criminals and be shot under Martial Law for many offences for which, if they had been wearing uniform and carrying arms openly, there would have been no penalty save imprisonment.

It was difficult to determine into which category the Boer Commandos fell. Certainly they were responsibly led, carried their arms openly and could be said to have observed the laws and customs of war remarkably faithfully for a people unused to formal warfare. And that they were not always identifiable at a distance was not always their fault. On the whole therefore the British were prepared to give them the benefit of the doubt and British commanders treated the Boers as part of a conventional army with the privileges of belligerents.

The position of the Boers or their families living on the farms was less clear and turned on the question of whether the area they lived in was occupied territory or not. If the territory was effectively occupied the inhabitants had of course no belligerent rights and were subject to Martial Law. On the other hand enemy civilians living in occupied territory have certain rights under the Hague Convention. They are not to be compelled to take part in military operations against their own country, and they are not to be pressed to take an oath to the hostile power. Family honour and rights, individual lives and property, as well as religious convictions and liberty must be respected. Private property is not to be confiscated. Pillage is prohibited. Finally, no general penalty pecuniary or otherwise, may be inflicted on the population on account of the acts of individuals, for which it could not be regarded as collectively responsible.

The British claimed in their Proclamations of Annexation that the Transvaal and Orange River Colony were occupied territory. Therefore any resistance could be dealt with under Martial Law. Equally however, if the territory was occupied, the British had no right, so long as the war continued, to make the Boers take an oath of allegiance or to inflict collective penalties on the innocent, or to confiscate, pillage or destroy their property, or to compel them to take part in military operations against their own country. Practices such as fining farmers for incidents committed near their farms but without their complicity would be clearly forbidden. So would pressing them to reveal the movements of 'the enemy', for this amounted to taking part in a military operation. Equally, under the Hague Convention, private property in occupied territory must be respected and not pillaged. If, on the other hand, the territory was not occupied but was being fought over, as was really the case civilians living there were unlikely to qualify for belligerent rights they must take their chance; and measures needed to win the war—which might include farm burning—were not excluded. Legal or not, the policy of farm burning was carried out extensively and in some cases without remorse.

A Munster Fusilier, writing to his mother from Honey Nest, December 30, says:

'We have a nice job on hand, going out to the farms for firewood, it doesn't matter what it is. The other day we brought in two pianos, a sofa, and two dozen chairs, what you would get £150 for at home—and Billy Jones made short work of them to boil our dinner with. All the people have left their homes, and we can do what we like with them.'

Murray Cosby Jackson in *A Soldier's Diary* covering the years from 1899-1901 wrote:

'Next day my company went out with orders to clear the two farms marked "H" on the plan, which we did pretty thoroughly; they were simply bursting with grain and all sorts of produce and pigs and poultry in hundreds. We wetted all the grain, burnt the forage, and killed the livestock, leaving merely enough for the family. The women couldn't quite make out Tommy, I think. A soldier, hot and grimy from burning their best haystack, and bloody with the blood of the old frou's pet Minorcas and Anconas, would go up to the back door without a trace of ill feeling and ask very civilly for a glass of milk, and then proceed to kill the pig.'

Others seemed less sure of themselves. Private Stanley, of the New South Wales contingent, wrote to the *Sydney Telegraph:*

'When within 800 yards of the farm we halted, and the infantry blazed a volley into the house; we broke open the place and went in. It was beautifully furnished and the officers got several things they could make use of. There was a lovely library—books of all descriptions, printed in Dutch and English. I secured a Bible, also a rifle, quite new. After getting all we wanted out of the house, our men put a charge under and blew it up. It seemed such a pity, it was a lovely house.'

In a Huddersfield paper, Mrs Bonsor, of Threshfield, published this letter from her husband, Private Fred Bonsor, of the Imperial Yeomanry:

'Captain Lane Fox is a splendid man to follow. Of course, all farms and houses on our way are looted, burned down and destroyed. It looks an awful shame, and the scenes are all along the sky-line, and shadows of women and kids running about trying to save something.'

Captain March Phillipps in his book *With Rimington* wrote:

'Soldiers as a class (I take the town-bred, slum-bred majority) are men who have discarded the civil standard of morality altogether, they simply ignore it. In soldiers' eyes, lying, theft, drunkenness, bad language are not evils at all... Looting, again, is one of his perpetual joys. Not merely looting for profit, though I have seen Tommies take possession of the most ridiculous things—perambulators and sewing machines, with a vague idea of carting them home somehow —but looting for the sheer fun of the destruction; tearing down pictures to kick their boots through them; smashing furniture for the fun of smashing it, and maybe dressing up in women's clothes to finish with, and dancing among the ruins they have made. To pick up a good heavy stone and send it *wallop* right through the works of a piano is a great moment for Tommy.'

Some of those who watched felt more strongly. The special correspondent of the *Manchester Guardian*, writing from Colonel Mahon's headquarters, Dry Harts Siding, en route for Kimberley, on May 8th said:

'In ten miles we have burned no fewer than six farmhouses; the wife watched from her sick husband's bedside the burning of her home a hundred yards away. It seems as though a kind of domestic murder were being committed. I stood till late last night and saw the flames lick around each piece of the poor furniture—the chairs, and tables, the baby's cradle, the chest of drawers, containing a world of treasure, and when I saw the poor housewife's face pressed against the window of the neighbouring house, my own heart burned with a sense of outrage.'

A letter published in the *South Wales Echo* from a telegraphist on Lord Roberts' staff read:

'We came across another farm richly furnished. The main body of troops had just passed forward unfortunately destroy-ing everything except a beautiful organ on which "Tommy" has been amusing himself. With grim humour he had placed a china dog near the door, firmly chained with the notice written in chalk "Beware of the dog".'

All this was tragic enough for the future relations between British and 'Dutch'. More serious still was the question of loot-ing. Unfortunately neither Lord Roberts' orders forbidding it, nor the Articles of the Hague Convention on the same subject were fully respected.

Sometimes the object taken was of mainly sentimental value as, for instance, in the case of Mrs Liebenberg, wife of the Minister at Bethal in the Transvaal, who complained that the Provost Marshal who came to burn her house in May 1901 purloined her husband's walking stick.

At other times something more material was involved. At Schweizer-Reinecke the Minister complained that an English officer had packed up the Communion Plate and carried it away in his suitcase. Mrs Van den Bergh of Witpoort declared that she had herself seen the Church plate taken by the English, one of whom scandalized the parishioners by climbing into the pulpit and imitating the preacher.

From May to September during the South African winter, the army was particularly short of fuel for their camp fires, and this was a circumstance that proved expensive for the South African farmer. 'At midday,' wrote Gaskell, 'we halted at a farmhouse which belonged to De Wet and his brother, and after picketing our horses outside, we went on collecting chair legs, window frames, etc., and we soon had a fire crackling merrily in the kitchen grate, on which we proceeded to cook our various delicacies.'

Later:

'On the way back we sighted a nice barbed wire fence, with wooden posts, and those who had hatchets, quickly clattered off to secure the coveted fuel. The custom was for each man to go for a particular post, and a race between two men would often ensue, the winner jumping off and commencing opera-tions at once, and the loser galloping on to the next post. I secured two posts this time and having successfully manoeuvred them on to the front of my saddle and got into it myself (no easy task with a rifle and horse that will move on directly your foot touches the stirrup) made off after the rest. I think every member of No. 3 had at least one post to show, so we had a fine blaze that night . . .

'. . . by hook or by crook we always manage to raise a fire behind the saddle-row. We commandeer the wood from anywhere we can, but generally by pulling down barbed wire fences. They have miles and miles of barbed wire fencing, stretching from post to post, and we cut the wire and pull up or chop down the posts, which make splendid firewood.'

Rudyard Kipling, as observant as ever, noted the same custom among the British Mounted Infantry, when he wrote:

> 'I wish my mother could see me now,
> with a fence post under my arm,
> and a knife and a spoon in my puttees that
> I found on a Boer Farm.
> Atop of a sore-backed Argentine, with
> a thirst you couldn't buy.
> I used to be in the Yorkshire's once
> (Sussex, Lincolns and Rifles once),
> Hampshires, Glosters and Scottish once!
> But now I am M.I.'

As early as February 1900 President Steyn of the Orange Free State and President Kruger directed a joint protest accusing the British troops 'contrary to the recognized usages of war, of destroying burning and blowing up farmhouses, devastating farms and depriving women and children of food and shelter.' This they claimed, happened not only in districts where natives had been encouraged by British officers but in other areas 'where white brigands come out from the theatre of war with the evident intention of carrying out a general devastation, without any reason recognized by the customs of war and without in any way furthering the operations.'

In July De Wet sent Roberts a list of farms destroyed in the Transvaal, adding, 'I trust that in the name of our common civilization and humanity your Excellency will have the culprits punished and prevent the perpetration of such acts in the future.'

A month later Botha complained that 'small bodies of (British) troops are captured far from their main force and who allege that they are scouts but who in point of fact go about to rob and that it cannot be expected that such robbers when captured will be in future treated as prisoners of war.'

By the autumn of 1900, despite the strict censorship to which the reports of British war correspondents were subjected, the news of farm burning and its consequences began to penetrate to Britain.

Margaret Hobhouse wrote to Mary Playne in November 1900: 'This burning of farms and homesteads (i.e. by the British army) is horrid and one doubts its wisdom.... The poor Courtneys are in despair ... I wish they were more moderate. It would be better for their cause.'

A letter from Charles Trevelyan published in the *Times* of November 26th called for some statistics of farm burning and pointed out that 'these men' (the Boers) were not enemies of a foreign state. He asked what happened to the women and children living on the farms that were burnt. It was a question that Emily asked herself more insistently as the days went by.

Leonard Courtney, in a letter published in the *Times* on November 28th, put farm burning on a par with poisoning wells, shooting prisoners or sacking undefended towns. He pointed out that not all Boer farms were forts. He might have added that sometimes they were hospitals in which women were either ill or pregnant.

More and more Britons began to doubt whether farm burning was going to prove effective. W. T. Stead, the British editor and publicist, was told by the Netherlands Minister for Colonies that the Dutch authorities had tried house burning as a means of reinforcing their authority in their colonies and had found it ineffective. No method was so certain to swell the ranks of the insurgents and extend the area of insurrection, the Minister said, according to Mr Stead.

General De Wet wrote in a letter to General Krion: 'My house cost me £700 to build. Its destruction will cost the English taxpayer two million.' Nor were the other Boers daunted by the destruction of their property. As Captain Phillipps put it:

'People who think the war can be ended by farm burning etc. mistake the Boer temper. I scarcely know how to convey to you any idea of the spirit of determination that exists among them all, women and children as well as men. The other day I picked up at a farmhouse a short characteristic form of prayer, written out evidently by the wife in a child's copybook, ending thus: "Forgive me all my sins for the sake of your Son Jesus Christ, in whom I put all my trust for days of sorrow and pain, and bring back my dear husband

and child and brothers and give us our land back again, which we paid for with blood from the beginning." Simple enough, as you see, and no particular cant about it, but very much in earnest.'

Later Phillipps reported:

'At another farm a small girl interrupted her preparation for departure to play indignantly their national anthem to us on an old piano. We were carting the people off. It was raining hard and blowing—a miserable hurried home-leaving; ransacked house, muddy soldiers, a distracted mother saving one or two trifles and pushing along her children to the ox-waggon outside, and this poor little wretch in the midst of it all pulling herself together to strum a final defiance.'

For a soldier in the thick of the fight, Phillipps showed himself remarkably far-sighted about the future of the country:

'The problem will apparently be when we have burnt these people out or shot them, and in various ways annexed a good deal of the land they now live on, how are we to replace them? What strikes one is that time and the country, acting on the naturally phlegmatic Dutch character, has produced a type exactly suited to this life and these surroundings... Indeed, it does not require any great knowledge of agriculture to see that a country like this, a lofty table-land, dry and barren, with no market handy, or chance of irrigation, is a wretched poor farming country. Hence the pity it seems of wiping out the burghers. They may not be a very lofty type of humanity, but they had the advantage in nature's scheme of filling a niche which no one else, when they are turned out, will care to fill in their place. The old dead-alive farm, the sunny stoep, the few flocks and herds and wandering horses sparsely scattered over the barren plain, the huge ox-waggon, most characteristic and intimate of their possessions, part tent and part conveyance, formed for the slow but sure navigation of these solitudes, and reminding one a great deal of the rough but seaworthy smacks and luggers of our coasts, that somehow seem in their rudeness and efficiency to stand for the very character of a whole life; all these things are no doubt infinitely dear to the Boer farmer and make up for him the only life possible, but I don't think it would be a possible life for anyone else.'

92

The women in particular did not visualize any other existence, and they were among the most vocal critics of the British farm-burning tactics.

'I never thought to be so badly treated in the Queen's name,' declared Mrs De la Rey, wife of the General. 'I could not have believed that, because you cannot get the better of our men you would set to work against the women.'

And Mrs Roos comforted Mrs Mocke, wife of a Veld-Kornet, who had been thrown into the Kaffirs' yard in Bloemfontein prison, by saying that they ought to feel specially proud since hundreds of women had suffered along with their husbands by being thrown into prison but none till then into the kaffir gaol.

In London Mr Chamberlain claimed that the war was being prolonged because of the encouragement which the enemy derived from the pro-Boers in Britain, and Mr Asquith was reported to have maintained that the policy of house burning had been carried out with the utmost humanity.

A letter to the *Times* of November 27th 1900 claimed that farm-burning was a penalty for oath-breaking. Another on December 4th pointed out that farmhouses were few and far between and were therefore normally the rallying points in each area and supply centres for water, forage etc. The writer added that the buildings were often mud-floored and roofed with iron and therefore not comparable to the traditional British farm house.

From a different standpoint the military leaders of Britain justified their conduct. General Roberts for example told the two Presidents who had protested to him that stringent instructions had been given to the British troops to respect private property:

'All wanton destruction or injury to peaceful inhabitants is contrary to British practice and tradition, and will, if necessary, be rigorously repressed by me.'

He added that it was an untrue statement that natives had ever been encouraged by the British officers to commit depredations.

'Why should the State which refused the aid of its own highly trained Indian army of 150,000 men avail itself of that of savages? I regret to say that it is the Republican forces which have in some cases been guilty of carrying on the war in a manner not in accordance with civilized usage. I refer especially to the expulsion of loyal subjects of Her Majesty from their homes in the invaded districts of this (Cape) Colony, because they refused to be commandeered by the invader. It is barbarous to attempt to force men to take sides against their own Sovereign and country by threats of spoliation and expulsion. Men, women and children have had to leave their homes owing to such compulsion, and many of those who were formerly in comfortable circumstances, are now being maintained by charity.'

He adds:

'I beg to call your Honour's attention to the wanton destruction of property by the Boer forces in Natal. They not only helped themselves freely to the cattle and other property of the farmers without payment, but they have utterly wrecked the contents of many farmhouses. As an instance I would specify Mr Theodore Wood's farm "Longwood" near Springfield. I point out how very different is the conduct of the British troops. It is reported to me from Modder River that farms within the actual area of the British Camp have never even been entered, the occupants are unmolested and their houses, gardens and crops remain absolutely untouched.'

'That a war should inflict hardships and injury on peaceful inhabitants is inevitable, but it is the desire of Her Majesty's Government and it is my intention to conduct this war with as little injury as possible to peaceful inhabitants and to private property and I hope your Honours will exercise your authority to ensure its being conducted in a similar spirit on your side.'

Nevertheless, that March Roberts did issue a proclamation limiting the scope of the fire-raisers. The proclamation ran:

'Notice is hereby given that all persons who within the territories of the South African Republic or Orange Free State shall authorize or be guilty of the wanton destruction or damage or the counselling, aiding, or assisting in the wanton destruction or damage of public or private property, such destruction or damage not being justified by the usages and customs of civilized warfare, will be held responsible in their persons and property for all such wanton destruction and damage.'

Commenting on this, Arthur Conan Doyle, who in addition

to creating Sherlock Holmes, had helped to run a military hospital unit in Bloemfontein, wrote in his book *The War in South Africa* that the military had not allowed empty villas belonging to Boers to be used to house patients for whom there was no room in hospital, that Lord Roberts had showed as scrupulous a regard for the right of property as the great Duke of Wellington in his campaigns and that in South Africa no hungry soldier was allowed to take so much as a chicken.

It was obviously a subject on which there could be two views.

Roberts' final word came in November 1900. He ruled that in future no farm was to be burnt except for treachery, or when troops had been fired on, or as a punishment for damage to the telegraph lines or railway or because the house had been used as a base for operations and then only with the consent of the General Officer Commanding 'which is to be given in writing':

> 'The mere fact that a burgher is absent on commando is on no account to be used for burning the house. All cattle, waggons and foodstuffs are to be removed from *all* farms; if this is found to be impossible, they are to be destroyed whether the owner is present or not.'

This meant that in almost every case, the families of Boers and others living on farms in the veld must become refugees. And it was their sufferings that drew Emily inevitably to South Africa. The vision of women and children without homes in desperation and distress obsessed her mind and never afterwards left her.

6

Miss Hobhouse said . . .

In the tidal wave of jingoism that swept over Britain in the early stages of the South African war, it was hard to find anyone who was prepared to tolerate criticism of the policy of Her Majesty's Government. Still fewer agreed that the war on two Republics with a population of the size of West Ham's was a disgrace to civilization and a scandal to Christendom, and that it was the duty of all Christians to endeavour to stop it.

S. C. Cronwright-Schreiner, husband of Olive Schreiner, the authoress whose name he took on marriage, was one of those who found the British unwilling to listen, although he came from South Africa largely at his own expense to speak to them.

Cronwright-Schreiner, who farmed in South Africa, and was a member of the Cape Legislative Assembly, was of English ancestry. His mother's forebears were among the South African settlers sponsored by the British Government in 1820. His father, also British by descent, had been Mayor of that most British of all South African cities—Grahamstown—and had represented it in Parliament.

When war broke out Cronwright-Schreiner was asked by J. A. Hobson to become war correspondent with the Boers for the *Manchester Guardian* and, later, to visit Britain to explain the views of the Cape Colonists (or some of them at least) to audiences at home. Cronwright-Schreiner's line was that the war was a blunder which might put Britain in danger of losing the whole of South Africa, unless she was prepared to hold it down by force with a permanent army in occupation. 'We might not all agree,' he said at Leicester in February 1900, 'as to what is the best means for securing the good of the Empire, but no one can surpass me in admiration for the men who are prepared to sacrifice their lives for what they conceive to be their duty.' (He then called for three cheers for the Queen and her soldiers.) Then he continued: 'Let us now consider whether these brave men are fighting in a cause and giving their lives for an end which will be beneficial to the Empire.'

But even this relatively inoffensive approach was unacceptable to the public at large. At Brighouse, the audience responded with rotten oranges, fish-heads and pieces of turf. At Edinburgh, potatoes and coloured powder were offered by the audience. At Dundee the meeting fixed for March 8th had to be abandoned, as also at Gateshead where the police said they could not provide protection.

At Sheffield the *Telegraph* printed the following in its leading article:

'We think it right that Sheffield should know that Mr Cronwright-Schreiner, the advocate of the Boers is coming to Sheffield today to plead the cause of men of the Kruger, Cronje, Steyn, Snyman and Leyds type. They are holding a very private meeting because they dare not hold a public one. Are they to be left to let England be deceived with the idea that Sheffield has aught in common with the Queen's enemies? Surely not. We are certain that the people of Sheffield would like to take part in this meeting, particularly as that champion of the Boers, Mr Cronwright-Schreiner is to address the gathering. It is possible, too, that Sheffield people might have several suggestions to give both Mr Cronwright-Schreiner and our local Little Englanders.'

The *Chronicle* wrote:

'Is it not about time that Mr Cronwright-Schreiner and his anti-English friends abandoned their persistent attempts to educate English audiences into thinking what they want them to think? The nation has shown unmistakeably that it does not want to hear the speeches of Mr C. Schreiner and his friends, and that its inclination is to take them as an insult to our honoured dead.'

At York, where Cronwright-Schreiner was the guest of Mrs Arthur Rowntree, they told him that he was lucky not to have put a label on his luggage, for the feeling about the war was particularly intense among the railwaymen.

Scarborough he had to leave secretly. At Leeds, where the *Yorkshire Post* described him as a talker from the enemy's camp, no hall could be hired and the meeting at Liverpool had

D

to be abandoned after a protest by the Chief Constable. And so, after six months, Mr Cronwright-Schreiner returned to South Africa to write the account of his experiences in a book *The Land of Free Speech*. In it he recalled Sir Wilfrid Lawson's story of the two clergymen, who were discussing the war in a railway carriage, one a Jingo and the other not. The Jingo clergyman could not get the other to state his opinions, so, after endeavouring for some time to draw him, he said: 'Well, what *are* your opinions on the war?'

'Well,' replied the peace man, 'I am trying to think what Jesus would have thought about it.'

'Oh, then, you are a pro-Boer,' hotly rejoined the Jingo.

The 'Stop the War' Committee which helped to arrange some of Cronwright-Schreiner's meetings was no more fortunate. The leading spirit in this organization was the editor and publicist W. T. Stead, of whom Walter Wellman, the London correspondent of the *Chicago Record Herald* wrote:

> 'the bravest man in the British Empire is not in South Africa fighting the Boers; he is right here in London fighting English public opinion. Though well-nigh single-handed, though opposed by a nearly unanimous press and people, he has started a current of thought which bids to run wider and deeper before many weeks shall have passed. The Government is obviously worried. It would like to close this man's mouth, but does not dare.'

Stead wrote a 70,000 word book *The Candidates of Cain* in six days in a vain attempt to prevent a Tory victory in the 1900 'khaki' election and his supporters at various times included organizations such as the Battersea Labour League, the Battersea Ethical Society, the Battersea Liberal and Radical Association, the Battersea Spiritualistic Society, the Clapham Labour League and in a wider field the Society of Friends. Individuals included Tom Mann, George Lansbury and John Burns. Keir Hardie, who first earned his living between the ages of seven and eleven by opening and shutting the draught gate in a coal mine, was another supporter. He was now an MP, after standing simultaneously for two seats in the same single election.

Yet one way or another the activities of the 'Stop the War' Committee were severely limited. 'Stop the War by all means,' fumed one imperialist circular; 'Stop the War by the only effective means. Stop Kruger. That is what our brave soldiers are now doing . . .' And the Tory election slogan was 'A vote given to the Liberals is a vote given to the Boers.' The windows of Stead's cottage on Hayling Island were duly broken.

The fight extended to the ranks of the Press where H. W. Massingham was forced to resign from the *Daily Chronicle*. The *Manchester Guardian* survived because its commercial news service was essential to the cotton trade, but in public men threw it away ostentatiously after they had read the cotton prices from the United States.

But a partially successful attempt to mobilize moderate opinion both at home and in South Africa was made by the South African Conciliation Committee. In Britain the movement included those who believed that the war could have been avoided and should have been ended, and in South Africa those who foresaw that, if Britain annexed the two Republics in the north, she would risk losing the loyalty of all those, including her colonists in the Cape, who had previously struggled to bring about a compromise settlement.

Emily's own feelings about the war at this time were probably more emotional than political. No doubt she agreed with her uncle's conviction that military conquests bring weakness rather than strength, that large armaments are a danger to the nation that creates them, and that those who take away the liberty of others are likely to lose their own. But she felt even more strongly that moral laws apply to nations as much as to individuals, that a true patriot is one who speaks out against his country when moral laws are broken, and that no government has the right to suppress criticism of its policies.

The Conciliation Committee was founded in November 1899, only three weeks after war had broken out, under the auspices of Frederick Selous, an Englishman who had made a name for himself as a big-game hunter, and at a meeting held at the Westminster Palace Hotel Leonard Courtney was elected its President.

On January 17th 1900 it made its public debut with a letter in the *Times*; its first public rally was held at Queens Hall a fortnight later. Emily undertook to act as Honorary Secretary of a Women's Branch of the Committee. But she was not yet completely dedicated to the cause and left after a few weeks to visit Italy with a friend whose health was said to require the change of air. The Women's Branch continued nevertheless to prosper and to proliferate drawing-room tea parties (into one of which the *Daily Chronicle* smuggled a woman reporter), educational soirées, and discussion groups, at which the iniquities of the Government met with righteous disapproval. But the difficulty was to find a practical course of action. The tide of public opinion was running so firmly in favour of the Government that any idea of seeking peace, particularly so soon after Britain's military recovery in South Africa, would have been howled down. But one evening after she got back from Italy Emily suggested at a small private dinner party at Collingham Gardens, at which the Courtneys were present, that it might be possible for the women conciliators to organize a protest meeting with relative impunity. To her surprise Leonard Courtney declared this to be a capital idea, and Emily, driving home with the Courtneys in her hostess' carriage, got definite approval for her plan. The Women's Branch was in favour too. The Queen's Hall was hired for June 13th, and sub-committees were formed in many different parts of London to 'bring out' the all-women audiences (for although admission was free it took some courage in those days for a woman to attend such a controversial meeting). As a protection against hecklers or worse, only those with tickets supplied by Emily were allowed to attend: and no men were allowed (though Mr Courtney was permitted to listen from behind a curtain outside the body of the hall). Emily was not billed as one of the speakers, but she proposed a resolution expressing sympathy with the women of the Transvaal and Orange Free State, and regret for the action of the British Government. The *Westminster Gazette* called it one of the most remarkable women's meetings held in London for a very long time and praised the excellence and brevity of the speeches.

By this time Emily had got the bit between her teeth and she decided to speak with Mr Lloyd George at a meeting at Liskeard which had once been the stronghold of the Courtney constituency. The meeting was under the auspices of the Women's Branch of the South African Conciliation Committee and was organized mainly by west-country Quakers. It had the dual purpose of supporting Mr Courtney and of promoting the policies he supported, but there was no peace or conciliation in the hall.

The account in the *Cornish Times* of July 7th 1900, with its headlines 'Peace Meeting at Liskeard ... Uproarious Proceedings ... Speakers Refused a Hearing ... Platform Stormed—Meeting Broken up in Disorder' has a familiar ring today, but the unsigned report is probably worth reproducing, for it shows not only the tension which prevailed in the relatively remote County of Cornwall on the rights and wrongs of the war, but the resource with which Emily tried to win over the hecklers, the courage with which she faced a hostile crowd and the scorn and contempt which she somewhat tactlessly measured out to her audience, when she saw that she was unsuccessful in getting a hearing:

'A public meeting was held at the Public Hall, Liskeard, on Thursday evening, under the auspices of the South Africa Conciliation Committee, in order to advocate an early close of the conflict with the Boers and a settlement which should conciliate the Dutch in the two Republics. Mr A. T. Quiller-Couch, of Fowey, the well-known novelist, presided, and the speakers were announced to be Miss Ellen Robinson of Liverpool; Miss Emily Hobhouse, secretary of the Conciliation Committee and Mr D. Lloyd George, the Radical member for Carnarvon. The announcement of the meeting caused great interest in the town and district, where political feeling has of late been unusually excited, and it was anticipated from the first that the proceedings would not pass off without some demonstration of opposition to the views set forth by the Committee. These expectations proved only too well justified. From the very beginning the temper of the large audience that filled the Hall was evidently unfavourable to the object of the meeting. The chairman had to bring his opening remarks to a hurried conclusion, and after this the crowd practically captured the meeting. Neither of the lady speakers could gain a hearing for more than a few minutes; Mr Lloyd George was unable even to utter a word, and after a scene of uproar and disorder unparalleled in Liskeard, the platform was stormed by a party of young fellows, many of whom bore miniature Union Jacks, and the meeting was broken up in confusion.

'Prior to the meeting "Imperialist" literature was freely distributed to those assembling in the streets around the Hall, and the expectation of a lively gathering attracted a crowded audience within the building. A good number of ladies were present, with numerous residents in the country districts, but quite half the Hall was filled with townsmen, who, even before the proceedings began, manifested their sentiments by singing and whistling patriotic airs, and vociferously cheering Private Webber, of the 2nd D.C.L.I. who came in from Hessenford to attend the meeting, wearing his khaki uniform. The waving

101

of a Union Jack was the signal for renewed cheering, and calls for cheers for Lord Roberts and Buller were readily responded to. The entrance of the Chairman and speakers was the signal for an outburst of shouting. "God Save The Queen" was started, and the whole audience, with the occupants of the platform, rose and joined in the singing of the National Anthem. Vociferous cheers followed for Her Majesty, amid the waving of the flag, and after this demonstration the audience settled down for a few minutes, and allowed the Chairman to open the meeting.

'The CHAIRMAN, who throughout his speech, had to contend with repeated interruptions, spoke under great difficulty, and often what he said must have been inaudible except to those in the first few seats. He said in an ordinary way, he supposed, his duty as Chairman would be merely to introduce the speakers, to whom they would listen with more profit than to him, and then sit down and efface himself They would agree with him, however, that the circumstances were not quite ordinary, and he hoped they would allow him to spend a few minutes in dwelling on the war—(three cheers for Tommy Atkins and disorder). The war in South Africa had brought several electors—many electors—into sharp opposition to Mr Courtney—(loud groans and hisses). Mr Courtney had served them long, and was one whom they had trusted long—("No more," and uproar). In the past they had been proud of him and he had reflected back honour on the constituency. They might tell him that all this was to come to an end, and even if it did so, he thought they could help feeling sorry, for sad the parting of the ways must be between old friends—(uproar). But Mr Courtney did not hide from himself that the war in South Africa, and the diplomacy which prefaced it, had magnified differences which in 1895 might have seemed unimportant to them. A great wave of what was called Imperialism had swept over the country. It had swept men off their feet, or off their heads, he was not quite certain which—("No, no" and interruption) —and the Liberal Unionist Association of South East Cornwall had turned their back upon Mr Courtney—("Quite right" and loud applause)—and had chosen another candidate for the next General Election—(applause). He did not know what the speakers who followed him would have to say, but he himself was not a member of the South Africa Conciliation Committee. He was merely a private citizen, whose judgement refused to approve of the war—(hisses). But the speakers who were to follow him came to them with higher credentials. Despising popularity and forgetting party they had come to speak the truth as they saw it. The Chairman appealed to the traditions of the borough, to that openmindedness and sense of respect for the opinion of others which had been the peculiar historical pride of Liskeard in the past, and which, together with their representative, they had the honour of handing over to South East Cornwall in 1885—(disorder and a VOICE: "Not in 1900"). Appealing to those traditions, he also put before them the fact that the war they were engaged in was costing them over 100 men and about £750,000 per day. Those shattered bodies would have to be mourned—(interruption, and a VOICE: "Spit it out")—the wounded would have to be maintained when they returned. They were told, and a great number in that room seemed to agree, that the time was not convenient for speech; but their political opinions, whether they were right or wrong, could only command the respect as they had the courage to enunciate them—(hear, hear). They had been going through a very dark time; they had been derided, menaced, heaped with vulgar abuse, and denied the name of patriots. This had been a very dark hour, and how many impregnable positions had been lost simply for the lack of a voice to call to them through the darkness!—(interruption and the blowing of a tin trumpet).

'At this point somebody started "Soldiers of the Queen", and the song was continued to an accompaniment of stamping feet, whistling, catcalls, and other noises. One prominent gentleman mounted a chair and waved a red, white and blue flag, and at times "conducted" the singing, using the banner as a baton. Cheers were loudly given for some of the Generals in South Africa, with hoots for Kruger, and further cheers for "Joe Chamberlain". Sheer fatigue alone put a stop to the "music" for a time. Taking advantage of the lull, the Chairman continued his speech. "Let me assure you," he said, but was interrupted by someone shouting "Give somebody else a chance." "When the day comes," Mr Couch continued, "and it shows the Liberal position still held, there will be plenty of you to do the shouting, but it will be the men who stand together now who will be able to look each other in the face." Here the whistling and stamping broke out anew, and the squeaking of the tin trumpet added another discordant element. Mr Quiller Couch remained standing for a minute or so, and then asked Miss Robinson to address the audience, and hoped they would treat her with the respect a lady deserved.

'Miss ROBINSON rose, and for a few moments comparative quiet prevailed. She said: "It is very evident that many of us in this room are of different opinions about many things, but I expect that there is one thing we are all heartily agreed on, and that is a love for our native land—" (loud applause). "I do not suppose there is a single one of the boys at the back of the room, who are making such a noise, who does not love his native country, but perhaps they have different ideas of what their native country ought to be. In my younger days we loved England because we thought she held the first place amongst the nations. We believed her to be the champion of justice, liberty, and humanity, because we thought Englishmen were always fair and just, and that our country was the refuge of the weak and oppressed. We loved her, too, because we thought England upheld the standard of religion, to do justice and love mercy, and . . ."

'Here someone walked up the hall and his raising of a flag was the signal for another outburst of shouting, which continued for some minutes. Proceeding, Miss ROBINSON said: "Although England was sometimes at fault, still we believed she was pursuing that high ideal and there were still many in her midst who thought this was the England they loved. We are sorry to see a different ideal springing up in the land—a different England springing up, which seems only to worship strength and bigness—" (interruption). "We see a country which has, during the last decade, added four million square miles to her territory—" (loud and continuous applause). "Many of you seem to think that this is the true ideal of greatness . . ." A long interruption took place here, whilst the chorus of "The Absentminded Beggar" was repeated several times. Miss Robinson went on: "Some think that is the only ideal of true greatness and we, alas, hear some of our leading statesmen and some of the ministers of the gospel, many of our poets and writers, a great part of the Press, and nearly all the 'men in the street', as they are called, boast of that ideal of England that she should be big and strong, but that she should be good and just and noble they have no comprehension—" (disorder). "There are a great many of our countrymen—"

'Miss Robinson was interrupted by someone at the back of the hall starting the National Anthem, followed by "Rule Britannia" and other patriotic airs. For some time there was a perfect hubbub. Cheers were given for the Queen, our Generals at the front, and Sir Lewis Molesworth. Someone called for three cheers for Kruger, and loud groans were the result. During a moment's calm, Miss Robinson was heard indignantly to remark: "I have spoken at some hundreds of meetings during the past winter, but this is the first one at which..." The noise which followed almost baffles description. On two or three occasions she attempted to speak, but each attempt led to a renewal of the disturbance. Presently someone started the Doxology, and it was sung with even more fervour than is often the case in chapel. When the verse had ended the undaunted speaker uttered a few words, but the humming of the Cornish ballad "Trelawny" was the next item on the programme. This was apparently encored, for the air was repeated, to the accompaniment of stamping feet. Many of the audience rose to their feet to watch the noisy proceedings at the back. The vocal efforts continued, punctuated with cheering, a white-haired old "Imperialist" encouraging the "Boys" at the back by waving his hat, while the gentleman with the flag beat time. For ten minutes or so, Miss Robinson stood regarding the unruly audience with indignation and contempt. It being manifestly impossible to gain a hearing, she at last resumed her seat. It was some time before the noise in any way abated; flags were waved, chairs knocked about, and as a khaki-clad soldier from the front tried to leave the building, he was lifted shoulder-high, and this led to an outburst of cheering for "Tommy Atkins".

'The whole audience were on their feet, and some timid ladies in the vicinity at once took flight into the ante-rooms. After some time an interval of quiet was restored. Mr Baron mounted a chair, and he was understood to ask for a fair hearing for the ladies, but the crowd had taken possession of the meeting, and refused to listen to him, and continued to sing the National Anthem and other airs. He then came to the platform and appealed to the audience to give Miss Hobhouse a hearing, she having been standing a mute spectator of the scene for some minutes. The disorder having decreased somewhat, Miss HOBHOUSE said: "I think you will agree with me that if Her Gracious Majesty the Queen, to whom

105

you have sung, were present here now, she would be heartily ashamed of her Cornish subjects—" (uproar). "I have a great deal that I am anxious to say to you—" (hisses and groans). "Will you sit down for a few minutes and listen to me? It seems to me a strange thing that Cornishmen will not listen to a Cornish woman."

'A deafening noise followed, and Mr Baron again appealed for "a hearing for the lady." The Chairman also endeavoured to restore order, and after some time Miss Hobhouse continued with "Is it your wish that I should address . . ." but was allowed to go no further. "I have addressed meetings lately," she continued after two or three minutes' interval, "all over England—in Leicester, Leeds, Bradford, Liverpool, and Manchester—but it has remained for me to come to Cornwall to see the worst behaviour of all. I am quite sure that it is not the best of the Cornish people—" (hear, hear from the platform). "It is only a few thoughtless and foolish spirits—" (derisive laughter and hoots, and a deep voice from the back of the hall shouted "How do you find 'em in London?"). Stamping of feet again ensued, and "Trelawny" was hoarsely voiced. Miss Hobhouse, when she was permitted, thanked the audience for having sung to her the old ballad of her family, but she had heard quite enough of it. If they wanted to serve the Queen, let them behave like subjects of the Queen should. It was not in the order of the meeting that she should speak first. Miss Robinson was to have first addressed them. Miss Hobhouse struggled bravely through these sentences, but at last she was ineffectual in making her voice heard. "Trelawny" and "Soldiers of the Queen" were again shouted and when this was done, Miss Hobhouse indignantly exclaimed, making her voice heard above the din, "It seems strange that the people of Liskeard should allow a few thoughtless and ill-mannered boys to spoil a meeting—" (disorder). "But this kind of behaviour," she continued under great difficulty, "will do more to advance our cause than the most eloquent speeches we could deliver. The account of this meeting will be printed far and wide through England, and Cornish people will be held up to shame because they would not give a fair hearing, especially to a lady, on this most complicated question—" (uproar). "One wonders that the people of the town and an old and respected town like Liskeard, should endure a handful of thoughtless boys to upset their meeting. It does not seem credible. You should not

106

have come if you did not intend to give us a hearing, but now that you have, will you give us a fair hearing, and when we have finished you can ask as many questions and talk as much as you like. Remember," she added, in a voice almost inaudible to the Press, that "Manners maketh man—" (derisive laughter). Generals Baden-Powell and Buller were again cheered at this point, as was also Mr Chamberlain. When quiet was somewhat restored, Miss Hobhouse said: "It is very strange to me, after so many years of absence—" (disorder)—"to come again into the old familiar town and to see around me so many familiar faces and be thus treated. It is a sad thought that I should be advocating what I am told are unpopular views in the town. But it is a still sadder thing for me to hear that Cornish people feel so differently on this subject from what I conceive to be the right and noblest thing. It is a very great satisfaction to me to have the opportunity of putting before you to some extent the views which I believe are correct—" (uproar). "But I ask you to give me a quiet hearing, and then go home and think over what I have said. We have respect for the feelings and opinions of our opponents, and we ask for the same—" (applause from the platform). "It is impossible, on an evening like this, to touch on more than one or two points on so great and complicated a question as that which faces us in the South African problem. I thought I should have spoken later and taken up just the shreds of what the other speakers left unsaid but it has fallen out that I shall be the first to speak and I shall put before you just one aspect of the great question as it appears to me. A few weeks ago there was but one word on the lips of the people of London, and in the hearts of the people of England. All those . . ."

'A tremendous noise arose, which made it impossible for the speaker to finish the sentence. Twice she made an attempt to speak, saying she would address the first few rows of people if they could hear. "Rule Britannia" was being sung when she made this remark, and when those in the back of the hall thought she was addressing a few in the front, they put more power into their singing, accompanied by a continuous stamping.

'The chairman rose to remonstrate, but this was only provocative of another wild outburst of shouting and cheering. Mr R. H. Lee mounted a chair and was understood to ask the audience to give the ladies a hearing. Mr T. Peters also addressed a portion of the meeting from the middle of the hall, and was understood to say that the reproaches of the lady speaker were themselves provoking the audience to disorder. Mr Baron attempted to quell the disturbance, but all efforts were useless. The Chairman shouted: "Do the respectable people of Liskeard wish the ladies to be insulted? Do they? Why do they allow the meeting to be dictated to by a lot of boys?" This appeal was unheeded and unheard by the noisy element, and it was not until four burly policemen took up positions near the main entrance that order was in any way restored.

'For about ten minutes Miss Hobhouse was allowed to continue without interruption as she spoke of the heroic defence of Mafeking and the sufferings endured by the besieged. Loud cheering for the defenders of Mafeking at last drowned her words, and Miss Hobhouse remarked: "Yes; you may well cheer them; they deserve a cheer." The noise increased, and as the noisy ones saw that the police made no attempt to check them, they resumed their endeavours to break up the meeting, "God Save the Queen", being once more sung. Miss Hobhouse continued, but only the reporters could hear her remarks; "This I say, that those who desecrate the National Anthem by making it the means of interrupting meetings are the very last people who would ever follow the noble example which has been set them by the people of Mafeking, and would be the last to uphold their country in time of peril."

'Once more the uproar swelled, someone starting "The Englishman" and "The Death of Nelson", but both proved unsuccessful, and popular airs were tried. Miss Hobhouse re-addressed her remarks as to the abuse of the National Anthem particularly to the Press representatives. After the storm had spent itself somewhat, Miss Hobhouse said: "I have been speaking at meetings—large meetings, to which this is nothing but a private party—in the North of England, and have had perfect attention. The rest of England will read the account of what has happened tonight with disgust. I shall take away from Liskeard . . ." From the back of the hall rose the strains of "Men of Harlech", with deafening stamping and shouting, and Miss Hobhouse, seeing that any further attempt at speech would be useless, resumed her seat.

'A few expressed a wish to hear Mr Lloyd George, but as that gentleman rose to speak, the riot broke out with increased

violence. In fact, it was afterwards stated by leading Conservatives that the whole of the opposition to the meeting had been
aroused by Mr Lloyd George's observations in the House of
Commons last Friday, when he attributed most unworthy
motives to members of the Government in connection with
the war. The Hon. Member, as he came forward, was greeted
with hoots, cheers, catcalls, shrill whistles, and booing,
followed by "Soldiers of the Queen". The crowd was
evidently getting dangerously excited, and many more ladies
left the hall. Messrs R. N. Clemens and Baron led further
cheering for Balfour, Chamberlain, Buller, and others, while
Mr Lloyd George stood smiling at the table, but did not
attempt to utter a syllable. It was perfectly evident that
the crowd would not hear the Welsh MP at any price.

'Then came the culmination of the disorder. About fifty
young men of the town, some bearing miniature Union Jacks,
gradually worked their way up the hall, happily on the side
farthest from the Press table. Shouting, cheering and whistling they swept up the stairs and surged upon the platform,
where they occupied half the space and kept up a continuous
noise of shouting, singing and cheering. Still Mr Lloyd George
refused to give in and remained standing by the table. Seeing
this, one of the storming party made a dash with a view to
overturning the table, but was collared by Mr Arnold Eliott,
the local secretary of the meeting, and the attempt was
frustrated. The youths on the platform were good-humoured,
though noisy, and no attempt was made to molest the
speakers. But most of the chairs were seized and piled in a
heap across the middle of the platform behind the Chairman,
who remained seated. Gradually the platform was invaded
from the other end, and people were standing on the Press
table and on the chairs all over the room. Meanwhile, Miss
Hobhouse was greeted by several old St Ive friends among
the audience, and, with Mrs J. Eliott and Miss Robinson,
took the opportunity of distributing "Conciliation" leaflets
among the people in front. Many of these were at once torn
up and the pieces tossed contemptuously into the air, while
"Britons Never Shall be Slaves" was sung by the stormy
party.

'Presently a further demonstration attracted attention to
the floor of the hall. The khaki-clad soldier from Hessenford
was hoisted onto the shoulders of half a dozen men, who
carried him around the hall to the steps leading to the oppo-

site end of the platform, with the evident intention of taking possession of that portion also. While the tour of the hall was being made the opposition cheered and shouted frantically. On reaching the platform steps, the men carrying the soldier found their way barred by a group of men determined to resist the capture of the platform. One of the group on the platform, a Sergeant of Police on leave from Devonport and a brother of the soldier, pulled him off the shoulders of the men and for a moment a free fight seemed imminent. No blow, however, was struck, and the disturbers relinquished the idea of storming that side of the platform and retired to another part of the hall. Meanwhile, those who had possession of the other part of the platform continued to sing and shout with undiminished vigour.

'The proceedings would have passed off without violence had not Mr Lloyd George and Rev. Nicholas moved to the centre of the platform with a view to taking down the barricade of chairs. In a moment they were surrounded and rudely hustled till the retreated again to the front. But this rencontre had stirred the passion of the crowd, and when some of the pro-Boer sympathizers on the other side of the platform attempted to pull away the chairs, an ugly rush was made at them. On both sides the chairs were pulled away and thrown in all directions and as the two parties got within arm's reach several blows were struck. At this point the police made their appearance on the platform, and the conflict at once ceased. The ladies, with Mr Quiller Couch, Mr Lloyd George, and their supporters, were then persuaded to leave the hall, and the crowd formed a lane and allowed them to walk to the ante-room without molestation. Cheers for Lord Roberts and leading statesmen followed them. The mob remained in undisputed possession of the hall and platform, and for a quarter of an hour longer continued to amuse itself with shouting, singing, and horseplay. One of the leaders, attempting a vocal solo, approached too near the edge of the platform, waving a Union Jack, and fell over into the arms of the people below. Hoisted up again, amid roars of laughter, he addressed an imaginary chairman and then proceeded with his song. About half past nine the uproar came to an end, and after once again singing the National Anthem, the gathering dispersed.'

Emily, at this time, still stoutly maintained that her activities were non-political. She detested the idea of being chained to a political machine—she was a cat that liked to walk alone. Politics, moreover, could well have divided the sympathies of those women members of the Conciliation movement, who were drawn to it by emotion rather than reason. Politicians, too, would have interfered with Emily's own ideas of how the Women's branches should be run. Nevertheless, woman-like, she was ready to make use of politicians after her own fashion— as they were of her, after theirs—and it is difficult for even the most well-disposed biographer to accept Emily's assurances that her meetings did not bear a political character. It was not merely that she was anxious and willing to appear on the same platform as Mr Lloyd George for the purpose of promoting the views held by Mr Courtney. The resolutions which the South African Conciliation Committee favoured not only condemned Britain's policy but even expressed regret about it to the Queen's enemies. They also condemned any settlement involving the annexation of the Republics which, though it might be regarded as a moral issue, certainly also had political elements. Emily afterwards claimed that her appearances at meetings at Liskeard and elsewhere lost her most of her girl-hood friends and led to a 'storm of abuse' from relatives, but there is evidence that this was an over-dramatization of what really happened. In fact Emily received from her relatives a good deal more tolerance than she might have expected in a time of strong political controversy.

Emily's next enterprise, however, was patently less political and more humanitarian and she rapidly succeeded in tunnel-ling through the Government's defences and getting qualified approval for her activities from Mr Chamberlain himself.

She conceived and founded the South African Women and Children's Distress Fund, the object of which was to bring help —and hope—to women and children whether of Boer, British, or any other nationality who were homeless as a result of Britain's policy of farm burning, by providing them with food, clothing, shelter and other necessities.

Among its supporters were men and women of high repute and respectability including Sir Thomas Acland, Canon Barnett, Sir Edward Fry, the Dean of Hereford, the Bishop of Nottingham, the Marchioness of Ripon, Herbert Spencer, Mrs Humphrey Ward, Lady Rendel, Lady Farrer and of course Lord and Lady Hobhouse, who was Honorary Treasurer. Soon Lady Hobhouse wrote to Lord Lansdowne and Mr Chamberlain and even these experienced politicians could hardly fail to approve of the idea, provided that the food and clothing distributed by the Fund did not reach the enemy in the field, and they promised to write to Sir Alfred Milner about it.

Not everyone reacted favourably to Emily's proposals and Emily preserved among her papers the name of one cleric who had refused a contribution lest keeping Boer women and children alive should serve to prolong the war. Others said that support might cast reflections on the honour of the British soldier.

In the meantime Emily had made her own preparations. While she collected money to be handed over to the Fund, she told her uncle and aunt that she was determined to go to South Africa herself to organize the relief; she let her flat and, before even the Executive Committee was fully formed, she had booked a second-class passage to Cape Town. Thus, when she handed over the money, amounting to £300, to the Fund, there could hardly have been any doubt as to who would be entrusted with handling it. It was not merely that Emily was a mistress in the art of presenting her friends and acquaintances with *faits accomplis*; in addition, her work with the South African Conciliation Committee had given her many contacts in South Africa, while at the same time she had received a good deal of information on where help was most urgently needed. Accordingly the Fund agreed to hand over her 'nest egg', as she called it, to a bank with instructions for it to be sent to Cape Town and held there at her disposal.

Emily's tactics of surprise—she sailed on December 7th—meant, of course, that she was obliged to pay her own fare to South Africa, and, although this gave her a measure of independence, she had to travel alone—with no maid or prospective bridesmaid on this occasion. She filled in her time during the cruise—for they called at the Canaries on the way—in reading up the history of South Africa and in learning something of its language.

Meantime, in Britain, the prolongation of the war continued to exasperate and humiliate the Government and led Chamberlain to urge that no supplies which would enable the Boers to carry on the war should be left, even in friendly hands. It was also a mistake, he thought, to allow Boers who had surrendered and had been released on parole, to return to areas which were still 'disaffected'.

Kitchener, who took over full command from Roberts at the

end of November, felt bound in turn to introduce stiffer
measures in the hope of bringing the war to a successful conclusion. In December, six months after the war was supposed to
have ended and a month after the *Times* had published *The
History of The Boer War*, Kitchener was asking for more troops
to be sent out from home. About the time of Emily's arrival
in South Africa, Lieutenant Morrison, an officer serving with
the Canadian Artillery wrote a letter home, extracts of which
were forwarded to the *New York Sun* (normally a pro-British
paper) by their correspondent in Ottawa. The letter described
the advance of the Imperial Forces through the countryside to
the north of Belfast, in the eastern Transvaal:

'During the trek our progress was like the old-time forays
in the highlands of Scotland two centuries ago. We moved
on from valley to valley lifting cattle and sheep, burning, looting and turning out the women and children to sit and weep
in despair beside the ruins of their once beautiful farm-
steads. It was the first touch of Kitchener's iron hand—a
terrible thing to witness.

'We burned a track about six miles wide through these
fertile valleys. The column left a trail of fire and smoke behind
it that could be seen at Belfast.'

Describing the sack of Dullstroom, the letter continues:

'Nobody who was there will ever forget that day's work.
about seven o'clock in the morning our force seized the town
after a little fight. The Boers went into the surrounding hills
and there was nobody in the town except women and children. It was a very pretty place, nestling in a valley. The houses
had lovely flower gardens and the roses were in bloom. The
Boers drove in our outposts on the flank and began sniping
the guns, and amid the row of the cannonade and the crackle
of rifle fire the sacking of the place began.

'First there was an ominous bluish haze over the town, and
then the smoke rolled up in volumes that could be seen for
fifty miles away. The Boers on the hills seemed paralysed by
the sight and stopped shooting.

'The town was very quiet, save for the roaring and crackle
of the flames. On the steps of the church a group of women
and children were huddled. The women's faces were very
white, but some of them had spots of red on either cheek
and their eyes were blazing.

'The troops were systematically looking the place over, and as they got quite through with each house they burned it.'

In earlier days an unsuccessful attempt had been made to offload women and children onto the Boer 'economy' and in July 1900 Major-General Maxwell issued a proclamation that 'in order to avoid the increase in destitution caused by burghers deserting their wives and children to continue hostilities, wives and children or relatives residing in the town of Pretoria or burghers in arms against the forces of Her Britannic Majesty shall, failing proof by them to the satisfaction of the Commissioner of Police on or before 19th July 1900 that they possess adequate means of subsistence, be deported to a place beyond the British lines to be hereafter determined by me.' Two consignments were indeed exported but the practice ceased abruptly when the Boers threatened to re-export the refugees to Europe.

In October the flow of refugees had been stimulated by an Order which said that the crops of men on commando could be reaped and carried off without the formality of a receipt, and the same month British troops were ordered to collect all farming gear within reach of their posts.

In his orderly, pigeon-hole mind, Kitchener divided the refugees into four different classes. There were the families of burghers who had surrendered, and who came in either voluntarily or were brought in to save them from reprisals by the enemy; there were dependents who were actively engaged in passing information to the enemy; there were families from farms which were used as sniper's posts and there were others from farms which were used mainly as food depots. And indeed, at first, attempts were made to distinguish between the states of mind in which refugees became refugees and to discriminate accordingly as to the food rations they should receive. When the first refugee camps were set up in September at Bloemfontein and Pretoria they were supposed to be for refugees who had surrendered voluntarily. But this distinction soon broke down. In Kitchener's own words, published in January 1901, 'I some time ago took measures for the establishment of properly organized camps at certain selected sites on the lines of railways, at which surrendered burghers are permitted to live with their families under our effective protection. The families of all burghers still under arms are as far as possible brought in from the adjacent districts and similarly lodged in these camps.'

But this 'bringing in as far as possible', Kitchener represented, was an act of mercy and not of compulsion or the result of capture. 'My column commanders,' he said, 'have orders to leave women and children alone unless it is clear that they must starve if they are left out upon the veldt.'

It is doubtful whether Emily would have appreciated any such distinction between the refugees brought in, and she certainly failed to make use of another distinction which was to become more and more important to her as the months rolled on—between the aims and objectives of Kitchener in the field and those of Milner in the seat of Government. The two men were mutually irreconcilable characters: Milner was scrupulous, sensitive, outwardly firm but withdrawn and sometimes without assurance of what should be his own guiding principles. 'He would have been made by being loved,' said Granville Barker, Fabian, and Manager of the Royal Court Theatre, after lunching with him in his later years. Kitchener, unlike Milner, had the complete contempt of the successful Army general for any authority other than his own. His authority was reinforced rather than diminished by his shy, awkward and nervous manner, his long silences and his apparent reluctance to look at the person he was addressing—so much so that Henry Nevinson during an interview, 'could not decide whether he was talking to me or Ian Hamilton'. His appearance, for in those days he had not yet become a figure of fun, was formidable; cheeks almost purple from sunburn and wrinkled with two gashes from abscessed glands, cold grey eyes, a mouth entirely hidden by a monstrous moustache and a heavy jowl that meant business.

It was not that Milner in his political attitude was any more friendly than Kitchener towards the Boers—indeed the Cape Dutch had been shocked to observe at a garden party given by Admiral Sir Robert Harris at the naval base of Simonstown, that Milner apparently glanced with approval at a coconut shy, in which the figures to be knocked down were crude representations of Kruger, Steyn and other Afrikaner leaders. They were unconvinced by the official explanation that Milner was known to be extremely short-sighted.

Nor did Milner see how some camps were avoidable. For, as he himself pointed out, the idea of boarding out thousands of Boers with loyal families would have been as unthinkable as it would have been to have boarded 10,000 French women and children with German *hausfraus* during the Franco-Prussian war. An arrangement of this kind in South Africa would, he said, 're-enact in thousands of families the fights which have

115

already been fought and would surely intensify the race hatred which all well-wishers of South Africa should desire to allay.' Camps, even large ones, could indeed be the sorting houses in which loyal citizens could be separated from the undesirables.

Milner would greatly have preferred that the loyalists should be protected in their own homes and not become refugees. Given a free hand his policy would, as he declared, have been:

1. to take all houses possible, area by area
2. to burn no houses except for treachery (homeless people become brigands)
3. to clear no areas of food supplies
4. to round up people and not cattle
5. to secure the cooperation of the inhabitants

His view was that by devastation 'we create more black-guards.'

The differences between Milner and Kitchener could however be summed up after another fashion. Kitchener's strategy was to restrict military occupation to an area which he could be sure of controlling and to lay waste the remainder of the Republics. Milner on the contrary believed that loyalty to Britain could best be maintained by insulating as much of the country as possible from the struggle, by extending the area under civil (his own) administration and by exempting it from Martial Law. He saw that this policy would help to speed the reconstruction of the country for which he himself would no doubt be responsible.

For some time, however, Milner's opposition to Kitchener remained fairly well concealed. One reason was that Whitehall's policy was one of finishing the war at all costs. Another was that Kitchener, wary of the fumbledom and bumbledom of authority, was sensible enough not to disclose his intentions to Milner any more than to the enemy. Thirdly, about the time of Emily's arrival, Milner had received a practical demonstration of the unwisdom of occupying more territory than it was possible to control.

Shortly after Kitchener took over, the Boers mounted a second invasion of the Cape, partly in retaliation for the farm-burning in the Free State, partly to get supplies denied to them by Britain's scorched-earth policy and partly in the hope of stirring up new resistance in the Cape.

The enemy, in Milner's words, 'have now marched two commandos right through the Colony and are hundreds of miles nearer Cape Town than they ever were before'.

This was the situation at the Cape when Emily stepped ashore on December 27th on a glorious summer's morning. She was at once charmed as thousands of visitors have been by the glory of the scene—the theatrically mauve and green seas spread before the towering rampart of Table Mountain, the cream-coloured houses festooned with purple and red bougainvilia, the stately avenues of eucalyptus and evergreen oak trees, the gardens ablaze with scarlet hibiscus, the natives dressed in weirdly striped blankets and, above, the blue sky stretching to eternity.

Almost at once she was snapped up, a willing prisoner of those as ready to tell her, as she was ready to learn, of the hardships which the war was inflicting on those living beyond the borders of Cape Colony. She learnt for the first time that refugee camps existed, other than those established in the Cape for loyalist refugees. In those she met, she found a reflection of her own feelings—a sense of bewilderment over the mother country's decision to make war on the relatives of her own subjects, and a sense of injustice over the fact that these subjects were comp-elled to remain neutral and were even debarred from offering shelter to members of their own families, lest the latter act as agents of subversion.

Sir Alfred of course had already heard as many complaints as he wished, particularly since most of them arose through a policy that was not his own. But, in deference to the fact that Emily brought personal letters of introduction to him, he invited her to lunch, hoping no doubt to pass the whole matter off some-time between the soup and the salad, as it were, more especially since it was a lunch at which there were eight men and no other women likely to chip in with frivolous comments. But when he began to broach the subject, Emily, a great believer in heart-to-heart talks, broke in and said quite firmly that she could not discuss the matter during lunch. Sir Alfred, who then was a bachelor and wary of all women, said that he would be too busy afterwards with his work. Emily countered that the welfare of refugees was part of his work and Sir Alfred, perhaps to avoid a scene (women in those days usually tried one if they did not get their way, and Emily seemed more tense than most), promised her an audience of fifteen minutes (the shortest known period of British Civil Service time) but no more. Once seated on Sir Alfred's sofa after coffee, Emily turned the full pressure of her moral authority on him and drew from him an admission that he was only too ready to make, namely that the policy of farm burning was mistaken. Emily pointed out that the refugee policy was turning women into martyrs and creating resentment that it would be impossible to wipe out for many years, perhaps for ever. She dilated on the sufferings of the women and children which she was able to affirm with greater authority than Milner was able to deny. And she spoke of details seldom, if ever before, mentioned in Sir Alfred's drawing room—and certainly not by an English spinster. Finally, she turned the screw by warning him how uneasy public opinion was getting, not only in Britain but elsewhere abroad, where Britain's good name was in jeopardy.

At the end of an hour, Sir Alfred, disconcerted, capitulated. He said that he would do everything in his power to arrange for Emily to go round the camps as representative of the English supporters of the Fund, together with Mrs Roos, the wife of a Dutch Minister and two railway trucks, one filled with clothes, the other with food.

Emily found Sir Alfred quite charming and came out from her interview certain that everything was going her way. It was perhaps a little risky on her part to have proposed that, in addition to Mrs Roos, she should take with her Mrs Ellie Cronje, whose knowledge of the country would be invaluable. And so indeed it might have been but Mrs Cronje was not perhaps the most unprejudiced person to visit British camps and reconcile the inmates to their lot. For indeed, as the daughter of General Cronje captured by the British, she was herself one of the 'martyrs'.

However, there was not much risk to the war effort, for Kitchener on this occasion was made of sterner stuff than Milner. In reply to Milner's letter of January 11th, he sent a telegram six days later, and four days after that Lord Milner communicated the contents of the telegram to Miss Hobhouse.

Kitchener, to put it mildly, was only half delighted at the prospect of having to look after two civilian women, one or perhaps both of whom might be pro-Boer sympathizers. He said that he had already been asked and had agreed to distribute funds among 'Dutch women kept out of their homes by the Boers' but that no funds had arrived. He assumed that Miss Hobhouse was the bearer. He had no objection to her coming as far as Bloemfontein, but no further north at present. 'I hope this will be clearly understood,' he added. He would also prefer that she was not accompanied by a Dutch lady. There were numbers of ladies in Bloemfontein who would give her every assistance.

Kitchener did not exclude the possibility of sending relief funds to the north for distribution by the Military Governors and the Controller of Refugee camps who would send Miss Hobhouse receipts for anything entrusted to them. One thousand pounds (more than three times what Emily had collected) would be very acceptable, Kitchener said.

While some of this news was anything but welcome to Emily, who was operating in a strange country speaking an almost strange language—she did not stay to argue.

A rush to Government House, a second interview with Milner and kind Mr Waldron, his Secretary, helped to speed Emily on her way. The military put a twelve-ton covered bogie-waggon at her disposal and it was loaded the very same day with groceries, bedding and bales of clothing—though the goods Emily had brought failed noticeably to fill it.

Emily set off the next day, armed with a letter of authorization from Lord Milner, with Lord Kitchener's somewhat ungracious telegram and the knowledge that Milner had also written in advance to General Pretyman, the Military Governor of the Orange River Colony, asking him to help Emily in any way he could. And so in brilliant moonlight on the night of January 22nd, she set off on a military train from Cape Town northwards through the Karoo desert, alone with bread, some melted butter, some apricot jam and a 'kettle lamp' for making tea and cocoa.

She was still believed by the British Government to be on the whole a 'Good Fairy'.

7

Miss Hobhouse saw

It was not the 'refugee' camps which first determined Emily to journey northwards. The very existence of any camps for Boer families had been unknown to her when she first landed (though she knew of one established in the Cape Province for 'loyal' refugees). She had however sensed from the course of the war that Boer women and children must be in want, and had always been determined to see things for herself, and what she learnt from letters from Afrikaners who had managed to evade the strict censorship operating made her doubly determined.

Mrs George Moll, the wife of a prisoner-of-war, had, for example, been able to write from Durban to Mrs Steytler in Cape Town as follows:

'You will no doubt be surprised to get a letter from me, who am quite a stranger to you, but I feel as if I must make our case known to you noble women of the Cape, so that you can publish it in one of the Cape papers. What I intend telling you I declare before God is the solemn and honest truth.

'My husband was taken prisoner at Elandslaagte thirteen months ago. I had to manage alone with my two children, which I did very well until the British came to Vrede the 23rd August. We lived about an hour from the town. At the time when they came I was staying in town, as I had just had a baby which was a month old. The British went out to the farm and destroyed all my furniture and clothing. From there they went to the veld and took all the cattle belonging to me. The herdsman told them that the owner of the cattle had been captured and that I was in town; but the answer was "She ought to have been here on the farm,"

and that they would take everything; so I was left without
anything.

'The second time the British occupied Vrede (a month
later), they first went to my sister's house (Mrs Cornelius
Moll) and drove her and her children out of the house
without anything, so she fled to my house. A little later they
came and told us to keep ourselves in readiness to go to
Standerton.

'We had only a few hours to get ready, when they sent
a bullock waggon to load us up for the journey. We didn't
go very far when the side of the waggon gave way. We almost
fell between the wheels. They shifted us into another old
waggon a very little better. So we had to travel to Standerton.
When we got there we were locked up in a dirty old schoolroom. The door was guarded by armed men. They brought us
food after we were almost starved, which consisted of six tins
of bully-beef and some biscuits (klinkers) in a dirty grain-bag,
which was thrown down in front of us; the poor children
could not eat the biscuits as they were too hard.

'Next morning early we were marched to the station, and
ten of us were packed into a third-class compartment and
the door was locked. We had to sit up straight for two whole
days and a night without being allowed to go out once. Our
poor children wanted to get out but they could not. They
were almost starved. They would not allow me to get food
for my baby, who was then little more than two months
old. She had to travel all the way, you may say, without anything. Miss Marie le Roux (who is now in Caledon) and I
warmed some water over a candle (as I wasn't allowed to
buy spirits or anything) to mix a little condensed milk for the
child.

'Along the road they told the Kaffirs to drive us nicely as
they were going to marry us when we got to Natal.

'When we got here we had to stand for ever so long with
our tired, hungry children, not knowing where to go. After a
lot of bother we were marched off to a private boarding-
house, and we were kept there for a week, when we got notice
that we would have to pay our own expenses in the future.
We had no money. We only left with a few pounds in our
pockets. You can never imagine what we had to go through.
We managed to hire a cottage, so we took in a few of our
people who are on parole here—Mr Enslin, our Dutch
minister from Vrede, and a few others, so we have to manage

121

along. We can hardly make ends meet. We heard from some of the inhabitants of Durban that the military say we asked them for protection, which is a falsehood—we never did anything of the kind. That's why they say we were sent down here. We have to report ourselves every day like the men. My sister was very ill just before we left Vrede. She was taken away sick and has been sick ever since. She asked the doctor here for a certificate to show the military that the heat was too much for her.'

Another similar letter had gone from Miss Ellie Cronje to Miss Hauptfleisch, whom Emily met in the Cape:

'Our farm lies three hours from Winburg. On the morning of the 18th two men came to the house and asked who the owner of the farm was, whether he was still fighting, who my mother was, and whether any of my brothers were still fighting. I answered these questions. They then asked if the Boers called at the house when passing, and whether any of them actually entered the house, and who these were. We told them the Boers did call when they passed; how could we prevent them, our own people, when we could not keep the soldiers out? Mother said she never asked their names, and added, "I do not ask you what your name is; you go away and I never know to whom I have been speaking." Then they tried to find out about the Boers from the Kaffir boys. Just before riding away they called the boy aside, and told him to tell mother to carry out her furniture because they were coming back with Colonel White's men to burn the house. We had about an hour to carry out furniture from the drawing and bedrooms, our piano and sideboard. While we were busy the troops came. They poured something over the floors to make them burn, and soon the dwelling-house and outside buildings were in flames, and soon our comfortable home was gone. My mother, our lady friend, and I remained outside amongst the furniture we had removed and watched the burning. One of the men asked where we intended sleeping that night. I said, "If I had burned the house I would have known where to have gone and what to have done." Others said, "You have to thank Presidents Steyn and Kruger for this. Why do they not come and give in, why do they go about like robbers?" So we said, "They will never, never give in; they are fighting for their country, and you are fighting women because you know they will not shoot

122

back." We also asked would they give in if we were fighting them and started burning their houses and sending women into the open veld without a morsel of food because their husbands and fathers and brothers would not give in? While we were still carrying out things the cutlery was taken from the sideboard drawers, along with a lot of things from the kitchen. A soldier helped himself from our butter-barrel with his hands, and when we asked him to leave that alone he replied we might be thankful we had saved something, by rights everything should have gone. That night we slept out among the furniture standing on the *werf,* the wind carrying sparks over our heads. Twice during the night the stables caught fire, and we got up to put it out so that we might have some shelter for the next night. Next day we had the stables cleaned and our goods carried in there and there we slept the second night. They now took our remaining horses, cattle and other things, and were going to send to gather the sheep. I asked for one cow to be left. The reply was, "Not one—not one." Thirteen waggons were sent to take all the homeless women to the town. On that day seventeen other families had been made homeless. Most of these are very poor and have a lot of little children. We did not want to go to the town, and asked to be left on the farm, hoping to be allowed to remain in the stables; there was no help for it, we had to go.'

Mrs John Murray, the wife of the missionary in the district of Waterberg, Transvaal, in a letter dated December 17th 1900 to one of her relatives, told a similar story. She said that when the order came to burn down her house, she protested, saying that the house was not her own but Church property. But the officers refused to listen. So she hurriedly collected a few clothes and put them on the stoep for loading on the waggon, but the soldiers tossed them all away. She had to come away in the old dress she was wearing about the house, and carried only a small parcel of a few necessaries for the baby. She and her neighbours with their children were placed on the waggon and driven through the British camp towards Warmbaths. Soldiers guarded the waggon with fixed bayonets both in front and behind. At Warmbaths they were put into a truck which had carried cattle the day before and had not been cleaned out, and sat in it in the cold without wraps throughout the journey from 10 a.m. to 10 p.m. when they arrived at Pretoria. Mrs Murray asked to be allowed to go to her aunt, Mrs Louis Botha, but this was refused. She protested that her children would perish of cold if they sat all night long in the cattle-truck. Upon this they were allowed to go into the ladies' waiting-room and were locked in. Every scrap of furniture had been taken out of this room, even the carpet, and there was nothing to sit or lie on but the bare floor. It was lighted above by a skylight, which was out of order and would not shut, and the night was bitterly cold. Mrs Murray lay down on the floor with her maid and the children, and the wind streamed down from the skylight and they could not sleep. She took off her own skirt and wrapped one child in that, the other was wrapped in the maid's skirt. The baby screamed all night from cold and hunger. In the morning Mrs Murray called out to the soldiers from the window, 'If you do not let us out this child will die.' At first they said she must stay where she was, for she was to be taken down to the Women's Camp at Port Elizabeth, but finally they allowed her to go and see her aunt. Mrs Botha took her at once to Governor Maxwell, and through her influence Mrs Murray was allowed to proceed to her parents in Natal.

The tribulations of the Afrikaners began days and sometimes weeks before they could reach the shelter of a British bell-tent. A typical experience that came to Emily's notice was that of Mrs Liebenberg, who was bathing the baby at half past five one evening when the British 'Khakis' called. She had to sleep in pitch dark on the side of a hill without a tent, after having watched her house burned to the ground. Distrust between the two sides led to needless cruelty, as for instance when the British refused to believe Catherine Labuschagne's story that her young child, who had died that week, had been buried, the day before, in a newly-dug grave. They suspected an arms cache and dug up the body. Similarly it was infinitely safer to kill a pet dog 'because it barked too much' than to risk pinpointing a British position to the enemy. Some cruelty which appeared wanton was in fact unavoidable. Thus, no ordinary military intelligence could have told the British in advance that some families who resisted the move really were suffering from measles, or that Mrs Hayns, who was turned out of her farm at Fouriesburg at ten minutes notice, with her four small children, was expecting a fifth. Nor did the military bother to explain to her that the reason she was not allowed to draw water from her own well was that they suspected she might throw salt into it.

Various ruses were adopted by the British to induce the

owners to leave their farms without too much fuss. Families were told, 'There's no need to take anything with you. You'll find everything you need at the camp.' Around Winburg, particularly, the British just waited until the mother of the family came in to do her weekly shopping—albeit with an official pass—held her under house arrest and sent the cart back with the driver and perhaps one child to fetch the rest of the family. A hint that 'the Kaffirs' (armed presumably with British weapons) might be planning a raid also helped to get the families out of their homes, the British found. Indeed the Kaffirs did visit Mrs Sue Nicholson while the British were still on her farm and made off with the bed-linen, after which the children had to be wrapped in the winter curtains.

At times the British appeared to be in league with the natives. For example Mrs Hans Fourie of Winburg claimed that the British had refused to allow her to get out her son's better suit of clothes. But later she saw a native with them, and when she begged him for them, he said they belonged to the British Government. A few minutes later he was wearing them.

For the children perhaps the saddest moment came when they had to part from their pets—from the horses, which, after being commandeered broke away from the military and came back to look over the garden gate—after which they had to be handed over once again. Sometimes the only record of a sad parting was a note in a child's handwriting pinned to the farm gate: 'Please feed my chickens and turkeys.'

A few families resolutely refused to give in. Mrs De la Rey, wife of the General, spent nineteen months on the veld with her four children, and her cows and chickens. Mrs P. Joubert of Wakkerstroom survived for ten months alone in a large wood.

For the others there was the journey first in mule or horse convoy and then on by rail. And the convoys limped on their way. Often the waggons were forced off the road and halted to allow gun carriages, ammunition carts or ambulances to pass. There were days when the convoy halted too late at night for meat to be slaughtered, and in this case food was handed out from no-one-knew-where and the women complained that they had to run from one waggon to another in search of scraps. Sometimes they had to harness up and start out again in pitch darkness when the enemy was said to be on the prowl. At other times the horses were so weak that all were compelled to walk. Occasionally, when no other arrangements were convenient, a family might be taken to watch the farmhouses of neighbouring friends being burnt.

A journey by train might be no more agreeable. The time of departure might be delayed—perhaps through the fault of the enemy rather than of the British—for anything from hours to days, while the women and children waited in the hot sun. At one station Emily recognized a contingent of women and children, whom she had noticed when her train passed through the same station ten days earlier. They were still waiting to be moved.

When the train eventually started—perhaps at night—often the only shelter provided consisted of the low walls of an open sheep truck coupled a short way behind the engine which belched sparks and coal dust. It was awkward, too, that a truck was held to accommodate exactly thirty-three people. Awkward because it often meant that a mother might be separated from her child. Also, the journey had to be completed under military discipline—which meant that in cases where a child died from one cause or another, there might be no time to stop and bury it.

Emily herself learnt something of the hardships of wartime travelling. Even in Cape Town things were abnormal. The docks were piled high with forage for the cavalry, the streets jammed with army waggons and men in uniform, and the shops charged wartime prices. Even with Lord Kitchener's blessing it took Emily the best part of two days to cover the five hundred miles from Cape Town to Bloemfontein, for the train had no restaurant car and, every so often, had to stop at a convenient station long enough for all concerned to have a meal. It was difficult for Emily to play the part of a lady of quality in a train that had travelled through an area of dust storms, and she found the refreshment rooms crowded with British officers who appeared not especially anxious to treat this middle-aged, none too fashionably dressed interloper as one of themselves. The food, too, was unappetizing, and Emily seizing as was her custom, the chance of living on her own terms, untrammelled by masculine muddle, contented herself with the remains of her melted butter, bread and apricot jam from a tin (as supplied normally only to troops, explorers or working-class folk).

Through the carriage window she viewed the Karoo in the height of summer, and like many of those who saw it for the first time, she considered it to be without sign of life. Here and there she saw the carcasses of horses and mules and burnt-out farms and others deserted with no labourers or livestock visible. Down the line she befriended the Tommies, yawning at their posts. They begged for newspapers at the carriage window. 'I gave them all I had, and all my novels,' Emily said in one of her reports to the Fund.

And now, on arrival at Bloemfontein on the afternoon of January 24th, the faintest signs of future trouble arose. In the first place, Emily, not having benefited signally from her position as the only woman on the train, began to resent the world of men, in which she found herself, and to rebel against the observances of Martial Law which required her to show her papers to some new military picket every ten yards (or so it seemed). Secondly, instead of presenting herself forthwith to General Pretyman, to whom she had an introduction and on whom she would depend for facilities, she took a room for herself in a private hotel and, next morning allowed herself to be fetched in the carriage of Mrs Fichardt (one of whose family, it will be remembered, had been designated as being a prominent resident of Bloemfontein, and consequently eligible for hostage duty aboard a military train). Mrs Fichardt lived in style in a cool and spacious house in the town and, since Emily already had an introduction to her, what could be more natural for a hospitable Afrikaner than to ask this charming English stranger to rest there a while? Emily, who was dependent on her own resources in South Africa, was not averse to saving money and was unwilling to recognize that this placed her under an obligation to 'the enemy'. On the contrary, she was only too pleased to have got into direct contact with one of the ladies who, Kitchener had promised, would be so helpful to her when he refused her permission to bring a Dutch lady with her from Cape Town. She was therefore deeply shocked when Mrs Fichardt told her that the military might consider her hospitality to Emily an act of subversion and visit their displeasure on the Fichardt family. She must insist that Emily get permission in writing from the General before taking up residence.

Emily was distressed, but all the more determined to stay with Mrs Fichardt.

Of all this General Pretyman was completely unaware when Emily presented herself at Government House, and he welcomed her warmly; he gave her a permanent pass to visit the refugee camp, introduced her to the Superintendent and told her that her suggestions would be considered, and that he would be glad to hear from her what she thought of the camp.

The General said that he had hoped to ask Emily to stay at Government House, but unfortunately they were in the midst of a bout of typhoid and the place was full of doctors and nurses. He was shocked to the core when Emily said she wanted to stay with Mrs Fichardt. 'Oh but she is very bitter,' he protested, for he was no doubt aware that her daughters in Cape Town had recently been refused permission to join her. 'Just so,' Emily replied, 'but my visit may have a softening effect on her.' Nonplussed (for he did not wish to offend a visitor who came to him with such good credentials) the General wrote out a pass while Emily stood triumphantly looking over his shoulder.

Then, having made arrangements for her truck of goods to be unloaded, she set out one afternoon in the blazing sun to make her first acquaintance with a refugee camp, her parasol at the ready. More shocks awaited her. She had come to South Africa prepared to hand out comforts and extras which the authorities could not have been expected to provide. In practice she found that the barest necessities were wanting. There was no soap provided (it was said that the British soldier got none). There was not enough water to go round; there was almost no fuel. Two miles outside Bloemfontein she found a village of two thousand people—nine hundred of them children and the rest, mainly women, with a few surrendered Boers. They were living six or more to a tent in conditions so crowded that there was no room even for the barest furniture. The atmosphere, even with the tent-flaps open, was indescribable. The refugees seemed to have become anonymous, for the camp had no streets nor the tents names or numbers. Few families had mattresses; most had to sleep wrapped in blankets on the bare ground—even the expectant mothers, who, if permitted, would have brought their own baby linen with them. The flies swarmed everywhere.

While Emily was on this first visit a puff adder crawled in under the flap of the tent and she attacked and 'wounded' it with her parasol. One could have expected nothing less of Emily. But a hardship more serious than the risk of snakes was the certainty of rain, which flowed in rivers through the tents. And the rain in South Africa deserves special mention. G. W. Steevens, the *Daily Mail* war correspondent, described it as 'a sheer sheet of water'. 'With the first stabbing drops,' he wrote, 'horses turned their heads away, trembling, and no whip or spur could bring them up to it. It drove through mackintoshes as if they were blotting-paper. The air was filled with hissing; underfoot you could see solid earth melting into mud, and mud flow-

Emily's childhood home in Cornwall

Archdeacon Hobhouse in old age

Jackson's Store in Virginia, Minnesota

An early shack-town dwelling in Virginia, Minnesota

The first fire engine in Virginia, Minnesota

Emily in South Africa

ing away in water. It blotted out hill and dale and enemy in one grey curtain of swooping water.'

Emily had not to look far in Bloemfontein for firsthand stories of personal tragedy. There was Mrs Pienaar, mother of six children, whom the war had separated from all of them, leaving her without news of whether they were alive or dead. There was Mrs Reintjes with two children in hospital with typhoid, and four sick in her tent, compelled to stay in the camp, though she had relatives in the Cape who would have welcomed the whole family. 'It is so pathetic,' Emily wrote home, 'they think I have come from England with magic powers to set them free, and it's dreadful to explain that there's no chance of that;' and on January 26th:

'I call this camp system wholesale cruelty. It can never be wiped out from the memories of the people. It presses hardest on the children. They droop in the terrible heat. Will you try somehow to make the British public understand the position and force it to ask itself what is going to be done with these people? There must be a full 50,000 of them. In one of two ways the British Public must support them—either by taxation through the authorities or else by voluntary charity. If only the English people would try to exercise a little imagination and picture the whole miserable scene. Entire villages and districts rooted up and dumped in a strange bare place. To keep these camps going is murder for the children. Of course by judicious management they could be improved; but do what you will, you can't undo the thing itself.'

It was not to be expected that the superintendent at Bloemfontein would escape Emily's wrath, and General Pretyman found himself no match for the woman who had subdued, not only the intemperate miners of Minnesota by 'giving it them hot and strong' but in the course of an after-lunch chat, Sir Alfred Milner himself. Indeed the camps were so poorly equipped and inefficiently run that it was the work of a few moments for Emily to convince those in charge of their own inadequacy, sinfulness, lack of understanding and thoughtless inhumanity, and to arouse in their minds a lively sense of what their fate might be when the British public got to know of the genocide that was taking place under their management.

In short, once Emily had got to know the true story of the camps, all who ran them were virtually in her power. News of all their failings came to her through the women who were her

E

friends. When sugar supplied to the camps by the contractors was suspected (correctly) of being mainly floor sweepings, or the coffee was thought to be adulterated, it was to Emily that the samples were brought and it was she who sent them on to the analyst in London. And it was obvious that Miss Hobhouse would not hesitate to expose the mistakes of British officials to her influential friends at home. She might even seek to hold some of them responsible for the deaths of women and children, if they did not carry out the measures which she considered were necessary—such as providing hay or straw for mattresses and wood and sacking for beds, and above all fuel, without which the rations of raw meat, meal and coffee, could not be cooked.

Soon, the Military Governor allowed Miss Hobhouse to procure a pail or crock for each tent at the Bloemfontein camp, and at her request issued a proclamation that all drinking water must be boiled. He also gave orders that she was to obeyed. He agreed to pay nearly £50 out of public funds and he put a Captain at her disposal with orders to do what Miss Hobhouse told him; and eventually she was given a free hand to ask for what she wanted. Her 'shopping-list' included an engine boiler big enough to boil all drinking water; she wanted forage for the cows, a boiler for the cow's milk, a wash-house with running water and soap; she wanted medical equipment, and nurses (for the camp had only one with two untrained girl assistants).

'Next I was called to see a woman panting in the heat, just sickening for her confinement. Fortunately I had a nightdress in my bundle to give her and two tiny baby gowns. Next tent, a little six months baby gasping its life out on its mother's knee. The doctor had given it powder in the morning, but it had taken nothing since. Two or three others drooping and sick in that tent. Next, a child recovering from measles sent back from the hospital before it could walk, stretched on the ground white and wan, three or four others lying about. Next, a girl of twenty-four lay dying on a stretcher. Her father, a big gentle Boer, kneeling beside her, while in the next tent his wife was watching a child of six also dying, and one of about five also drooping. Already this couple had lost three children in the hospital, and so would not let those go, though I begged hard to take them out of the hot tent. "We must watch these ourselves," they said. Captain H. had mounted guard over me—he thinks I am too sympathetic—

but I sent him flying to get some brandy and got some down the girl's throat. But for the most part you must stand and look on helpless to do anything, because there is nothing to do anything with. Then a man came up and said, "Sister" (they call me Sister), "come and see my child, sick for nearly three months." It was a dear little chap of four, and nothing left of him except his great brown eyes and white teeth from which the lips were drawn back too thin to close. His body was emaciated. The little fellow had craved for fresh milk, but of course there had been none until the last few days, and now our fifty cows only gave four buckets, so you can imagine what feed there is for them. I sent Captain H. for some of this and then made them lay the child outside on a pillow to get the breeze that comes up at sunset. I can't describe what it is to see these children lying about in a state of collapse—it's just exactly like faded flowers thrown away. And one hates to stand and look on at such misery and be able to do almost nothing.'

To the Committee of the Fund she wrote letters which were sometimes chatty—of how long pinafores were much worn by women of all ages up to about forty and 'kappies'—a kind of glorified sunbonnet, so that the women looked like magnified children and rather picturesque. In general she found Afrikaner women 'simple . . . calm and composed in manner, but always brimming over with hospitable impulses. They possess shrewdness and mother-wit in abundance, and they are wrapped in suspicion like a coat of mail. Once succeed in piercing that armour and the trustfulness below is as complete as a child's. Betray that trust and it will never be forgotten. The women have a natural homely dignity which becomes them well and commands respect.'

But in private she deplored the overthrow of moral standards and decencies as a result of the war and the surrender of the better instincts of the individual to those of the herd. She hated to see lies, treachery and meanness and other 'virtues of war' replace those of Christianity. It depressed her to think, for at times she was a melancholy person, that every tent contained a family in trouble, a family with loss behind them, poverty in front and sickness, privation and death in the present.

'It is such a curious position,' she wrote home, 'hollow and rotten to the heart's core, to have made, all over the state, large uncomfortable communities of people whom you call refugees and say you are protecting but who call themselves prisoners-of-war compulsorily detained, and detesting your protection.'

Sometimes, when she had convicted the camp superintendent or his accomplices in the Army of sin, and had rendered them contrite and humble, she became almost motherly towards them and felt impelled to treat them like small boys caught stealing jam out of the pantry. But when officials told her that the cost of laying on water supplies would be prohibitive or that forage for war-horses was too precious to be given to cows, a strong streak of feminism became apparent and she raged against the hopeless confusion created in the camps, as in the world at large, by men in their ignorance and stupidity.

In an attempt to set out the size of the problem Emily devised a series of questions to be answered by each family, on their previous circumstances, their present needs and the prospects of satisfying them. It was before the days when 'means test' meant humiliation.

Bloemfontein was only one camp and others needed to be visited too. There was Springfontein about ninety miles south west of Bloemfontein and Norvals Pont still further south and just across the Cape Border, and others. For Emily this meant unsponsored travel under military control without civilian station masters or rail officials to appeal to. Instead of normal tickets, she needed permits and passes. The fact that she was a woman was no help. 'I should get on much better,' she wrote, 'if I were shaped like a truck and ran on wheels.' By day she faced almost intolerable heat in trains which, because they were military, were uncared for and filled with dust. From the Tommies, however, she learnt which tap to turn on the side of the engine if you wanted boiling water for a cup of tea. By night there was the danger of being ambushed or blown up. At one time, Emily wrote, Miss Hobhouse and De Wet struggled for who should use the line. Often the train was held up and Emily had to sleep in it. Once, travelling from Springfontein, she had to sit bolt upright for fifteen hours alone in the guard's van while the train was shunted to and fro all night long, and at Norvals Pont she had to wait seven hours for her train, and was completely stranded when it failed to arrive.

Sometimes she was able to get a bed in a so-called hotel— probably above the drinking saloon or the commercial travellers' writing room. Occasionally she was able to undress and spend the night in the guard's van. She was quite overcome and burst into tears after one railway station officer had allowed her to use his bed and bath while he slept nearby in a van. At

Springfontein she stayed with a German Lutheran missionary and his wife. Here Emily found the people were in greater need than in Bloemfontein for the camp had been set up in an area where there was not even a bush that could be used for fuel. She had brought three cases of clothes with her but they were nothing like enough to go round—as she found when family after family came to her on the verandah of a farm house.

'All day I have sat on a farmhouse stoep, and had each family in succession brought to me from the tents, fitting each in turn with clothes as far as possible, just to cover their nakedness. Each woman tells me her story, a story which, from its similarity to all which have gone before, grows monotonous. But it is always interesting to note the various ways in which the great common trouble is met by divers characters. Some are scared, some paralysed and unable to realize their loss, some are dissolved in tears; some, mute and dry-eyed, seem only able to think of the blank, penniless future; and some are glowing with pride at being prisoners for their country's sake.

'A few bare women had made petticoats out of the brown rough blankets—one had on a man's trousers. Nearly all the children have nothing left but a worn print frock, with nothing beneath it, and shoes and socks long since worn away. Shoes we must leave—it is hopeless—until we can procure rolls of sole leather and uppers, lasts and sprigs, and then the men can make *veld schoone,* a simple kind of rough shoe. . . .

'I clothed about fifteen families today, or about sixty persons, and hope to do the same tomorrow, and I may collect some old clothes from the residents here to help us along.

'In despair I went to the one village shop, but it is long since cleared out, and I came away empty, save for some packets of needles. I had been giving some material for women to make their own boys' clothing, but we are stopped by the utter famine of cotton or thread. Scissors are handed round from tent to tent; thimbles are very few. Everything here is so scarce that the sight of my rough deal packing cases created quite a sensation—not for what was inside, but for the actual wood. They are destined to make low bedsteads, tables and a few bits for firing.

'Mattresses, I fear, are out of the question here on account of the lack of material, but we thought low beds might be made if a little wood could be found and strips of sacking nailed across. This would lift them off the ground for the winter. Perhaps we shall manage a few. The crying need in this Camp is fuel. Wood there is none; a little coal is served out, but so little that many days the people cannot cook at all, and their rations are raw meat, meal and coffee, so each of these needs fire. If you could peep at Springfontein you would at once realize the hopelessness of getting any fuel—a bare veldt, covered with short sparse vegetation, ringed by barest kopjes, stony, and without even grass. Except at the farm where I sat there are no trees, and these have been grown with greatest pains. So there is nothing to burn.

'Women to whom I have given nothing nor offered to, and who neither ask nor wish for charity, express deepest gratitude for the bare tidings that any English people feel for them. They are very sore at heart, and are really helped by the knowledge that we understand at all the aspect of affairs as it appears to them. They are tired of being told by officers that they are refugees under the "kind and beneficent protection of the British". In most cases there is no pretence that there was treachery, or ammunition concealed, or food given, or anything. It was just that an order was given to empty the country.

'One woman told me today that a waggon load of her goods was brought away by soldiers, and followed their convoy. She begged hard for a favourite chair of hers, but was refused.

'One afternoon a poor young Tommy came to the door of this house to buy eggs. He was from Somersetshire, near Taunton, and "zo Zummerzet" in his talk that I had to go out and interpret. Poor boy, he was very sorry for himself and longing for home. Never, never, never would he go to war again; he had had a "sickener". He was just out from hospital and an attack of slow fever, and was jealous of the C.I.V.'s going home so soon. I gave him my pot of cocoa, which he said would be a great treat. He had had to sleep in six inches of water, and all his rations were swamped and those of his companions.

'I just want to say, while it's in my mind, that the blouses sent from England, and supposed to be full grown, are only useful here for girls of twelve to fourteen or so—much too small for the well-developed Boer maiden, who is really a fine creature. Could an out, out woman's size be procured? and for camp life dark colours are best. It's hard to keep clean and soap is a luxury, water not superabundant. You would have realized the scarcity and poverty a little had you seen me doling out pins and needles by twos and threes, and dividing reels of cotton and bits of rag for patching. A few combs I brought up from Capetown were caught at with joy.

'There is very little time here for letter writing, as I am busy in Camp all day, and then we all have to be in bed and lights out by 8.30 p.m. It's rather nice living with the sun in this sort of way.'

As far as possible she made allowances for the obstacles and difficulties that were unavoidable, particularly if a camp had been recently set up at a time when the materials needed for it had become more and more difficult to get. At Norvals Pont she was agreeably surprised to find the camp well sited with a view of the Orange River, and the tents were properly laid out in rows with street names and numbers. There was furniture in the tents, including some beds and mattresses, though most of these had to be dried every day as the heavy autumn dews sank through two layers of canvas and dripped on them. There was water from a fresh spring which no-one could reach to contaminate. There was the beginnings of a tennis court and an effort to arrange classes for the children. Mr Cole Bowen, the Superintendent, impressed her so much that she urged that he should be allowed to go to other camps to show them his methods.

At Aliwal North, she was pleased to note that the camp had no soldiers or sentries and that the inmates could walk into town and receive visitors without a special pass. They were encouraged, too, to help themselves by making extra rooms. Here, too, she cemented her friendship with Mrs Tibbie Steyn, wife of the President, who although a Scot by birth was treated as an enemy and followed everywhere by a trooper.

From Kimberley she wrote:

'Today (March 15th) I got the mother's black clothes (all hers are burnt), and took them up. Another child had died in the night, and I found all three little corpses being photographed for the absent fathers to see some day. Two little wee white coffins at the gate waiting, and a third wanted. I was glad to see them, for at Springfontein, a young woman had to be buried in a sack, and it hurt their feelings woefully.

'Today (March 16th) I bought and presented some clothes

135

and combs, and soap, and towels to the women who tried to run away. They are, of course, in disgrace, and I felt so sorry for them that we had long talks, and I was sure the best thing was to make them a little happier in camp.'

Towards the end of March, Emily returned to Cape Town to get permission to visit Mafeking and to return to Bloemfontein. To the discomforture of British officials she lost no time in telling her Dutch friends of the pitiable fate of their fellow Afrikaners, whom she had seen in cattle trucks by the railwayside in suffocating heat, bitter cold or in cataracts of rain, hungry, sick, dying or dead. Resentment was not long in showing itself among the 'British' Community at the Cape. In particular, Emily incurred the wrath of Miss Dora Fairbridge, a third generation 'British' South African who had helped to found, and was Joint Secretary of, the Guild of Loyal Women of South Africa, of which the Princess of Wales had become the patron. The Loyal Women were said to be 'non-political save for their determination to uphold the Imperial Supremacy in South Africa'. According to Mrs K. H. R. Stuart of Whyteleafe, Surrey, their delegate in Britain, 'They felt that a crisis had come which called on all women true to Queen and Country to bestir themselves and to throw their womanhood's loving gentle influence upon the right side.' Mrs Stuart thought fit to add in her letter to the *Times,* that 'the stand taken by the so-called "Conciliation Women" who declared their undying hatred of Great Britain and their wicked resolve to bring up their children to swear vengeance against her, made the Guild of Women feel more than ever the necessity for their labour of love and loyalty, believing as they do that love must be the conqueror and finally break down the barriers between Boer and Britain.'

Miss Fairbridge reported to Sir Walter Hely-Hutchinson, who had become the Governor of Cape Colony, that 'Our Guild members at Bloemfontein write that she (Emily) has sown discontent and dissatisfaction among the women she is supposed to benefit. They were all satisfied and grateful to the English Government until she came amongst them and taught them to invent grievances where none existed.' Miss Fairbridge added: 'This lady is a member of the "Conciliation Committee" at present being formed in London under the auspices of Mr Leonard Courtney, Mr Mackarness and Mr P. J. Molteno and we feel that she is the agent of the Conciliation Committee.

Miss Hobhouse is at present in Cape Town but I believe she leaves for the north tonight.'

Sir Walter did not take the hint and cancel Emily's pass, for indeed it had been the military who had issued it. But he wrote to Mr Chamberlain that the Guild had reported 'that Miss Hobhouse exercises a bad influence on the Boer Women in the Refugee camps'. And although Emily was able to reach Mafeking (in the back of beyond), she was not able to wheedle Major Sir Hamilton Goold-Adams, the Lieutenant Governor of the Orange River Colony, to allow her to visit the camp at Kroonstad. In explanation he said that Emily was reported to have shown 'personal sympathy' with the Boers, when doling out clothes and food. 'I replied with astonishment that that was just what I came to do—to give personal sympathy and help in personal troubles.' Sir Hamilton was of the opinion that the gifts to the women and children could and should be handed out mechanically. But Emily told him that she could not work like that, that she must treat people as fellow-beings and share in their hardships. Sir Hamilton also said that news had reached him that a letter from Emily had been read in London, at a political meeting, and although Emily insisted that the meeting referred to was a private gathering held in her aunt's house, she left him unconvinced.

At Mafeking she formed a Committee to deal out clothes and to visit the tents regularly, section by section, for she knew now how camps should be organized.

At the same time however, she realized that there were limits to what she could do in South Africa. It was not only the difficulties created for her by the Guild of Loyal Women or even the fact that Kitchener was still preventing her from visiting the newly-established camps in the Transvaal. She had become alarmed by the death rate in the camps, so horrific when compared with those of an English country parish that she was reminded of a disaster such as the Black Death or the Great Plague. Moreover, with Kitchener's drives becoming more and more ruthless, she felt that conditions were getting worse rather than better. Springfontein, which at the time of Emily's first visit, had held 500 people, was endeavouring in April to shelter 3,000 and when Emily's train passed south she saw a trainload of 600 more. Camp superintendents were continually getting telegrams telling them to expect 500 or a thousand refugees on such and such a date but no tents were provided to house them, or food to revive them, when they arrived tired and exhausted after their journey.

At Bloemfontein (where Mrs Fichardt's pass to drive to her farm had been taken away, partly because she had 'harboured' Miss Hobhouse), Emily found that rations were not being met and sixty-two had died, including two of the nurses:

'The population had doubled, and had swamped the effect of improvements which could not keep pace with the numbers to be accommodated. There was more sickness, and the people looked forlorn. Disease and death were stamped upon their faces. Many whom I had left hale and hearty, full in figure and face, had undergone such a change that I could not recognize them. I realized how camp life under these imperfect conditions was telling upon them, and no impartial observer could have failed to see what must ensue, unless nurses, doctors, workers and, above all, extra food, clothing and bedding, could be poured out in abundance and without delay. I sought the Deputy Administrator, and represented to him the death-rate already worked out in the adjoining camp at 20 per cent, and asked if nothing could be done to stop the influx of people. He replied that he believed that all the people in the entire country, with the exception of towns on the line, were to be brought in.

'My fund was but a drop in the ocean of such a need. There were two courses open to me. To stay among the people, doling out small gifts of clothes, which could only touch the surface of the need, or to return home with the hope of inducing both the Government and the public to give so promptly and abundantly that the lives of the people, or at least the children, might be saved. It seemed certain that in South Africa itself adequate expenditure would never be authorized.'

Two days after returning to Cape Town she was sharing a two-berth cabin on the *Saxon,* preparing the horror story with which she would awaken the people of Britain to a sense of their responsibilities. Alfred Milner, who was on the same ship, told her that he had received more than sixty complaints about her conduct. She was unperturbed. Perhaps what stirred her most of all was a message from Lord Kitchener read in the House of Commons by Mr Brodrick, Secretary of State for War, which said, according to the *Times* of March 2nd, that the people in the camps had 'a sufficient allowance and were all comfortable and happy'.

8

Not without Honour

Back in London, Emily found the world's opinion of Britannia to be no higher than her own. A cartoon in the Netherlands *Amsterdammer* was captioned: ENGLISH OFFICIAL TELEGRAM: 'We have taken a great number of prisoners,' and showed a platoon of British troops with fixed bayonets escorting their captives—an old grandfather with a stick, four small children, a man on crutches and two women with babes in arms. In June Madame Waszklewicz, President of the Women's League for the Promotion of International Disarmament, pleaded to Mr Brodrick for Boer women and suggested in the name of the women of Europe and America that all Boer women be moved to neutral ground. A pro-Boer Committee had been formed in Germany, and a similar group in Paris sent out the Abbé Espil as Chaplain of the French volunteers. 'Bold youths of France,' cried the Abbé in one of his appeals, 'The Boers hold out their hands; come to their help.'

The Boers themselves proved able propagandists. A Boer Peace Mission led by Abraham Fischer had arrived in Naples in April 1900 with sealed orders; its members announced that their object was to 'Treat for peace without diminution of political rights or independence.' During a tour of Europe they were received by the Queen of the Netherlands and afterwards departed for the United States, where a 'Dutch' Committee was already in existence.

Kruger himself, still claiming full rights as President, landed at Marseilles in November 1900 and told his audience: 'The war which is being waged against the two Republics has reached the utmost limits of barbarity. In my life I have had occasion many times to fight with the savage tribes of Africa but the barbarians with whom we have now to fight are much worse than the others. They have gone so far as to arm the Kaffirs

139

against us. They burn our farms which we have built with so much difficulty. They hurt the women and children whose husbands and fathers have been killed or taken prisoner. They leave them without protection, without wood, often without bread. But whatever may happen we shall never surrender.' In Paris he was accorded an address by the Irish Independence Committee: 'Our enemy is yours,' it read. 'Our prayer for vengeance mingles with the prayer of your people before the Throne of the Almighty; and the arrows which at the proper moment will avenge our sufferings and those of your people are from the same quiver.'

Kruger made a deep impression on those he was willing to receive. Mrs Ernest Luden, writing in the *Pall Mall Gazette*, found him not unlike the Kruger of the cartoonists—'The tall chimney-pot hat, the "apple-pie" boots, [pies in those days were often baked in long narrow pie-dishes], the short trousers, the Bible, the long pipe, the oyster eyes, the Newgate frill, the flattened hair,' she wrote, 'are as well known as Mr Chamberlain's eyeglass. Will no-one arbitrate?', she quoted Kruger as saying. 'Will no-one give us a fair hearing, a chance of defending ourselves? We may have done wrongly; we may have had our faults; we declared this war, but our hands were forced—we can prove it. Let someone judge between England and ourselves. Let someone judge.'

Mr Van Hamel, who was entrusted with the arduous duty of interpreting for Kruger in France, was equally impressed. Kruger told him that he had come to France to ask for the conflict to be settled by the only honourable means—namely arbitration. He declared that the barbarities of the English 'had attained their ultimate limits'. The Boer farms were burned and their women and children left without a roof over their heads and often without bread, he maintained.

On another occasion, he told Mr Van Hamel to say that the English had forced the Boers to retreat not by superior military skill but by the superiority of numbers. 'We have not been conquered,' he said, 'we have been submerged.'

Asked to lay a wreath on the statue of Joan of Arc, Kruger demurred. 'I understand very well what you want,' he said, 'but all these statues are idolatry. When Moses consented to accept homage for himself, God carried him off and no-one can find his tomb.' Then, when someone told him that probably after his death, if he had succeeded in driving the English from the national soil as Joan of Arc had done in France, posterity would put up a statue to him, he said: 'No, no statue for me—never. You know well that they wanted to put up one to me in Pretoria; there was never more than a pedestal—nothing else.' Future generations, of course, have overruled his wishes.

The British in one way or another supported Kruger's charges, as for instance when they compelled the citizens of Cradock to attend the public execution, ordered by the military, of one of their own countrymen. A similar public execution had already been staged in Middelburg and on May 18th Chamberlain told Mr Flavin (Kerry North) in the House that the Government had no intention of rebuilding the farmhouses burnt by British troops.

The British refused, too, to accept food or clothing offered by the Swiss and Dutch philanthropic societies, despite, or perhaps because of the fact that the *Times* had printed on July 10th a letter from a Boer pastor in Pretoria saying that the children in camp there were 'living skeletons', and that people were starving by hundreds. The Pastor added (for the letter was directed to the public of the United States) that England was guilty of a terrible iniquity which Americans, rising as one man, should forbid.

But while this might be exaggerated, Lady Maxwell, the American wife of Britain's military Governor of Pretoria, appealed in the *New York Herald* of April 16th 1901 on behalf of the children in the camps, who, she said, were 'living in open tents without fires and with only the scantiest of clothes.'

Inevitably the British public were bewildered. They did not know what to believe. From the start the war had had support from the highest quarters. The Queen herself in the dark days of December 1899 had decided to entertain the wives and children of serving soldiers and to hand out presents from a Christmas tree 25 foot high. The Transvaal War Fund sponsored by Lady Chesham and Lady Georgiana Curzon reached £465,000 by the end of that year. On a slightly less exalted level, hymns, calling on the Deity to favour the British cause, were published by Novello & Company at 2d a copy, for the benefit of the War Fund. Prayers were said in many a parish church and the Bishop of Chichester in due course published a letter from his son alleging that while he lay wounded a Boer had tried to drag a ring from his finger while others set fire to the veld without regard to the safety of the wounded. Yet the accounts of the war correspondents gave a totally different impression. For example, the *Daily Telegraph* correspondent with General French's column wrote:

'Our burying party was received by the Boers sympathetically. They rendered assistance also to our men. Over the grave they sang a hymn, and some of the leaders made impressive speeches, expressing abhorrence of the war, regretting the heavy losses on both sides, and declaring the hope that the war would soon be ended.'

The *Daily News* correspondent wrote on April 2nd 1900:

'Our men, when wounded, are treated by the Boers with manly gentleness and kind consideration. . . . They brought us cooling drinks, or moved us into more comfortable positions; women with gentle fingers shifted bandages, or washed wounds, or gave us little dainties; while the little children crowded round us with tears running down their cheeks. In every solitary instance, our countrymen declare that they have been grandly treated.'

And if some sceptics urged that the *Daily News* was a pro-Boer paper and might have been expected to write in those terms, they could hardly say the same of the *Daily Mail*, whose correspondent reported:

'No army every had more serviceable allies than the Boers have in their wives. I have seen them taking delicacies to the English prisoners at the race-course. Both the officers and the privates have received more games, books and even pigskin footballs than ever before fell into the hands of military prisoners.'

The days when the Boers could look after English prisoners ended with the capture of Pretoria, but the impression left by their chivalry must have lingered on, despite Kitchener's report in the *Times* of January 14th 1901 that De Wet had shot one of the delegates of the Boer Central Peace Committee and flogged others.

Thus a tide of opinion began to flow, slowly at first, but later more powerfully away from those who felt that the soldiers of the Queen could do no wrong and the Afrikaners no right.

Meanwhile, the South African Conciliation Committee had not been idle in Emily's absence, and Leonard Courtney, who had not hesitated, even on Mafeking night in Liverpool, to speak out against annexation, continued, despite threatening

letters delivered to his house in Cheyne Walk, to lead the
campaign.

Many a pamphlet bearing the Conciliation Committee's
imprint winged its way along the corridors of power and even
overseas. One of the earliest titles was *Some authoritative
sketches of the Boer* by Distinguished Englishmen. *How the
War affects our fellow subjects at the Cape* by a Dutch girl
was number eleven in the series. 'A Boer Parson' and Sir Robert
Reid both wrote on the rights and wrongs of the war, and
A. G. Hales described *The Life of the Boer in a Fighting Laager.*
The *Times* of March 1901 reported: 'A well-attended meeting of
the South Africa Conciliation Committee was held yesterday
afternoon at the Westminster Palace Hotel. Mr Leonard
Courtney presided, and those present included Sir Robert Reid,
MP; Mr Channing, MP; Mr H. J. Wilson, MP; Prebendary
Barker, Mrs Courtney, Mr F. Debenham, Mr C. P. Scott, and
Mr Keir Hardie, MP.' At the end a motion was passed rejecting
the policy of unconditional surrender.

The 'Stop the War' Committee continued to raise its voice.
The Committee declared in their annual report of February
1901 that:

'Their policy in the future, as in the past, should be one of
uncompromising opposition to the war. The formula "stop the
war and stop it now," is as sound today as it was when the
committee was constituted, and the war can be stopped only
in one of two ways. Either the Dutch must be exterminated
or we must complete our evacuation of the two Republics
and concede that demand for arbitration which the Boers
have made from the first. At present Lord Kitchener is
evacuating the country on lateral lines. That is to say, he is
retreating from all positions except those on the lines of railway. It is a confession that he has not conquered the
Republics; he has only seized their railways and the towns
through which they pass, and to hold them and nothing else
is the task for which he regards 200,000 men as all too few.
The Committee, therefore appeals with confidence for a
renewal of subscriptions to enable it to keep up a *mitraille*
of pamphlets, broadsheets, and leaflets for the purpose of
driving conviction into the public mind as to the insanity and
criminality of this war. The time is not one which calls for
mealy-mouthed utterances. The committee believes that this
war, which from its beginning was a crime without justifica-

tion or excuse, has now degenerated into a campaign of extermination, carried out by a policy of systematic devastation,
the like of which for atrocity can only be paralleled in our
time by the operations of the Turks in Armenia and Bulgaria.
Never before has the British nation attempted the extermination of an entire nationality. Never before have we waged
unrelenting war upon the women and children of brave men
whom we are unable to subdue in battle. This professedly
Christian nation is now proceeding in a policy of murder,
wholesale and retail, which renders our religion a hollow
farce, and exposes us to the contempt and execration even of
the heathen world. Face to face with such phenomena of
unprecedented crime there is only one thing for us to do,
and that is to stop the war and stop it at once, and stop it
in the only way in which it can be stopped—by ceasing to
murder and to steal, by retiring within our own possessions,
and making such amends as we can to the people whose homesteads we have burnt and whose country we have converted
into a blackened wilderness.'

Groups of 'Friends of Peace' had been formed in various
parts of the country and a vast quantity of leaflets distributed
including 'between 20,000 and 30,000 among workmen travelling by the early morning trains'.

In Parliament the subject had not been allowed to drop. On
the day that Emily sailed for South Africa there had been a
debate during which Government spokesmen had been obliged
to give reassurances on farm burning, the deportation of Boer
women and children and other matters about which the opposition showed concern.

Campbell-Bannerman, leader since 1899 of the Liberals in the
House of Commons, was able to quote all the arguments put
forward by Joseph Chamberlain twenty years earlier *against*
the earlier war in which Britain annexed the Transvaal, and
went on to justify the motives of his party in opposing the
prosecution of the present war:

'Some members have invented a convenient theory by which
opposition is silenced in the presence of foreign complications.
If we attempt discussion before war breaks out, we are hamp-
ering the government in negotiations and endangering peace.
If we wait till the war is upon us, then it is said we are dividing
the country in the presence of the enemy, while if we post-
pone the discussion until the war is over, we are told we are

guilty of fault-finding and unnecessary introspection. The thing in fact comes to this, that it is not the business of the House of Commons or the people to express an opinion on foreign affairs. This should be left to the responsible advisers of the Crown.'

He was echoing the words of Lloyd George who asked:

'Is every politician who opposes a war during its progress a traitor? If so, then Chatham was a traitor, and Burke and Fox especially, and, in later times, Cobden and Bright and even Mr Chamberlain.'

On February 25th Mr John Ellis, Liberal member for the Rushcliffe Division of Nottingham, who had travelled out in the same ship as Emily to visit 'loyal' refugee camps asked Mr W. St. John Brodrick, Secretary for War in the House of Commons, how many people were under guard in the refugee camps; where these camps were situated; who was responsible for supplying them; what kind of shelter was provided and whether relatives were allowed to visit them. He learnt that the numbers and situations of the camps, the numbers of protected persons in each and the nature of the shelter provided had not been reported to the Secretary of State for War but the number was believed to be 'about 15,000'. The Secretary of State also explained that the inmates of the camps were 'protected persons' and not prisoners-of-war. A fortnight later the persistent Mr Ellis again raised the question. On this occasion he learnt from Mr Brodrick that no more information was available. It was then that members learnt that Lord Kitchener 'had telegraphed to me that he himself has gone into the question and finds that the people in the *laagers* are all contented and comfortable and we must rely on his assurance.'

The following month (March) Mr John Dillon, who twenty years later was to become leader of the Irish Nationalist Party, proposed an amendment to the address. It ran:

'And we humbly represent to your Majesty that the whole-sale burning of farmhouses, the wanton destruction and looting of private property, the driving of women and children out of their homes without shelter or proper provision of food, and the confinement of women and children in prison camps are practices not in accordance with the usages of war as recognized by civilized nations; that such proceedings are in the highest degree disgraceful and dishonouring to a nation professing to be Christian, and are calculated, by the intense indignation and hatred of the British name which they must excite in the Dutch population, to increase immensely the difficulty of restoring peace to South Africa. And we humbly and earnestly represent to your Majesty that it is the duty of your Majesty's Government immediately to put a stop to all practices contrary to the recognized usages of war in the conduct of the war in South Africa; and to make an effort to bring the war to an end by proposing to the Governments of the two Republics such terms of peace as brave and honourable men might, under all the circumstances, be reasonably expected to entertain.'

In April Mr Brodrick rejected a report from Dr McKensie, brother of the Military Governor, which declared that the food at the Refugee Camp at Johannesburg was unfit for human consumption and that the death rate there was abnormally high. In June he told the House that the rations allowed in the camps had 'been pronounced sufficient' by medical authorities and it was not proposed to increase them and that there was 'no reason to believe' that medical arrangements in any of the camps were unsatisfactory.

But as for seeking peace there could be no question of that. Indeed the men in the field were calling for stronger measures, for on July 25th Mr Chamberlain received the following urgent cable from Sir H. E. McCallum, Governor of Natal, to the effect that:

'If burghers now in the field do not surrender by given date, say within one month, cost of maintenance of all women and children will be chargeable against the immovable property of burghers in the field; also that Boer generals and leaders in the field should be informed that unless they and their commandos surrender by date specified they will be banished from South Africa for life, when captured.'

The *Times* on August 24th reported that three Boers had been executed on a rising hill outside Semelspoort and that forty civilians had attended 'voluntarily'.

In view of the eminence of those involved in the crisis, it would have been quite unlike Emily to put her case through an Opposition MP in Parliament if she could make a direct approach to a Cabinet Minister, and this she proceeded to do. Lady Harcourt, wife of the prominent Liberal leader, Sir

William Harcourt, had already shown some of her letters to
A. J. Balfour, who was leader in the House of Commons of
Lord Salisbury's Tory administration.

'I am quite overcome by the responsibility resting on me
and by the importance attached to every word I speak,' she
wrote to Mrs Charles Murray at the Cape. 'My letters, too, are
regarded as strong documents and are to be printed in some
form as soon as I break from the Authorities—but first I am
to appeal to them and give them their chance.'

Authority's chance came on June 4th when Emily saw Mr
Brodrick. Her interview with him went smoothly and Emily
spoke with her usual persuasive eloquence, so much so that
it was nearly two hours before she rose to leave the War Office.
But it seems likely that part of Mr Brodrick's willingness to listen
was due to the realization that this spinster of forty-one
possessed information which, if widely publicized, could endanger
the Minister's own position if not that of the entire Government. No doubt he felt certain in his own mind that Emily
was telling no more than the truth when she said that, once
they knew of it, the people of Britain would never tolerate the
suffering of the women and children in the camps. She, in turn,
was unimpressed with Brodrick's well-brushed hair, luxuriant
moustache and dapper drainpipe collar. She thought him gentle-
manly but incompetent, pleasant but slippery, agreeable but
mediocre; a man of indecision.

Brodrick asked Emily for her suggestions (she had already
roughed them out in advance) and at the end of the interview
she hoped, despite her first impression, that at last something
had really been accomplished. Her requirements were indeed
far from exacting. They called for the release from the refugee
camps of women who had money enough to support themselves, or who possessed houses near the camp, or who had relatives willing to support them; and she suggested that free passes
from the camp should be given to those who could earn their
living in the nearest town. Emily asked for English philanthrop-
ical societies to be allowed to organize and carry out the distribution of clothing and other supplies. She called for a resident
minister in each camp who could hold religious services—
including of course funeral services, and urged that in view of
the overcrowding that already existed, no more women and
children should be brought in from the veld to existing camps
and that any new ones formed should be in a healthy spot in
Cape Colony, closer to ports where supplies were landed.

After some delay an official answer came; the women, it said, could be freed if there were no objections either from the military—or, if numbers were large—from the Cape Colony Government. Those who wished to work in nearby towns were already receiving passes allowing them to do so. Every camp, the letter said, has a trained matron, a qualified medical officer and a superintendent with efficient staff, the whole staff being chosen 'with a special view to their knowledge of the Dutch language'. All refugee camps had ministers resident in or near them and so on. In some respects, however, Mr Brodrick did not accept Emily's suggestions. In the first place the authorities could not undertake to limit the numbers of those who, for military reasons, might be brought into concentration camps (in point of fact the Boers and the rigours of the winter made it difficult to move large numbers of civilians from one part of the country to another). They were prepared to sponsor an appeal by the Victoria League to provide Dutch women and children with something more than the bare necessities, but the Government thought it would be better to work through local committees and through people chosen and sent out by the Government in London. They obviously did not like the idea of giving philanthropic societies a foothold in Government camps.

The Government's reply was a neat way of evading charges of inhumanity. It also evaded for the moment Miss Hobhouse, for she was inclined to believe on most occasions that she knew best and was not the kind of person to work willingly under Government supervision—particularly when the Government was opposed to her own Liberals. But the Government could justifiably argue that any idea that the relief would be distributed by 'pro-Boers' would have been fatal to the success of the appeal. They could also conclude that there was now no possibility of making use of Emily as an ally. For much had happened during the three weeks between her interview with Mr Brodrick and his reply. In the first place Emily decided without more ado that selections from her letters should be printed and circulated to members of both Houses of Parliament. Then on June 14th at a dinner given by the National Reform Union, Sir Henry Campbell-Bannerman widened the split in the Liberal Party by describing British tactics in South Africa as 'methods of barbarism'.

A week before Mr Brodrick's answer reached Emily, the Committee of the Distress Fund for South African Women and

Children published her report of her visit. In it, she referred, naturally enough, to the overcrowding, poor water supplies, defective sanitation and shortages of fuel, soap etc. 'There are,' said the *Times*, 'some pathetic instances of children dying amid the comfortless and unfamiliar surroundings of these camps. At the end of the report is an appendix, containing a number of narratives from Boer women of how they were ordered off their farms and brought in, and of the hardships undergone by them, though it would not appear that the narrators were subjected to any searching cross-examination by Miss Hobhouse.'

It was the start of a battle between Emily and that newspaper which ended only 25 years later with her death. The paper, however, did publish all the recommendations put forward by Miss Hobhouse, including one with which she had not favoured Mr Brodrick. It read:

'That, considering the growing impertinence of the Kaffirs, seeing the white women thus humiliated, every care shall be taken not to put them in places of authority.'

We cannot be sure whether Emily would have said the same today but these few words summed up perfectly her attitude at the time. And, as for bringing relief to the Kaffirs suffering from the hardships of war, that was a matter which in her view should best be attended to by the Society for the Protection of Aborigines or other similar bodies.

Only a day after Emily's report had been published there was a memorable meeting at the Queen's Hall, Langham Place, which was held to hear speeches from two former members of the Cape Colony Government—John Xavier Merriman and Johannes Sauer—on the war and its evils. Six MPs including Mr Lloyd George and Mr Keir Hardie were on the platform and the Chair was taken by the famous Henry Labouchere, founder of the magazine *Truth* and part proprietor of the *Daily News*. Admission was by ticket only and the stewards had orders to stand no nonsense. Indeed, according to the *Times*, crashes of glass were several times heard in various parts of the hall as some unfortunate individual was being summarily thrust out of the building'; and at one point the Chairman exhibited a soiled Union Jack on the end of a broken stick, saying: 'I have been asked to state that this is the battle flag of the Stock Exchange contingent which was sent here to disturb the meeting, and which has been captured.' Loud cheers greeted

Lloyd George when he declared 'The Herod of old sought to crush a little race by killing all the young children. It was not a success, and he would commend that story to Herod's modern imitator.'

These attacks provoked of course, counter-attacks, notably a letter to the *Times* signed by Lord Hugh Cecil, castigating Campbell-Bannerman.

'Sir,

It is right to protest against Sir Henry Campbell-Bannerman's assertion that he has made no attack upon British generals and soldiers, but only upon the Government. His charge is that the South African War is being conducted by "methods of barbarism". But the methods of a war are the concern, in the first instance at any rate, of the generals in command. . . . And why does Sir Henry seek to pretend that he has made no attack upon these generals? Can the widest charity suggest a more favourable explanation than that he shrinks from the unpopularity of such an attack? If what has been done be really barbaric Sir Henry ought to clamour not only for the resignation of the Government but also for the recall, or at least the severe reprimand, of Lord Kitchener and the other South African commanders. But this would be bad party tactics. Humanity is all very well, but one must not forget the ballot-box nor the unity of the Radical party. And so in defiance of common sense Sir Henry attempts to confine his accusation to the Government. . . . Would not all the suffering involved in devastating and concentrating be considered quite allowable if inflicted not on dwellers in the open but on the inhabitants of a besieged town? Surely all, and much more. We hear of food supplies being destroyed. In what siege has this not been done? We hear of houses being destroyed. A besieging army may bombard till not one stone stands upon another. We hear of women and children falling sick and dying form insanitary conditions, from insufficient or unsuitable food. Has not this happened in every blockade? I remember hearing during the siege of Kimberley that babies were dying for want of milk. Yet I did not blame the Boers for so sad a consequence of their operations. But if these terrible sufferings may for military objects be rightly inflicted on those who live in fortified towns, why is it wicked to inflict them for the like objects on those who live in the open country? Morality cannot depend on fortifications. There cannot be one duty to your neighbour when he is the other side of a wall and another when he is not. Certainly in both cases suffering ought to be economized as much as possible consistently with the success of military operations. But the example of a siege plainly shows that all that has been done—and very much more—is justifiable if it be necessary to achieve the object of the campaign. And that it is necessary we must accept on the authority of the best military advice at our disposal.

I am your obedient servant,
Hugh Cecil'

In time Emily herself became the target for attacks not only through letters to the Editor and reports by the *Times* Correspondent but through Editorials by the newspaper's leader writers. One published on August 27th read:

'Sufficient time has now elapsed for matured colonial opinion on the statements made by Miss Hobhouse to have reached us by mail. We publish this morning a communication from a correspondent at Cape Town and a letter from Mr Sampson, a member of the Cape Legislative Assembly, which agree in substance in their view of that lady's pamphlet. Our Correspondent feels the sympathy we all feel for the suffering brought upon the wives and children of our enemies by the war. But he insists with force and point on some considerations which the pro-Boers here and the foes of England abroad deliberately and persistently ignore in their treatment of this subject. Miss Hobhouse's pamphlet, our Correspondent complains, has been siezed upon in Cape Town as a weapon of party warfare. It has been used as such a weapon wherever the name of England is hated, and even in the dynamite Press of America. In these circumstances our Correspondent thinks it worthwhile to examine the competence of the compiler of these charges against us and the nature of the charges themselves. Miss Hobhouse, he points out, as men of common judgement pointed out long since at home, is deficient in one of the first qualities of an investigator into such a subject. She has no knowledge and no previous experience of the habits of the people whose conditions she undertook to examine. Our Correspondent, who has that knowledge and experience, affirms that the overcrowding which impressed her, like many of the other alleged hardships of which she complains, is habitually practised by the Dutch

151

in ordinary times of their own free will. This statement is fully confirmed by Mr Sampson, who laughs at Miss Hobhouse's complaint of the want of sufficient towels at Green Point.'

A few days later another unfriendly editorial followed:

'Miss Hobhouse, it is true, accuses us of raising every obstacle to prevent all knowledge of the truth from reaching the nation, but this is an ill-considered ebullition of temper, such as ladies sometimes imprudently indulge in, which we are sure she will herself in cooler moments regret. The fact that we have published all Miss Hobhouse's own communications ought surely to have suggested to her that this charge was as foolish as it is ungenerous and untrue. Upon the situation disclosed by such evidence as is available to us we have not hesitated to express our judgement and our sentiments in free and plain terms. They are not the judgement or the sentiments of Miss Hobhouse, but we shall be greatly astonished if they are not those of sensible and patriotic Englishmen. We hold, with Major Davies, that the women and children of our fellow-countrymen and fellow-subjects who have stood true to us have a far stronger and better claim upon us than the wives and daughters of our foes.'

About this date the *Times* correspondent in Cape Town had written:

'The report to which Miss Hobhouse has signed her name is full of heart-rending accounts of these hardships, which are bound to make a great impression on a public such as the British, who have all their necessities at their own door and no small amount of luxuries. A Dutch farmhouse cannot be compared in comfort for a moment to the house of the ordinary English working-man. Certainly the Dutch farmer has space and air and cattle, but he has none of the smaller comforts to which even our poorer classes are accustomed at home. I have seen farms where, during the winter, it has been impossible to get a drop of milk. I have seen whole members of a family huddled together in damp rooms, with closed windows, affording no fresh air and no comfort. In one farm I have seen a common bedroom in which the father, mother and four children slept. These experiences are common out here, and it would not be necessary to touch on them were it not for the fact that Miss Hobhouse dilates upon the misery of overcrowding, as though it were something unknown before in the lives of the inmates of the camps. I do not for a moment wish to say that life in these concentration camps has all the comforts of a sojourn in a stone-built house, but it must be remembered that the climate of South Africa is a most genial one, and it is the only one, perhaps, where it is possible to live in the open air all the year round without much risk of illness. That there are hardships, and terrible hardships too, I cannot deny, nor indeed, do I wish to, but these hardships are the result of war. Miss Hobhouse has had no experience of South Africa before the war, nor has she ever had any experience of war itself.

'The second question I would attempt to answer is this: Are camps of concentration necessary? After all, the whole question hinges on this. Could we have carried on this war without herding together the women and children in canvas or tin camps? To this question neither Miss Hobhouse nor anybody else who has not been through this way has any qualification to offer an answer. Space is too short to take up the arguments in favour of it, but from every man in the British Army to whom I have spoken I have received the one answer, that it was an absolute necessity in most cases. Regret was expressed that such a necessity did exist. The heads of departments regretted it all the more because it threw on their shoulders an enormous amount of work. The Army Service Corps hated it, because they were called upon suddenly to feed a couple of army corps. The commandants disliked it, because they are responsible for the lives and safety of these people within their lines. But it was an urgent military necessity, and as such it had to be undertaken and carried out.

'In case, however, Miss Hobhouse and her friends would not recognize this argument as a good one, there comes the third question: Would the women and children be better off in their own homes? Miss Hobhouse often suggests this in her report, but her knowledge of the condition of things prevailing in war time is so small that no heed should be paid to these suggestions unless the question is thoroughly examined from the standpoint of those who have had the experience of military operations. Suppose for a moment these women and children were returned to their houses: we could not leave them to starve there. The military authorities would be obliged to provide them with stock and sheep and with a certain amount of food. Then each house would again become a Boer depot whence our enemies, who, it must remembered, are every day killing our kith and kin, would draw supplies for their operations. This, as any military man would acknowledge, is an impossibility. Therefore, the alternative remains of leaving them there on their farms, a prey to Kaffirs, with just sufficient food for themselves, to be renewed weekly or monthly, as the case may be. Does Miss Hobhouse for a moment believe that it is possible that a British army, now operating over an enormous extent of country, and meeting with tremendous difficulties, should be turned into a sort of glorified Army Service Corps to keep alive the women and children of our enemies? The thing is absurd, and it is only Miss Hobhouse's ignorance of war and its evils which is responsible for the suggestion.'

Another correspondent wrote:

'When Miss Hobhouse laments over the removal of families into concentration camps she is ignorant of the fact that the Boers under arms hailed their removal as a special boon. They said justly that their women and children would be far better off than if left at their homes, and that the knowledge that they were being protected by us from the severest evils which inevitably accompany war would enable them to fight us with a better heart. Nor is this approval confined to the men still in the field. I will cite one instance as an example. A nephew of Paul Kruger, a man named Caspar Kruger, whom I know well, surrendered about a year ago and has been for months anxious to have his family brought from their home to a concentration camp. At his urgent request I more than once brought his very natural desire to the notice of the authorities in Pretoria, but it was only when I was leaving, about the middle of June, that military exigencies allowed of an attempt being made to do so. He left Pretoria with a column of our troops about the same time that I left for England.

'Miss Hobhouse, is, I conclude, unaware of how well the Boer women have served, and are still serving, the commandos as intelligence officers, spies and even as decoys. If she knew this she would hardly consider their being kept under some supervision a hardship, or wish them to be left at liberty. They cannot appeal to sympathy on the plea of harmless womenhood, for they have proved themselves to be very dangerous enemies. We may admire their courage, but they have forfeited the right to be considered non-belligerents.'

R. B. Douglas, Presbyterian minister in Johannesburg, gave the camp there a glowing testimonial:

'Sir,

In the last issue of the *Times* that arrived here I see a report of the debate in the Commons on the burgher camps in which so much ignorance of the real facts is manifest that I think it right to give my personal testimony as to the way in which these camps are conducted. I have walked through every department of the camp at Johannesburg and seen nothing to suggest hardship and privation. In the tents there are not only beds, tables, chairs etc. but often carpets, sewing machines, and even organs. The women are kept busy cooking and sewing, the children are taught in school, the men work in the grounds or at carpentry. Everywhere there is evidence of cheerfulness and contentment. The unfortunate epidemic of measles early in the year took its origin in the country, not in the camps and now the general health is wonderfully good. Sufficient proof of the comfort of the camp is afforded by the fact that, though the whole male staff in charge consists of five unarmed civilians, there is no difficulty in keeping order, and also by the fact that, though there are 400 able-bodied men in camp and there is nothing to prevent them escaping, only 13 have gone off to commando since the middle of February. The gentlemen in charge of the camp are Johannesburg merchants of good standing and high character, and they spare no effort to do their best for the 4,000 people committed to their care. And the superintendent informs me he has never asked the authorities for anything and been refused. I am sure no unprejudiced person could visit the camp without being convinced that everything possible is being done for the comfort of the families of the enemy. Would that charitable persons at home were as sympathetic to the families of our own people waiting so patiently and in such distress to get back to their homes!'

One indignant correspondent quarrelled with Emily's statement that while £240,000 had been subscribed for British refugees in South Africa only £20,000 had gone to the Dutch. The correspondent pointed out that British tax-payers were contributing £40,000 per week for the camps.

Mrs M. J. Moon, a British subject formerly resident in the

Transvaal and later a refugee from Johannesburg, wrote from Sea Point Cape Town: 'Among the Boers the men openly chuckle that they have no encumbrance; that they are able to enjoy the "picnic", as they term this guerilla warfare. And their women— well, one expression will suffice. "Where is your husband?" I asked of a well-dressed prosperous Dutch woman I met in Doornfontein the other day. She replied "He is on commando." "Don't you want him back?" I asked. "If he comes back I would spit in his face," she answered.'

Of those who wrote personally, Mrs K. H. R. Stuart, delegate in Britain of the 'Guild of Loyal Women' of South Africa was perhaps the most persistent:

'If the hearts of English women are weighed by the inevitable sufferings and sorrow which war always brings, not only upon the combatants but upon women and children, how much more is this the case with the hearts of loyal South African women like myself, who have loved ones on both sides; and one is glad that Miss Hobhouse is eager to alleviate these sufferings, as far, at least, as the Boer women and children are concerned. One realizes the inherent goodness of her heart; but her report is apt to give wrong impressions to those who are unacquainted with the habits of life and conditions of things in South Africa, where intense heat, crowded tents, flies, scarcity of milk, snakes, etc. are every-day occurrences. We South Africans wonder to hear so much made of things which we have always had to put up with.

Snakes are often found in the houses, even more so than in tents, because of the stone walls, and what South African has not seen the ceiling and floor of an up-country Boer house black with flies, which it requires the utmost cleanliness, coolness and darkness to keep out of doors?

'In my native village and district of Fraserburg, in the karoo, Cape Colony, cow's milk is hardly ever seen, black tea and coffee being the usual beverage, saving where condensed milk can be had. When mother's milk fails, babies are reared upon a home-made kind of Benger's food called "meal-boll", or upon condensed milk.

'Camp life must be very hard for those Boer women who have been accustomed to live in better homes, but the ordinary women of the bywoner class are accustomed to a life somewhat similar to that of the gipsies in this country. This same class never have extra clothing for their babies, and generally tuck up what little clothing the babies have on under their arms and let them crawl about semi-naked on the ground.

'It is always disagreeable to be in a tent when it rains, as it generally leaks until the canvas is soaked, but it should not be forgotten that in Africa these discomforts are usually of but short duration, as the heaviest showers are speedily followed by sunshine and warmth.

'No South African who has been foolish enough to walk two miles between 3 and 4 p.m. in summer but will sympathize with Miss Hobhouse's feeling of heat and exhaustion; but why state that the camp was "dumped down on the southern slopes of a kopje" thereby attaching indefinitely some blame to the military, who in this instance have decidedly proved themselves more *au fait* than Miss Hobhouse is with the needs of a country lying in the southern temperate zone, where the southern side of a house and the southern slopes of a hill are always the coolest?

'On the whole, Miss Hobhouse's report is unintentionally a marvellous testimony to the exceeding care our military have expended upon the women and children of the very men who are shooting our brave soldiers down, and she admits that some people in South Africa regard "the camp as a haven of bliss". She begs us to "let them go," but she forgets that all the towns and villages are forsaken and that they would only go back to poverty and destitution, and altogether overlooks the fact that they could all get back to their homes at once if war ceased.'

This was not an opportunity that Emily could let slip and her reply, written in white heat, conjures up the picture of her as she might have spoken to Mrs Stuart, if they had ever met:

'Sir,

'In your issue of July 2nd appears a long letter from Mrs K. H. R. Stuart relative to my report to the committee of the South African Women and Children Distress Fund.

'May I be allowed a few words in reply?

'Mrs Stuart seems an adept at reading into simple phrases meanings which do not exist. For instance, in paragraph 15 she takes exception to my innocent description of a camp which lies "on the southern slopes of a kopje". She says I "hereby attach indefinitely some blame to the military, who in this instance have decidedly proved themselves more *au fait* than Miss Hobhouse is with the needs of a country lying in the southern temperate zone, where the southern side of a house and the southern slopes of a hill are always the coolest." What right has Mrs Stuart to deduce blame from my simple words? Does she seriously believe the English people so ignorant that they do not know the difference between the Northern and Southern Hemispheres? Is it Mrs Stuart's mission to give uncalled for instruction in physical geography?

'It would be tedious to reply categorically to all these superficial criticisms; but in paragraphs 5 and 17 Mrs Stuart expresses surprise that I made no allusion to suffering endured in the sieges of Ladysmith and Kimberley, and that I tell no stories detrimental to the conduct of our soldiers.

'Sir, what have these topics to do with my narrative to the Distress Fund Committee? I understand keeping to the point, even if, as her letter indicates, Mrs Stuart does not. I repudiate such criticism.

'I have not the advantage of knowing Mrs Stuart, but I do know intimately scores of South African men and women from north and south who know as much of their country and the habits of their people as Mrs Stuart can do, and who feel and testify to the truth of my presentment of the subject.

'Does Mrs Stuart fancy that English people need her to tell them that snakes, flies etc. are common in hot countries? I have not dwelt on such details, or I might have spoken of scorpions which infest one camp and ants which eat the bedding in another.

'Does Mrs Stuart imagine we do not know that tentcloth leaks until it is soaked, or that bell-tents are often resorted to in England as well as South Africa for a summer holiday?

'Sir, this is playing with a serious subject. And why once more bring politics into this question? I have protested once against that. I will protest again and appeal to you, Sir, to use the great influence of your paper to keep this matter free from party strife. It is only remotely connected with politics. It is far, far removed above them, as far as the blue sky above the clouds which obscures it. Let us keep it so.

'Mrs Stuart is, I understand, in England collecting money to put gravestones over the victims of the war fallen on either side. Hers is a sacred task. She cares for the dead; I care for the living. I do not interfere with her work; why should she seek to criticize mine? At any rate, before offering further criticism, will she not visit the camps and learn their condition at first hand?

'The great fact of the death rate she totally ignores. No one in their senses knowing these camps will or can deny that the suffering there is very great and likely to be greater. In my opinion it is a subject upon which all can write and work under the sanction of the Government, which has been already accorded.

July 3   I am, etc.

EMILY HOBHOUSE'

An effective piece of debating but one which unfortunately gave the impression that Emily, after having visited only half a dozen or so camps, considered that she was the person best qualified to supervise all.

In addition to writing letters, Emily herself was speaking here, there and everywhere at meetings. She was nervous at first and inclined to burden her audiences with too many detailed statistics. But with practice she grew more confident and she learnt that the art of emphasis lay in knowing what to leave out. She continued, however, to rely on logic rather than on eloquence for her effects. On June 25th, she held a meeting attended mainly by women in the Master's Lodge at Balliol College, Oxford, in an effort to correct the widely held impression (given in fact by Mr Brodrick in the House of Commons) that the camps were voluntary, that people went into them of their own free will and could leave them when they liked. At Hull on June 28th she held a private meeting at the Friends' Meeting-house with Sir James Reckitt in the chair, at which she questioned whether the British had the right to bring women and children by force into the camps if they could not supply them with the necessities of life. On June 29th at Scarborough where, as in Hull and York, she had been refused a public hearing, she again addressed a private meeting under the chairmanship of Mr Joshua Rowntree at the Friends' Meeting-house. At Southport on July 3rd, where Emily spoke in the Temperance Institute, she was greeted with shouts of 'traitor to her country' and 'where's Kruger?' (the suggestion being that he should subsidize the camps). On July 1st she was at Leeds. On July 8th she returned to the West country and addressed a meeting at Redland Park Hall, Bristol, where it was suggested to her that British soldiers had been treacherously shot while taking food to Boer women on the farms. Sticks and stones flew through the air despite attempts by Quakers to lower the tension by singing hymns. At Plymouth it was the vegetable marrow season and the ammunition, as Emily put it, was less durable. At Northampton on July 17th a hall was let to her only on condition that no resolution was proposed beyond a vote of thanks. She and her supporters on the platform sat in silence for one and a half hours (the time the speeches would have taken) face to face with an equally silent audience. On July 21st, however, she spoke in the drawing room of West Lodge, Darlington, the home of Sir David and Lady Dale.

In later years Emily was inclined, perhaps understandably, to adopt the role of a minor martyr. For example to her friend Mrs Steyn she wrote:

'My work for the camps in South Africa has brought nearly all my people to look on me with contempt and suspicion. The Press has singled me out and I am branded as a rebel, a liar, an enemy of my own people, and accused of hysteria and a lot worse. One or two papers such as the *Manchester Guardian* have raised their voices in my defence, but the struggle was not even, and most people have a totally false impression about me. This has done much to sour my life. I am banned from society. People turn away when my name is mentioned. It has been so for years and has meant losing many old friends of my youth.'

But the 'suspicion and contempt' did not extend to her own family. True, Charles Hobhouse, the Liberal MP for Bristol East, complained that Emily's statements should be made on evidence of 'persons whose names are given in full and whose assertations are verified and corroborated by others and not upon the *ex parte* statements of people whose identity is veiled behind initials and blanks.' But on the other hand it was with banter rather than protest that he told her that she had added lustre to the name of Hobhouse in so far as everyone now asked him, 'Are you related to *the* Miss Hobhouse?' Emily gave him a characteristic look. 'I thought I was really THAT Miss Hobhouse,' she said.

Anyway the discouragements she might find in her public and private appearances in Britain were to some extent compensated for by the support that came to her from abroad. Her own report had been translated into French and sold for the benefit of the Boer Independence Committee. Despite strict military censorship, letters from Boers in South Africa supporting Emily's

Boer inhabitants of a bell tent shortly before their arrival in a concentration camp

Emily with General Beyers and General Smuts at a reception in Heidelberg in 1903

' "Anything in sight, General?"
"Certainly, congratulations and expressions of sympathy from
everywhere – for our enemies." '

'John Bull: "Open fire: they certainly won't shoot back." '
Originally reproduced in *De Amsterdammer* weekly in
Holland

'QUEEN VICTORIA: "Oh God, Joe! – I wash my hands in Innocence."'
Originally reproduced in *De Amsterdammer* weekly in Holland

Emily in her last years

statements were reaching sympathizers in Europe through Dr Williamson, U.S. Consul at the Hague, and the Boer Delegation in Europe delivered a lengthy plea on behalf of their compatriots to the Permanent Court of Arbitration at the Hague. President Kruger himself helped by giving an interview to William Redmond which was published in the August 17th issue of *Freeman's Journal* in which he said, between numerous thumps on the table, that surrender was unthinkable: 'We know England's promises. We should be slaves.' The aged President added: 'All we want is to enjoy our own. Even now, if we got our independence we would still manage to rebuild our country. But to enable us to do so we want our full independence.'

About this time the lead stories in British newspapers several days a week concerned the train wrecking by the Boers, examples of which were becoming more and more frequent. This was not of course Emily's affair except in so far as she regretted both the loss of life and the increasing bitterness to which this led in the closing stages of the conflict.

But in the public mind all pro-Boers were birds of a feather, and when Mr Mackarness argued in Parliament that, if train wreckers were, as the Government alleged, brigands, they were unlikely to be deterred by the practice of compelling respectable old gentlemen to travel as hostages in the trains, it was as if Emily herself had spoken; and when one correspondent questioned whether it was legal for a Government to use its own subjects as hostages in this manner, Emily herself might have been the inquiring Christian.

For the Government, the awkward thing was that, no matter what measures were or were not tried, the war was becoming hideously expensive. For example Lord Stanley, Financial Secretary to the War Office, disclosed, in a supplementary statement to the budget, that the cost of the fighting for the four months between April 1st and July 31st was £25,750,000 and that during July the cost had continued to run at £1,250,000 per week.

The concentration camps were, perhaps, a less urgent problem, especially as Kitchener had once more telegraphed on August 3rd from Pretoria to say that 'Goold-Adams has made a tour of inspection refugee camps Orange River Colony and reports people well looked after and completely satisfied with all we are doing for them. Bad outbreak of measles at Kroonstad among those brought on by Elliot from Reitz. Male refugees

F

at Kroonstad presented most loyal address and peace movement is spreading fast in all camps.'

Emily meanwhile found herself on the horns of the dilemma which confronted her throughout the war. In June 1900 she had guessed that all was not well with the refugees but could not be certain without seeing for herself, so she went to South Africa. Then, having seen for herself, she had to return to England to correct the false impression that the British were getting from their own Government. Now, having been away from South Africa, she could no longer be certain what was happening there. She wanted to carry on the work she had begun, yet, from what had been said in Parliament and elsewhere, it began to look as though the Government was not only prepared to dispense with her services but had acquired a positive aversion to her activities.

Emily endeavoured to keep her delicate foot in the door by means of a letter to Mr Brodrick in which she suggested that since he had adopted most of her recommendations she could hardly imagine there could be a valid objection to her resuming her work. She also suggested that 'some of the persons whom you propose shall be sent by the Government . . . should be persons nominated by the committees of the several funds raised in England and submitted to the Government for approval. I am not in a position to speak for the other funds, but with regard to the South African Distress Fund, I am authorized to state that such a mode of distribution would meet the approval of the Committee. For obvious reasons they would not feel justified in delegating to others the entire responsibility of distribution.'

Early in July Lord Ripon, acting as Chairman of the Distress Fund, followed this up with a suggestion that 'ladies should at once be sent to the camps' and added that Emily was prepared to go on this mission.

Mr Brodrick, however, was unmoved. He wrote:

'I am directed to assure you that His Majesty's Government view with satisfaction the readiness of various philanthropic associations to supply funds and give service for the amelioration of the conditions of those suffering by the war; though they would regret that such efforts should be confined to one part only of those who have been rendered homeless or penniless by the course of hostilities. But these proposals, by their number alone, make it impossible for the Government to accede to them. The Secretary of State for War has three such proposals before him at this moment, and it is obvious that it would be impossible to introduce a variety of authorities into camps organized and regulated by the Government.

'The Secretary of State has every reason to believe that, allowing for the obvious difficulty of temporarily accommodating so large a population as is now congregated in the camps, all proper arrangements have been made for the food, clothing, medical attendance, and spiritual supervision of those in the camps. Schools have been established, and a properly qualified matron has been appointed in each camp. Beyond this the Government will shortly send out certain ladies to visit the camps and co-operate with the local committees in the distribution of comforts or gifts of money which may be entrusted to them.'

From this rosy description of the camps it was evident to Emily that she had failed to present the matter in its most urgent and serious light to Mr Brodrick. The long delay before sending workers and the rise in the death rate combined to make her seek and obtain a further interview with the Secretary of State.

The conversation between Emily and the Minister took place on July 18th and was confidential in character, but the ungallant gentleman repeated the refusal of the Government to let Emily return to the camps and, to use Emily's words, 'as it was confidently expected by the public in many parts of England that I should so return, I asked for and was promised a letter containing the Government's reasons for this refusal.' Not having received this letter by July 26th she wrote as follows:

'Dear Mr Brodrick,
When we parted on the 18th you promised to send me a letter giving the reasons why you could not allow me to return to my work in South Africa. Such a letter has not reached me, and I hope you will forgive me if I rather urgently press that it should be immediately sent. I am continually asked on all sides when I am going out again. It is generally expected I shall soon start, which is, indeed, my own desire. Since you have adopted, in principle, almost all my recommendations, I can scarcely think any ground of objection can be regarded as tenable against a proposal to resume work the results of which have been accepted by yourself. It has occurred to me that you might say that any help on my part was unnecessary, because you have yourself selected certain ladies to visit and report upon the Concentration Camps. In

relation to this, may I be permitted to urge that the number you have sent is really quite insufficient for the work entrusted to them, considering the largely increased number of refugees now found in the camps, unless they have supplementary assistance; that they must spend much time and labour before they will have acquired the preliminary knowledge necessary for useful action; and, if I may speak of myself, that my experience in the camps, my acquaintance with the people, and to some extent with their language, ought to enable me, and I trust would enable me, to be a useful auxiliary to them in the discharge of their duties. I would fain hope that the delay in sending your letter may mean a disposition to reconsider my appeal for leave to revisit the camps in South Africa. In spite of improvements that have been made, there is much suffering and misery still wanting alleviation, and I do most earnestly press you to grant me permission to return at the earliest possible moment to the work in which I have become so deeply interested—I have, etc.'

The reply which came by return was an uncompromising 'No'. It ran:

'Dear Miss Hobhouse,

I am sorry if there has been any delay in writing you a letter on the subject which, with others, you mentioned when I saw you on the 18th, but as I was forced to refer to the matter publicly in reply to questions in the House of Commons, I hoped I had done what was necessary to explain the action of the Government. The only considerations which have guided the Government in their selection of ladies to visit the Concentration Camps beyond their special capacity for such work, was that they should be, so far as is possible, removed from the suspicion of partiality to the system adopted or the reverse. I pointed out to you that for this reason the Government had been forced to decline the services of ladies representing various philanthropic agencies, whose presence in an unofficial capacity would be a difficulty in camps controlled by Government organization. It would have been impossible for the Government to accept your services in this capacity while declining others, the more so as your reports and speeches have been made the subject of so much controversy; and I regret, therefore, we cannot alter the decision which I conveyed to you on the 18th instant. Yours, etc.

ST. JOHN BRODRICK'

Having failed with her technique of 'almost in confidence', Emily decided, for better or worse to write an 'open letter' to the Minister.

'Dear Mr Brodrick,

Three months have passed since I approached you on the subject of the Concentration Camps in South Africa, three terrible months in the history of those camps. Can the appalling figures just shown in the Government returns for August and the preceding months pass unnoticed by the Government and by the great mass of the English people? Will you bear with me for a moment if I approach you again on this sad topic, and with these latest figures before us make one more appeal to your clemency, and through you to the humanity of the country?

'If we leave for the present the coloured camps and speak only of the white people, the returns show that the population of the camps has increased gradually during June, July and August from 85,000 to 105,000 souls. In the past month of August 1,878 deaths occurred among the whites, of which 1,545 were children. The total number of deaths for the three months for which we have returns is 4,067, of which 3,245 were children. We have no account of the hundreds who passed away in the first six months of this year and part of last year. What is there to indicate the probability of any abatement in this fearful mortality? The cold winter nights are happily passing away, but rains are falling in many parts, and the increasing heat will bring sicknesses of other kinds. Scurvy has appeared. Daily the children are dying, and unless the rate be checked a few months will suffice to see the extermination of the majority.

'Will nothing be done? Will no prompt measures be taken to deal with this terrible evil? Three months ago I tried to place the matter strongly before you, and begged permission to organize immediate alleviatory measures, based on the experience I had acquired, in order thus to avert a mortality I have plainly seen was increasing. My request was refused, and thus experience which I could not pass on to others, rendered useless. The repulse to myself would have mattered nothing, had only a large band of kindly workers been instantly dispatched with full powers to deal with each individual camp as its needs required. The necessity was instant if innocent human lives were to be saved. Instead, we had to wait a

165

month while six ladies were chosen. During that month 576 children died. The preparation and journey of these ladies occupied yet another month, and in that interval, 1,124 more children succumbed. In place of at once proceeding to the great centres of high mortality, the bulk of yet a third month seems to have been spent in their long journey to Mafeking, and in passing a few days at some of the healthier camps. Meanwhile, 1,545 more children died. This was not immediate action; it was very deliberate inquiry, and that, too, at a time when death, which is unanswerable, was at work; nay, when the demands of death, instead of diminishing, were increasing. Will you not now, with the thought before you of those 3,245 children who have closed their eyes for ever since last I saw you, on their behalf, will you not now take instant action, and endeavour thus to avert the evil results of facts patent to all, and suspend further inquiry into the truth of what the whole world knows?

'In the name of the little children whom I have watched suffer and die, and whom I cannot for a moment forget, I make bold to plead with you once more. In the name of our common humanity I urge that immediate steps may be taken by those qualified and empowered to act, lest one day we are bowed down by the humiliating and grievous thought that we have sat still and watched calmly the extermination of a race brave and strong enough to have kept the British Empire at bay for two long years. I need not recapitulate the proposals which I made to you, some of which you seemed to adopt, though, alas, even your adoption has appeared to be powerless to secure the effectual employment of the most important. I ask at least for effectual amelioration.'

The letter continued for some time in the same strain and ended: 'In the earnest hope, that you will listen to my appeal.' But as often happens the letters about which one feels most deeply when writing appear almost Dickensian in their sentimentality, and occasional lapses into 'fain would I' style clichés did not improve Emily's effusion. The 'open answer' that appeared in the *Times* was typical of the reaction among the *Times* readers:

'Sir,
In a letter published in today's issue of the *Times,* Miss Emily Hobhouse makes an impassioned appeal to Mr Brodrick on the subject of the mortality and suffering among the Boer

children now congregated in the concentration camps provided by the English Government. As to the accuracy of her facts and figures, or to the extent to which the suffering, great as it may be, has been mitigated by the humane efforts of our people, I have nothing to say which you would think worthy of place in your columns, where the matter has been debated and elucidated with more knowledge than I can pretend to. But I confess that among the many amazing utterances which the war in South Africa has inspired, not one seems to me more amazing than Miss Hobhouse's assumption that, although the Boer men—and I understand her to add the Boer women also—are not moved one hair's-breadth in the direction of surrender by the sickness and death of their children, yet it is very barbarous on the part of the British Empire not to end the war at all costs because there is sickness and death among the offspring of these people! She clearly has not the slightest hope that the fathers of these children will give up a losing cause to save the little ones, but we—we British—are not to be "deaf to the cry", etc! A more severe indictment against the Boers, male and female (from Miss Hobhouse's point of view) could scarcely be framed. I am glad the accusation comes from so enthusiastic an advocate on their side, and is not brought by any prejudiced patriot in these islands. A charge of inhumanity such as this is perhaps deserved, but would certainly be passionately denied and vehemently resented if made by, Sir your obedient servant,

AN INSIGNIFICANT ENGLISHWOMAN

October 3'

In her open letter Emily referred to six ladies chosen by the Government to go to South Africa. This was in fact the famous Ladies' Committee, which, the Government had decided, should go to South Africa to inquire whether the camps were properly organized and sited, and to consider the way in which the funds raised in England could best be spent.

Its most prominent member was Mrs Millicent Garett Fawcett widow of the late Professor Henry Fawcett, who, although blind, rose to be Postmaster General of England. Mrs Fawcett was a scholar, an orator and an authoress and derived some reflected glory from her sister Dr Elizabeth Garrett Anderson. Politically Mrs Fawcett was a strong feminist and an ardent suffragette, and cynics said that her absence from the country might be a convenience to the Government. She was also an old friend of Leonard Courtney, but, in the matter of South Africa, her views did not march with his. She was in sympathy with the 'uitlanders' whom Dr Jameson had planned to liberate from the tyranny of President Kruger, and gave no credit to the reports that the Chamberlain Government had contrived the war in order to seize a rich territory. Also she had written an article strongly critical of Emily in the *Westminster Gazette* of July 4th 1901.

Another of the chosen six was Dr Jane Waterston, South Africa's first woman doctor, whose portrait shows a handsome, if somewhat masculine figure wearing a man's butterfly stiff collar, a white bow tie, jabot shirt with a rose tucked below. Mrs Fawcett as a feminist was somewhat put out when the doctor's male colleagues, while praising her professional work, referred to her as 'the best man among us'. Though beloved by the natives —she had originally come out as a medical missionary—Dr Jane was not one to be led astray by false sentiment. Her feelings were clearly expressed in a letter which appeared in the *Cape Times,* whose editor was by coincidence a near relative of Mrs Fawcett. 'Judging by some of the hysterical whining going on in England at the present time, it would seem as if we might neglect or half starve our faithful soldiers and keep our civilian population eating their hearts out here as long as we feed and pamper people who had not even the grace to say thank you for the care bestowed on them.'

Miss Lucy Deane, another member of the party was experienced in infant welfare work but was also an Inspector of Factories in the U.K.—and therefore perhaps a little beholden to the Government that employed her. Miss Katherine Brereton, who had been in charge of a yeomanry hospital in South Africa and knew how well or badly our own troops were cared for, was a trained nurse and had formerly been a sister in Guy's Hospital. Lady Anne Knox was the wife of General Sir William Knox. She had nursed in Ladysmith and could be expected to be aware at least of some of the workings of the military mind. Dr The Hon. Ella Campbell Scarlett was the sixth member of the Committee. All of them could be expected, once they had visited the camps, to speak with more authority than Emily Hobhouse and most could be expected also to disagree with her findings. But they were hardly the unprejudiced witnesses for whom Brodrick, on his own showing, had been seeking.

It was against this background that Emily decided to return to the heart of the matter in South Africa. For one thing her friends in both countries continued to ask her when she would return and, although she realized that there would be no place for her in the concentration camps, her experience might yet be useful in the camps in Cape Colony in which the 'loyal' refugees, which she had been accused of neglecting, were sheltered.

Before leaving home, however, she set out in an article published in the *Contemporary Review* of October 1901 her considered thoughts on the issue which had absorbed her attention and which had now become the major motivation in her life.

The article was for Emily surprisingly moderate in tone.

'The public mind has been distracted by so many diverse statements that it will be useful to gather up the straying threads of thought and fix them on a few central ideas connected with the camps. I have never, and do not now, put forward any criticism on the policy (be it military or civil) which led to the formation of these camps. Seeing, however, that it is a new departure in our own history to have placed 93,000 white women and children (besides 24,000 natives) in camps after total destruction of their homes, it is also for us a new as well as difficult problem to learn how to carry out so serious an undertaking without undue suffering and loss of life. Since the days when Nebuzaradan acted for Nebuchadnezzar in a similar undertaking, it is doubtful if the world has seen such a sight; but in his days the number carried away was comparatively small. Everyone must admit that, whether right or wrong, the task now undertaken is a vast one, embracing a host of difficulties. My object was simply to explain these difficulties, and, after close study on the spot, to suggest means of meeting them.'

After drawing attention to the death rate in the camps which she considered alarming in spite of government efforts to prove otherwise Emily continued:

'Other critics admit the high mortality, but lay the whole blame upon the Boer mothers. That is singularly unfair. A Boer woman brought to camp, smarting under the recollection of what she has just undergone, the sight of her burning home, her lost goods, her ignominious captivity, looks at first, naturally enough, on the khaki-clad officials of the camp as "the enemy". It is so difficult to us as a nation to realize that we are regarded as "the enemy" by others, being so sure of our best possible intentions for the welfare of all. The official attitude, variously expressed, is as follows: "It is very kind of us to have burnt your farms, destroyed your goods, deprived you of food-stuffs and above all, to have brought you here to feed at great cost and trouble to ourselves; it is all for your very highest good, and will end by placing you under the best of all possible rules." The two attitudes of mind cannot at once coalesce, and a Boer woman's first instinct (like that of our own poor, even where their own countrymen are concerned) is to keep her children beneath her own eye. Moreover when she sees but a rough hospital—and for months most rough they were, if they existed at all—and finds that many sick die there too, she doubts the benefit. Time and a little gentle explanation would, and does very soon, work wonders, but doctors who swear at the women and call them "murderers" to their faces because they do not at once put their sick children in the hands of strangers and "enemies" are hardly likely to inspire confidence. . . .

'In the little sketch of his camp given by Mr Caldecott in the July number of the *Empire Review,* one is sorry to see that it is proposed to make the women eventually pay for their own food and clothes. A debit account for daily food and for any article of clothing provided is being prepared. That may be just if a credit account is also allowed, showing clothing burnt and food and furniture destroyed on their side. But if they are, many of them, after all, living at their own expense, then surely they should be free to choose their own abode if they have friends or relatives to whom to go. Mr Caldecott says they are not prisoners. Yet the camp is enclosed with barbed wire, they are confined within certain bounds, their letters coming and going are censored, and they live by rule. It is difficult to see how they are *not* prisoners, except that they are in the end to pay back for food and clothing provided.

'Passing to the other points, the one really solid concession in the reply made by the Secretary of State for War to my recommendations is that which grants permission to leave the camps to women having means or friends or children from whom they are separated. The added clause, "Unless there is any military objection" is a grave one. Under martial law objections of the most trivial nature spring up like weeds, and under that same martial law there is no means of redress, of explanation, or investigation. But apart from the difficulties hanging round that clause, the concession is likely to remain on paper only, unless, first, the tidings of it are brought to those concerned, and, secondly, the applicants are put in the way to appeal, and thirdly, help is given them for travelling arrangements. This alone needs detailed personal work. Will the Ladies' Commission have time to attend to it? There is a note of gloom in advices from South Africa, giving information that since the joyful news was cabled out, many well-to-do people have applied for the release of their friends and relatives in camps, hitherto, it is believed, without success. . . .

'It is surely wise to take some note of the mental attitude of the captive women. They are many and influential, and their consolidated opinion an important factor in the problem of the future. Though the majority are bywoners (a class nearly equivalent to our agricultural labourers) yet a large number are women of education and refinement, holding positions of influence in their country. The present method of keeping them in semi-disgrace till they acknowledge their husbands and sons to be rebels is futile, and it is worse. A recent telegram from the Orange River Colony stated that strict methods were going to be taken to put down seditious language in the camps. What does that amount to? It means that women cannot talk together of the prowess of their men or express amongst each other hopes for their success, but some spy (and the camp is full of such) reports these most natural utterances, and punishment is enforced. One woman with several children, who made a remark, boastful in character, of their national hero De Wet, was sentenced to £5 fine, or a fortnight's imprisonment. Having no money, she was sent to prison, even though she was nursing an infant. Feeling was intense, and a number of women subscribed and paid the fine, hating thus seemingly to admit the principle of the thing, but feeling more keenly the separation of mother and infant; and by their generosity she was brought back in two days. Latest advices from Bloemfontein camp speak of one section as being now a "prison camp" where those men and women are placed who openly express patriotic sentiments; it is said the *Volkslied* (Boer anthem) is frequently heard from this quarter. As would be the effect upon ourselves, treatment of this nature only antagonizes a race, somewhat independent and determined like the Dutch, and we are our own worst enemies in allowing it to continue. . . . Shall we rest content with merely keeping these people alive, or shall we extend to them also a kindly treatment, freed from any suspicion of coercion. It is the *one* chance of forging fresh links between ourselves and them. We must confess, as we sorrowfully examine the death rates, that so far we have not succeeded very well in the attempt to keep them alive. . . .'

Having put her case, Emily booked her passage in the *Avondale Castle* and prepared to enjoy the relaxation of the voyage and the sunshine of the Cape Spring season at the end of it.

But she was in for a bitter disappointment.

9

That Miss Hobhouse

After three weeks at sea the *Avondale* dropped anchor in Table Bay at tea time on the afternoon of Sunday October 27th. Emily and her companion, Miss Phillips, a nurse whose skill could have been useful in South Africa, had packed in readiness for leaving the ship but when the tug came out towards them, Emily espied a khaki uniform which told her that Martial Law, which had formerly prevailed north of the Orange River only, had now been extended to Cape Town. Furthermore the officer in charge of the tug, Lieutenant Lingham R.N., brought with him orders enjoining him to examine every passenger—and there was some 450 of them—individually before allowing any to land.

It was clear, therefore, that there was little chance of the passengers being cleared in time to go ashore that evening; moreover, when it came to Emily's turn in the queue, the officer recognized her name and told her that he wished to speak to her later, when he had attended to all the other passengers.

Emily, according to her own account, bowed, withdrew and resigned herself to the inconvenience of unpacking once more. The dinner gong had rung before she was summoned again and, at her suggestion, interviewed out of the hearing of the other passengers in the cabin of the Master of the *Avondale*, Captain Brown, with whom she had already become good friends. The Captain, having received her, prepared to withdraw but the Naval Officer stopped him saying that what he had to say concerned Captain Brown as well as Miss Hobhouse.

Turning to Emily he said: 'I have to inform you that you are not to be allowed to land in Cape Town, that you are to remain on the *Avondale Castle*, under strict supervision, that you are to hold no communication with anybody on shore either by word or letter, and that it is proposed you should return

173

by the *Carisbrooke Castle* leaving on Wednesday afternoon.'

Then, turning to Captain Brown he said, 'You will be held responsible, under martial law for guarding Miss Hobhouse; you are not to allow her to leave the ship or receive or speak to anyone from shore; you are not to allow her to send or receive letters.'

This was rough stuff for a lady liberal, for in two sentences Emily had been cut off from the friends in South Africa who were waiting to welcome her and precluded from carrying out the work which she had planned. Her passage money had been wasted and she was being treated in public as an enemy of her country.

On the first occasion on which Emily landed in South Africa, Leonard Courtney, who was in a good position to judge, had given her four words of advice: 'Be prudent, be calm.' Emily did her best to follow this counsel.

Her first care was to ask who had issued the orders to Mr Lingham, and the officer replied that he had got his orders from Colonel Cooper, Acting Commandant in Cape Town. 'And from whom did Colonel Cooper get his order?' pursued Emily.

'Of that I can say nothing.'

Emily flared up then, protesting that when she left England no martial law had been declared in Cape Town and adding that it was incredible that people should not be allowed to land, after having made such a long voyage. To this, according to Emily, the officer had nothing to say, but, in response to questions, he told Emily that she would not be allowed to land at any of the other ports in Cape Colony—East London or Port Elizabeth, nor at Durban in Natal, nor anywhere in South Africa. Her nurse (for Emily had now slipped effortlessly into the role of an invalid) would probably be able to land but must allow herself to be searched if she did so.

Emily continued to object. She pointed out that Lieutenant Lingham had brought no warrant with him or statement of any offence that Emily might have committed; he had given her no chance of answering objections to her landing or of explaining why she wanted to visit the country. And she complained that the ban on communications with the shore deprived her of all help. She insisted on writing to Colonel Cooper and prevailed on Lieutenant Lingham to take the letter on her behalf. In fact she was making things as difficult as possible for the authorities, telling them that it was out of the question for her to return to wintry Britain in the *Carisbrooke Castle* and

they had answered that the only alternative was to stay where
she was. Then she went in to dinner and made small-talk as
if nothing had happened. Afterwards, with the help of Miss
Steedman, a fellow-passenger who was on her way to take up
the post of headmistress at a girls' school in Bloemfontein, she
wrote a number of letters. One was to Colonel Cooper and read :

'Lieutenant Lingham kindly undertakes to be the bearer of
this note. It was a matter of immense surprise to me when that
officer brought me your message forbidding me to land or to
hold communication with friends ashore, and stating that
I was to be made a prisoner on board the ship.

'He had no reason to offer me for this communication, and
he did not even wish to hear what my reasons were for visiting
South Africa. I therefore deem it wisest and due to myself
to approach you direct in order to gain some information
concerning the matter.

'I could understand the rigour of martial law being applied
to me if I had in the past taken or even now intended to
take a political part of any kind. But this I have never done.
Both in South Africa and in England my words and work
have been purely and consistently philanthropic in character.
I have left politics severely alone. My intentions in revisiting
South Africa were simply to carry on this philanthropic work
amongst all classes of sufferers of all nationalities in the various
coast towns where, when I left England, no martial law
existed. I have been urged from end to end of England to
ascertain the exact needs of the British refugees of whom so
much has been heard, and I have come here simply for that
purpose, being in a position to obtain considerable sums for
them in England when I have been able to satisfy myself of
the extent and nature of their needs.

'If we are to believe the outcries of the papers, much needs
doing in that direction. Still if, for any reason, the Government objects to such useful and necessary work I am of
course willing to forgo it; but what objection can be offered
to my living quietly in Cape Town for a while where I have
many old friends? I have been out of health, and shrinking
from the cold of an English winter came to this warm climate.
I do not feel equal to the strain of an immediate return voyage
which you offer me, nor the alternative of remaining a
prisoner on board the *Avondale Castle*.

'I am enclosing a letter which I earnestly ask you to convey

175

to the Governor, also one to Lord Milner and one to Lord Kitchener. I must further appeal to you on behalf of my nurse, a young woman who came as my attendant and masseuse. She intended living with me while nursing the needy sick under direction, and hoped eventually to settle in the country. Will you allow her to land, and be the bearer for me of a letter from Lady Ripon to Lady Hely-Hutchinson, also from myself to that lady? In any case, I trust you will in the just exercise of your office give full attention to this letter. It cannot but seem to me that the summary arrest of an Englishwoman bound on works of charity, without warrant of any kind or stated offence, is a proceeding which requires explanation.

I am, Sir,

yours faithfully.'

Having dealt with Colonel Cooper, Emily wrote as well to Lord Milner and Lord Kitchener saying perhaps over-optimistically that she could not believe they knew of her arrest. She made a further appeal to Sir Walter Hely-Hutchinson to 'protect' her and also asked Colonel Cooper to read and forward a letter to a lady friend. (Emily's habit of cloaking the identity of her friends and informants is irritating but perhaps understandable in circumstances where contact of any kind with Miss Hobhouse might bring attacks, protests, and even official reprisals on the head of the person named.)

To Sir Walter, she said:

'I have been repeatedly urged in England to return to South Africa and take up the cause of the British Refugees from Johannesburg etc. and acquaint myself fully with their needs with a view to the collection of funds on their behalf when I return home.

'I am satisfied I could obtain considerable sums for their relief when I have taught myself the true extent and character of their need, in such manner as to be able to present it before others.

'On arriving in Table Bay today I am astonished to find myself placed under arrest—forbidden to land or hold communication with any old friend on shore.

'This summary arrest of an Englishwoman bound on a charitable errand appears to me so astonishing that I cannot believe you are cognizant of it.

'If for any reason you or the local military authorities object

176

to my doing the work indicated I will of course desist from it but I must beg you to allow me to land if only for a few weeks in order to obtain rest and change. I feel quite unfit for another long voyage. If it will enhance the honour of England that I remain a prisoner I am quite willing and ready, but I beg you to let this prison be on *land* and not on sea. I cannot sleep here. I do not care how poor a cell or how meagre a diet provided only I can be on land. I hope to send Lady Hely-Hutchinson a letter entrusted to me for her from Lady Ripon—Lord Ripon with whom I was staying just before sailing sent you his remembrances I believe.

'It amuses me *now* to think Lord Ripon said that in *his* opinion I had done a great public service and ought to be received wherever I went with "a cannonade". Consequently his surprise at my present treatment will surpass my own.

'I trust however that our older English notions of justice and common sense will prevail and I hope therefore I shall not appeal in vain to England's representative in Cape Colony for leave to rest a few weeks on shore at least in prison if not free.'

These letters, read even seventy years later, bring Emily into focus almost as if she were standing in the room. There is the judicious use of temper over the issue on which her case was weakest—namely whether it was reasonable to apply martial law to someone who happened to have been on the high seas when it was declared. There is the hint that she had been exhausted by the voyage and needed 'several weeks' for recovery despite the fact that when in England she had looked forward to it as a relaxation. There is the proposition that she was unable to stand the English winter without an explanation of whether 'stand' meant 'survive' or 'enjoy'. There is the statement 'I have been out of health' which is true if we take into account that Emily had been receiving massage from Miss Phillips on the boat, but less convincing if we consider her plans for a strenuous programme in South Africa. And it is fair to ask whether her desire for a land prison was just good tactics since she apparently did not suffer from sea-sickness. Also would she, if allowed to land, have confined her activities to 'loyal' refugees? Again, Emily's plea that her life was non-political meant less in those days when women could neither vote nor enter Parliament than it would today.

During this crisis the presence that had sudbued Lord Milner was brought to bear on the young lieutenant to get him to convey Emily's 'missives' ashore while profuse name-dropping was resorted to as a form of scare-tactics.

But nothing it availed her and the following morning she watched in dismay while the other passengers made their way ashore, leaving her behind in solitary state.

In solitude, she continued her plans for causing as much trouble as possible. To embarrass the authorities she would make her plight known in Cape Town. She would refuse to give her parole and insist on a guard (because soldiers hate guarding women); she would require to be given her instructions in writing. She would persist in asking to be confined, if at all, in a land prison (where visitors could hardly be refused).

That day it blew a south-easter as only it can blow at the Cape, but Emily decided that she would like to paint and did two scenes in oils of Table Mountain and the Lion's Head peak nearby. Captain Brown was ashore most of the day, when he returned aboard in the evening, and told Emily that he had orders to take the ship into dock the next day to unload, all kinds of possible ways of communicating from ship to shore suggested themselves to Emily. But she did not wish to give the authorities extra grounds for complaint.

Moreover Colonel Cooper had not been entirely unco-operative. His reply to Emily's 'missive' had been sent at once from The Castle, Cape Town, and read:

'Madam,
I am in receipt of your letter of this date and regret it is not in my power to allow you to land in South Africa. The letters you enclose will be forwarded to the High Commissioner, the Commander in Chief, the Governor and Mrs Murray. There is no objection to your nurse landing.

I am, Madam, your obedient servant,
    H. COOPER
                        Colonel Commandant.'

So Emily decided to write again to the Colonel:

'I have to thank you for your kindness in giving prompt reply to my letter, and am obliged to you for forwarding my enclosures. My nurse, with your permission, will land to-morrow, and take the letters (Lady R's and mine) to Lady Hely-Hutchinson. I feel it my duty to ask you to let me have in writing exactly the regulations to which you wish me to conform whilst a prisoner on this vessel. Word of mouth is vague at the best, and as we are moving into dock tomorrow, I can foresee many occasions may arise where it will be difficult to guide myself without written instructions. As we move early I should be obliged to receive these at once. Moreover, I conceive that it would be wiser to appoint a regular guard to see that I do not pass the limits of these regulations. May I ask you to send one for that purpose? A guard will not only be a satisfaction to your mind but he will be a witness also to my adhesion to your regulations, until such time as you see fit to intern me in a land prison.

P.S. Do you allow me to communicate with a washer-woman, or is uncleanliness part of the régime to which I must submit? A bath here is also impossible.'

The following day a full gale was blowing with too much wind to set up an easel. Too much, even, to take the ship into dock or to communicate with the shore except by signal. So Emily pinned her drawing paper to the deck and did a sketch lying down. Not perhaps the act of an invalid, who in her report later claimed to have been unwell and sleepless, but character-istic, none the less, of Emily herself.

Of that day, Emily wrote :

'I sought the ship's library, in the hope of finding books which would show me how other people acted under similar circum-stances. By a curious chance I hit upon a volume of Macaulay's history, and found some stimulus in reading again how Bishop Trelawny (who happens to be an ancestor of mine) resisted with his colleagues the despotism of James II. I wished I, too, had six companions, but except that he refused to pay the bill for his keep while under detention in the Tower, I could find no hint for my guidance.'

But that one hint saved her a bushel of money. It gave her the courage to refuse to pay the ten shillings a day that her maintenance was said to cost, and it reassured her that, although she might have wasted the fare for her passage out, she would not, being an 'undesirable', have to pay for the return journey.

On Wednesday the *Avondale Castle* duly moved into dock and Emily was allowed a few visits from her friends Mrs Charles Murray and Mrs Curry, perhaps because the military thought she would be sailing on the following day in the *Carisbrooke Castle*.

In other respects, however, the day was less propitious. The letter from Sir Walter at Government House declined in an almost jaunty manner to accept any civil responsibility for Emily's plight:

'Dear Miss Hobhouse,
Your letter of yesterday was delivered to me this afternoon. I presume that you have been detained on board the *Avondale Castle* under the powers conferred on the military authorities by martial law, and I will therefore lay your complaint before the General. In the meanwhile I may assure you that the care of the British refugees is in safe hands, and that you need have no anxiety on that account.'

Neither did Colonel Cooper give her the satisfactory reply she had hoped for. Instead, he called at 4 o'clock. Emily wrote in her subsequent report to the Committee of the South African Women and Children's Defence Fund:

'The interview was short.
'He said, "I am sorry Miss Hobhouse, to make your acquaintance under these circumstances."
'I said: "I am sorry, too."
'There was silence awhile, then Colonel Cooper asked if I did not think it best to leave on the *Carisbrooke* that afternoon. I replied as before that I felt unequal to it and needed rest; that no reason had been given me for my detention, and I knew of none which could warrant a proceeding so arbitrary on the part of the authorities. He inquired what then were my plans. I answered they had been to land and, after rest, do my work in the town, but now my plans appeared to be somewhat in his hands, that I should naturally prefer the alternative of remaining on the *Avondale,* where I knew the ship's crew, to being sent on board any other vessel in the Bay, until answers had come from Lords Milner and Kitchener, who I hoped were unaware of my arrest. If it would enhance the honour or add to the safety of England that I should be imprisoned I was willing, but I begged it might be a land prison. Until justice could be obtained any cell and any fare would do on land. Colonel Cooper remarked on the unpleasantness of a ship unloading in dock, noise, dirt and smells prevailing. I assured him it was not my wish to remain in it, but disagreeable as it was anything was preferable to another immediate voyage. I further said it was incredible

to me that English officers or Englishmen could insist on imposing on me a long sea voyage immediately following on a previous long voyage. I had not felt well since leaving England, was overdone when I embarked, my arrest had been a great shock, and I shrank from further strain; I considered that both in reason and justice I was entitled to rest if not to freedom.

'The same evening Lieutenant Lingham came, mainly in reply to my letter demanding a guard rather than the gaoler-ship of the captain. He seemed to have some objection to this, and wished me to give my parole that I would not escape. I said it appeared to me a disagreeable and unfair position for Captain Brown, who was my personal friend, and that I could not understand interfering with people's liberty, detaining them in prison, and yet not taking the trouble to guard them. Giving my parole not to escape was tantamount to keeping myself in prison, and why should I do that? I was detained at their wish, not at my own. He said parole was a usual thing, and I answered I believed that was so only in quite different cases, for I understood people were let out of prison on parole, not detained thereby. Further, he was asking for a thing which by their own actions the authorities deemed worthless. I had told them repeatedly I had come on no political errand, that such work as I should do would be philanthropic merely and open to supervision. If, therefore, they refused to believe me or trust my word on shore, how could they trust my word afloat, the value being the same on land or sea. Mr Lingham appeared to have no answer to this argument, but pressed for parole, though sorry to trouble me.

'I assured him I attached no blame to him, regarding him merely as a mouthpiece of a tyranny and injustice higher than himself. I inquired what alternative he proposed failing my parole, but this he refused to reveal beforehand.

'Dreading therefore being forcibly placed on a strange ship out at sea I resolved to compromise by agreeing to give my parole until I received answers from Lords Milner and Kitchener, and then I must reconsider my position. The interview was protracted, but Mr Lingham expressed himself satisfied with this, and departed.'

That night Miss Phillips had to give Emily a sleeping draught to calm her.

181

By Thursday, the day after the *Carisbrooke Castle* had sailed, the authorities felt more sure of themselves. They sent an officer to Emily with written instructions informing her that a berth had been booked for her on the *Roslin Castle* which was leaving that very afternoon. Emily claimed to be too unwell to read the paper or to take in the contents of a telegram from Kitchener, who in agreement with a recommendation made by Lord Milner several months earlier, had ordered her immediate deportation.

'The officer told me the meaning of it, and I said, "I am not strong enough to entertain the idea." This he demanded in writing, and I roused myself to scrawl a pencil note to Colonel Cooper, saying I was sorry I could not face the proposed voyage.

Later Mr Lingham returned saying the orders must be carried out. My reply was necessarily the same, and that if I left in peace to recover strength, I might be fit to take the mail the following week, if still compelled. He said he should then be obliged to use force. I answered, "I cannot help what you do; that is your affair; I can only judge what is right for myself to do. Why not take me on shore and hang me? Why torment me so?"

'He pleaded his orders. I replied that I believed the whole British public would exonerate him if he refused to carry out such orders as forcing a sick, overwrought woman to take a long voyage without even a few days for rest.

'A card was brought me with the name Lieutenant-Colonel Williamson, R.A.M.C., which I returned, saying I was too unwell to see a stranger. In a few minutes the owner thrust himself upon me, saying he was a medical officer, and had orders to examine me. In vain I refused examination by a stranger, saying I had asked to see my friend and medical man in Cape Town. He would not go, and at length for very weariness, I submitted to a superficial examination. He said I had not heart disease, which I knew before. Under martial law the stewardesses were ordered to pack my clothes, and the chief officer was told to get my trunks from the hold. He rightly insisted on written orders before doing this.

'Throughout I maintained the same attitude, that I did not feel able to go, that this made it more unjust I should go, but that I would do my best to be well enough for the mail should respite not come, and I would let Lord Kitchener know as soon as I felt fit. I said repeatedly I still had faith enough in English men and English officers to believe that they would not force a sick woman on a long journey against her will, and that I should retain that faith as long as possible.

'Finally Dr Williamson brought two Army nurses, Sisters MacKillan and Nicholson, to take me by force. The chief officer of the ship was present at my request, besides the military men, and I spoke quietly to the women asking them to lay no violent hands upon me. They answered they were under military orders, and this I said I understood, but I put before them that the laws of humanity and nature are, or should be, higher than military laws, and appealed to them not to mar their sacred office as nurses by molesting a sick woman. I had appealed in vain to the men, but hoped I should not appeal in vain to my own sex. Both Sisters turned, and silently left the room, and I thanked them as they went. They behaved like true English women. I was left alone.

'It must have been an hour later, about 7 p.m. when Dr Williamson returned, followed by two soldiers. He approached, and, touching me on the shoulder, said, "Will you yield to technico?" I said, "I don't know what you mean." He explained, "Will you yield of your own free will, otherwise there are the soldiers." I could only say, "Sir, I cannot and will not give other reply than what I have said from the beginning. My refusal was based on principle, and principles do not alter in a day; nor can they be frightened out of me by force. I am weak and ill, unfit to take this voyage. It is not a right thing in my case, and especially unreasonable to ask it without giving me previous rest. I will not go one step voluntarily towards the *Roslin Castle*. I beg you to leave me."

' "Madam," he said, "do you wish to be taken like a lunatic?"

' "Sir," I replied, "the lunacy is on your side and with those whose commands you obey. If you have any manhood in you, you will go and leave me alone."

'He signed to the soldiers to come forward. They looked at me and hesitated a moment, and I took the opportunity of appealing to them to afford me the same respect as they would like shown to their own wives and mothers in similar condition. One man turned and was making for the door when Dr Williamson, fearful of losing his last chance, urged the other forward, and reluctantly they did their work. My shawl was wound round me, confining my arms, and I was forced on to the deck where several soldiers were waiting.

They carried me away through the ship and on to the dock where a carriage was in readiness. I spoke a few words to the men who bore me, otherwise there was silence. The stars were brilliant, and the fresh night air revived me a little. At the dock where the *Roslin* lay I was asked to board her voluntarily, but I refused as a matter of principle. Even had I possessed the strength to do so I would not move one step towards the vessel. My whole strength was centred in the resolution to refuse acquiescence in the injustice of the order, and for the time it deprived me of power in other ways. Orderlies were summoned who carried me, as before, to a cabin, where I lay till placed under charge of Colonel Clowes, officer in command of the transport, whom I begged to release me or appeal to Colonel Cooper to do so. He spoke kindly and said he would see Colonel Cooper in the morning.

'Next morning the medical man I had wished to see succeeded with difficulty in getting a permit, not, however, until too late; when he arrived the vessel was gliding from the quay.

'The voyage took twenty-four days, and my weak condition at starting made it one of great suffering for me, lightened only by the devotion of my nurse; there was no stewardess on board.

'My nurse, Miss Phillips, altered her plans and most unselfishly refused to leave me, judging me unfit to be left to strangers.

'From the moment I was arrested till the present time, I have never been informed what was the ground of complaint against me, or by whose original authority I was subjected to the treatment I have described.'

But she was well enough on November 1st before leaving to send a parting shot to Sir Walter in her best 'melo' style, a document which is still treasured in the Public Record Office but which has not, so far as I know, been previously published.

'I am obliged to you for your note, and am sorry you could lift no finger to help an Englishwoman brutally treated.

'I shall make the whole affair very widely known in England that the people may realize the sort of things done in their name. One blushes for the name and honour of England.

'I am glad to have in writing from you a statement so authoritative as to the welfare of the British Refugees. It seems a pity, if what you say is true, that some official statement of the kind has not all these past months been made in the *Times* to allay the anxiety in the public mind. I will gladly quote you.

'Excuse a pencil scrawl but I am weak and exhausted.

'It seems to me if I were a Governor without power enough to protect one sick Englishwoman from torment and brutality, I would resign a post so useless.

I have the honour to be,

Yours in bitter shame for England'

It was unfortunate for Emily that the *Roslin Castle* was a troop ship on which the standards of cleanliness and order fell far below that of any civilian mail ship, but Kitchener's orders, specifying immediate deportation, left no alternative. The only women aboard—apart from Miss Phillips—were two officers' wives. Neither of them spoke to Emily.

Her friends could well have thought that Emily had disappeared over the deck-rail of the *Avondale Castle*. The Cape Town papers, under censorship, printed hardly anything of her arrest, and her friends in England had to rely on a cryptically worded cable from one of Emily's friends in Cape Town and on two letters which she had managed to persuade an officer on the *Avondale Castle* to post for her. They were addressed to Lord Hobhouse and Lord Ripon in the hope that officials would not dare to interfere with the correspondence of persons of such eminence.

So it was with a sense of relief that Emily, on landing in Britain after seven weeks away, was met by friends.

For a matter of days, if not weeks, Emily and her supporters considered whether to go to law about her arrest. Her uncle Arthur, Lord Hobhouse, put the matter in the hands of Lewis and Lewis, an eminent firm of solicitors to find out whether her detention aboard the *Avondale Castle,* her removal by force to the *Roslin Castle* and her deportation to England were illegal.

Letters were actually sent to Mr Brodrick informing him of Emily's intention to bring an action against Lord Kitchener and Lord Milner as well as against the officers who had helped to detain her in the first ship and to take her aboard the second. The action would be for false imprisonment and assault and the Court would have to decide how far an English subject could be deprived of his or her liberty by martial law.

In Lord Hobhouse's view this question had never been dealt

185

with since 1865, in the days when martial law had been declared in Jamaica in connection with the rebellion there.

Mr Isaacs, K.C., better known as Lord Reading and as Viceroy of India, was to have been Emily's Counsel. But Mr Brodrick refused to give instructions for the Solicitor to the War Office to appear on behalf of Lord Kitchener and Lord Milner and the Hobhouses reluctantly concluded that if the action looked like succeeding—which was doubtful—the Government would introduce a bill to idemnify them from the consequences of their misdeeds. Only the years ahead would give Emily the verdict, they thought.

Soon afterwards, Emily who knew how to make herself comfortable, as well as how to rough it, departed to Talloires, on the lake of Annecy in Haute Savoie, a picturesque resort which, even then, was earning a reputation for the manner in which its local trout and crayfish were cooked and served.

IO

What the Other Ladies saw

W hat would Emily have discovered in the concentration
camps if she had been allowed to visit them?
More, perhaps, than those who compiled the various
Command Papers published by the Government.

But even these official accounts were lurid enough.

There was for instance, Command Paper 819 entitled *Reports
on the Working of the Refugee Camps in the Transvaal, Orange
River Colony, Cape Colony and Natal,* published in November
1901; it ran to more than three hundred pages. There, we learn
that in order to avoid making the camps a target for attack
general instructions had been given that stocks of food should
be kept as low as possible 'consistent with safety'; that, at
Potchefstroom, the refugees had to be housed in reed huts as no
tents could be provided, that ten of the camps when first set up
had no stores, and that, as a result, 'these people are bare-footed
and in rags.' At Irene it was noticed that the water was drawn
from an open furrow over which sheep and cattle frequently
strayed. There, too, the refugees arrived wearing sacks tied round
them. At Johannesburg families living in the converted stables
of the racecourse had to hang up blankets to get privacy. At
Pietersburg and Volksrust there was no wood for fires. Of Bloemfontein, which Emily *had* visited, the report said that 'cleanliness
at this camp is a great source of anxiety,' and that the hospital
was 'excessively cold and draughty'. The report added: 'The
children are mostly not well or warmly clad. There was a shortage of boys' clothing and material for shirts. Boots are very
badly wanted.'

Of Middelburg it was recorded that, in July 1901, at the height
of the South African winter, some families had one blanket
only and several hundred children were without shoes or stock-
ings. Some girls had only one garment. At this camp, too, there

187

was a great shortage of wood for coffins; and packing cases and planks had to be used instead. 'I have just managed to keep going, but with the greatest difficulty,' the British official reported with unconscious irony. At this camp, where influenza followed an outbreak of measles, there was no isolation ward, and mothers took their children with them when they went to town or carried them in the open while they cooked. They refused to tell the dispenser the numbers of their tents lest their children be taken away to hospital. They believed that patients there were starved (enteric cases were). They also feared that they might be called on to pay for the cost of the treatment. Seven hundred refugees, some of them suffering from measles, were moved by orders of the General Officer commanding to Heilbron where they infected other patients. At Kroonstad, the military had installed a crematorium close to the refugee camp and refused to move it.

But Command Paper 819 was not the only report to reach the Government from their own officials. In December 1901, a month later, *Further Papers Relating to the Working of the Refugee Camps in the Transvaal, Orange River Colony, Cape Colony and Natal* were published as Command Paper 853. This mentioned that as late as October 1901 there were still water shortages at Winburg, Kroonstad and Vredefort Road, and Command Paper 934, issued in February 1902, noted of the Orange River Station in November 1901: 'It is a most extraordinary thing that there is not one trained or qualified nurse either in the hospital or camp.' The same report noted that at Mafeking in October there were only two 'medicals', one Austrian and the other German, who could speak but little English and no Dutch. They were supposed to visit between 800 and 1,200 patients.

Certainly there were difficulties which were no fault of the camp superintendents. In some cases the Boers in the field cut the water supplies on which the camps depended; or they interfered with the trains that could have brought fuel. Sometimes, on the pretext of military necessity, the British Commanders would seize supplies that would otherwise have helped to relieve hardship in the camps.

It was difficult if not impossible to arrange for effective isolation of infected patients. For example, a child in the measles ward would often develop chicken pox or whooping cough at the same time. Moreover, camp officials discovered that mothers had a habit of substituting a healthy infant for their own between

188

the visits of matron and doctor in order to avoid its removal to hospital.

And then the 'Dutch' were so difficult to deal with. Those with relatives who had surrendered could not live in harmony with those whose husbands were still in the field. Others refused to grow vegetables or help in the running of the camp on the grounds that the British had taken them prisoner and were therefore entirely responsible for their welfare.

Boer assistants to matrons were also found to be unsatisfactory and 'great artfulness in concealing hidden resources and displaying assumed indigence is exhibited in many cases and the kindly matron needs much to wit to detach the truly indigent from the impostor.'

There was also the fact that the Dutch distrusted hospitals run by the enemy and had developed their own remedies which they had used with success on their remote farms, where there were no doctors nearby to advise them.

Dr Pratt Yule, British Medical Officer of Health for the Orange River Colony, was particularly critical of the Boer hygiene and methods of self-help:

'The great majority of the people are filthy in their habits, though probably not to blame for this under ordinary circumstances. They live far apart; there are no sanitary conveniences of any kind (on the majority of farms latrines are unknown, and every kind of refuse and slops is disposed of in the immediate vicinity of their houses). They have naturally introduced these habits into the camps. When the camps were first formed it was extremely difficult to get the refugees to use latrines; they were unaccustomed to them and preferred the open spaces round their tents. The camps had to be strictly policed to prevent this.

'Dutch mothers have no ideas as to how a child ought to be fed and none as to how it ought to be nursed when sick. They cook their food very badly and it is common to see a baby feeding on meat, heavy dough bread and stewed black coffee . . . Every available aperture by which fresh air might enter is stopped and the windows are kept shut . . . As long as water can be obtained, they do not care what it may have come in contact with.'

Dr Kendal Franks, Consulting Surgeon to Her Britannic Majesty's Forces also had some hair-raising tales to tell of Boer medicinal practice. From Bloemfontein he wrote:

189

'There is here a Mr J. Kruger, a nephew of the ex-President. Being a man of superior intelligence he has been selected for one of the higher offices of the camp. One day he told the superintendent that his wife was suffering a good deal from rheumatism and he requested Mr Randle to use his influence with Dr Beaumann to allow him to give his wife a cow-dung bath which he stated "was the best thing for rheumatism".'

From Bloemfontein in January 1902 Dr Franks wrote:

'Mr Randle one day visited Abram Strauss, a man who had been selected as one of the head men of the camp and in virtue of his office was housed in a marquee. Mr Randle was surprised to see a cat running about the tent with all its fur clipped off. He inquired the cause and was told that the fur had been cut off and roasted and then applied to his child's chest as a remedy for bronchitis.'

But however satisfactory these explanations might sound to the medical profession in England, they failed to reassure the Government, and on November 16th, Chamberlain telegraphed to Milner to express anxiety about the mortality rates, the shortage of nursing staff, water supplies and other problems of the camps. It was not a complete answer, Chamberlain argued, to say that the situation was inevitable with crowds of people liable to infectious disease. The shortage of milk did not seem inevitable to him. 'The military captured thousands of cattle,' he said, 'in December 1901. Are there no milk cows among them?'

Milner, for his part was so concerned that he replied to Chamberlain in language that bordered on the mutinous. 'Every attention is being given to the matter (of the camps),' he averred. 'It absorbs for the moment in fact, practically the whole of my time, to the great detriment of other business. Indeed I should be glad if someone else could take it over but I do not see who there is.'

Meanwhile an attempt was made to compare the mortality in the camps with those which normally obtained in Cape Colony, especially in the Boer country districts, where, as Milner put it, 'I understand that the ordinary death rate of children is exceptionally high.' But Dr Gregory, the Medical Officer of Health for the Colony, had to admit defeat. The last census in the colony had been taken back in 1891 and, besides, the farmers in the more remote country districts were allowed a period of three months grace before they need declare deaths, by which time, of course, it was far too late to ascertain the cause. It was alleged, however, in Command Paper 934 that the death rate in the camps could be expected to fall as the weaker members died out. There would also be fewer of them coming in and the improved measures of cleanliness and hygiene would be certain to have a favourable effect.

Milner himself was prepared to argue that in any case the responsibility for deaths should have been put on the enemy. 'The problem was not of our making,' he said in a despatch preserved in the Milner papers, 'and it is beyond our power to grapple with it.'

On top of this came the invasion of the Committee of Women —their official description, though they were often dignified by the title of Commission. They had been recruited in July, were ready to sail in ten days, and arrived in Cape Town in mid-August. There the ladies found themselves in a highly delicate situation. Cape Town, they discovered, 'was riven into hostile sections', so much so that Lady Hely-Hutchinson thought it better that they did not call at Government House. The loyalists in the Cape deeply resented added concern being shown for the welfare of those whose relatives were killing their own sons and husbands.

The Afrikaner community in Cape Town, on the other hand saw the women as the 'Whitewashing Commission', and Mrs Fawcett was asked, 'How can you expect Boer women to make you their confidante when they know just as well as we do too that you have been sent to South Africa for the express purpose of whitewashing the administration of the Concentration Camps?' The ladies nevertheless sought and got an interview with 'the committee of ladies in Cape Town who were ardently in sympathy with the Boers.' The 'English ladies' told the 'Dutch that private sources in England had provided a moderate sum of money and asked how it could best be used? They at once answered 'Send them calico to wrap their corpses in.' This startled the English ladies, but they took the request seriously and added a twenty-second question to the list of those they had already drafted. It did not apparently occur to Mrs Fawcett that the request could have been in any way ironical or sparked by resentment because the friends of the refugees were the only ones forbidden to visit them.

Then, after leaving Cape Town, the Ladies Committee lived for four months in a special train consisting of a second-class carriage fitted out with berths, a saloon car for meals and a travelling kitchen staffed by a Portuguese cook named Gomez.

Meals were served by a young batman named Collins. 'We each have a little hole of our own,' Mrs Fawcett wrote, 'but it is a very small one, and the saloon in which we eat and have our meetings is of such dimensions that each must go to her place in turn; there is no passing one another in the saloon. An equable temper is of primary importance for getting on in such a life.' They pursued an unpredictable course and paid a number of surprise visits to make sure that they were seeing the camps under 'normal' conditions.

Thirty-three camps were inspected and, in addition to inquiring about the supply of shrouds, the ladies put questions about water, sanitation, housing, rations, kitchens, fuel, live-stock slaughter, beds, clothing, shops, hospitals, camp matrons, resident ministers, discipline and morals, education, employment, treatment of orphans, the death rate, absconders, servants and local welfare committees.

They appear to have made an investigation in depth although Dr Jane alone seems to have volunteered to look into the less attractive problems such as the slaughtering arrangements, the camp drainage and sanitation. 'She was an out-and-out Britisher by instinct and training,' wrote Dame Millicent, with an approval not to be shared by Emily.

In general, the ladies, in their reports, steered a realistic, middle-of-the-road course. They did not allow themselves to be exploited by the Government and refused to endorse a despatch which Milner proposed to send home saying that the Head Administrators and officers under them had left undone nothing that they could do with the means at their disposal. The Committee conceded that they had discovered no cases of cruelty or of harshness; they were, however, strongly critical of officials who, for example, were satisfied that they had done everything to get fuel when they had requisitioned it.

Kitchener consented to see a delegation of two of the ladies (but no more), and agreed to provide one extra truck a week in addition to the sixteen that already went to the camps in the Orange River Colony.

Familiarity did not breed admiration among the ladies for the Boer character, and Dame Millicent recorded in her memoirs the answer she got when she told a Boer Committee that their fuel ration in camp was the same as that of the soldiers, and that they should be able to make do with it if they cooked their meals in common. 'Honoured ladies,' the reply came, 'what you say is very true but we Boer people could not do it; we should all have to be born again and new love would have to be created among us; each one of us must boil his own pot.'

Sometimes, camp inmates were detected selling rations on the black market and one woman was found leaving a camp in the Orange River Colony with 240 lbs of flour, 40 lbs of salt, 28 lbs of rice, 22 lbs of coffee, together with tea, candles and soap which she had saved from her rations. The Boers at the time were only a few miles away.

In their report the ladies did help to explain why the phenomenal rise in the death rate was not due solely to the callousness of the British. Horses and mules, the ladies noted, were killed in large numbers during the fighting, or died of over-work and their bodies poisoned the water supplies. Cattle disease was prevalent and the sick beasts crawled to the nearest stream to die.

The ladies confirmed that at times no fresh meat, milk or fruit could be got in some districts and that in many cases sheep were down to 11 lbs in weight.

The children died, not because they were in camps, but because of the poisons outside, the ladies said.

The ladies were duly critical when British arrangements did not meet with their approval. They pointed out that while soldiers might normally sleep sixteen to a tent, more than five amounted to overcrowding if the family concerned had to live there under concentration-camp conditions. Telegrams were sent to India asking for more tents. They noted that Vredefort Road camp was sited two and a half miles from its water source, that Kroonstad had an 'extremely bad' water supply and that Standerton's was even worse. At Bloemfontein the washing arrangements were also 'extremely bad' and the woman had to wash their clothes in dirty puddles. At Aliwal North, the ladies discovered that all water had to be carried up steep banks from the river and that there was no private latrine for the nurses. In this camp it took seven hours to serve out the meat rations. The Zastron section of the camp was the worst. 'It would be difficult to imagine any dirtier dwelling place than some of the tents in this part of the camp. Everything was filthy. The floors were of loose earth scattered over with every abomination, the bones of the day before yesterday's dinner, apple rind and tops, banana husks of doubtful antiquity ... In many of the filthy tents there were sewing machines, in one a piano.'

At Bethulie, more than a year after the first camps had been set up, four-fifths of the people were having to sleep on the

193

ground, and those that died had to be buried in their blankets for want of wood for coffins. Food in the area was scarce and people in the village were living on half rations.

At Kimberley the ladies noted five sick children stretched out on the ground on mattresses. Their mother would have been willing to send them to hospital but there were no beds for them. Four epidemics (measles, pneumonia, influenza and whooping cough) were raging simultaneously.

At the Orange River camp several old women of sixty-five to seventy were without bedsteads, and there was no trained nurse. At Springfontein, the ladies found some of the inmates sleeping on the ground and having to eat half-cooked food because of the shortage of fuel. Winburg provided no separate latrines for women. At Heilbron there was less than a gallon of water per head per day and no bath houses. Here the burgher families were lodged in town houses, in the church vestry, in a blacksmith's forge and 'what must have been intended as a refuge for Kaffirs or pigs.' Here, the civilian population in the town had not tasted meat for two months and complained that all supplies were taken by the camp but they were healthy until some hundreds of patients infected with measles were sent to Heilbron from Kroonstad. Shortly after the ladies had visited the camp, a party sent out from this camp to cut fuel was captured by the Boers.

At Johannesburg the ladies found that half the people were sleeping on the ground and at Irene that there were no bath houses. Here the English ladies met a formidable Committee of 'Dutch' ladies who, between bouts of knitting and eating double rations, had apparently got the camp under their control.

At this camp the ladies from London were astonished to see children watching sheep and cattle being slaughtered for the meat ration—a sight which they might well have seen at any time on their family farm. 'It should have been impossible for such a savagely brutal scene to take place in a professedly Christian camp under British rule,' the British ladies commented.

At Potchefstroom Dr Jane found the bones and skulls of oxen, old tins, boots and rubbish and a dead crab in the water supply, in which, incidentally, a large dog was bathing. Here, there were no baths for the women, and they had to wade through ankle-deep mud to bathe in the same river in which clothes were washed. Here, families were still so short of clothes that they had to use flour bags for underwear. An old church, the walls of which had not even been whitewashed, served as a hospital. At

Klerksdorp the hospital had no matron, no sheets, no pillow cases, few beds and no provision for sterilizing instruments.

Middelburg camp was 'one of the most unsatisfactory we have seen,' the ladies said. They found it 'difficult to get accurate statements as to matters of fact from the Superintendent, or any definite information as to who is responsible for carrying out the details of camp work. There is complete want of order, method and organization, and there is hardly one department of the camp life which can be reported as being in a satisfactory state.'

And so the story continued. At Vereeniging the supply of disinfectant had run out. At Standerton drinking water was still being taken in buckets from the polluted Vaal river. There were no bath rooms, and the women had to do their washing in the river near the body of a dead ox. Forty more nurses were needed for the camps in the Orange River Colony alone and fifteen matrons from the Transvaal.

In short, the ladies committee had discovered almost exactly the kind of situation which Emily Hobhouse had believed they would find but in doing so had succeeded in pleasing nobody. Milner had originally instructed that the ladies' recommendations, even if mistaken, were not to be set aside without references to Headquarters but it was awkward, to say the least, when they recommended to him that no camp should hold more than 3,000 inmates, and aired a feminist, if unpractical, opinion that every able-bodied male should be subjected daily to three hours compulsory labour.

British officials rejected some of their recommendations and Milner had to tell Chamberlain that their condemnation of the site of Merebank camp as too damp was 'opposed to local advice'. The verdict of the medical board appointed to inquire into the matter 'does not bear this criticism out except as to a small part which has been cleared of inmates'.

Nor was Emily herself satisfied with the labours of the ladies. She had been dismayed by the delay in sending them—had not 576 children died in the month while the six ladies were being chosen? Had not the preparations and journey taken another month during which 1,124 children had died? And the bulk of a third month, had it not been spent at the more healthy camps and en route for Mafeking, during which 1,545 more children had perished?

She felt hurt and indignant in so far as her own opinions and experience were discounted, merely because she had been known to feel sorry for the sickly children and because she had shown personal sympathy to destitute Boer women in their personal troubles. 'What I chiefly regret about this commission is that it is one of inquiry (since it was the Government's wish for the commission to be impartial) rather than one of work and that no place was found on it for representatives of Colonial Cape Dutch.' 'Why inquire into something that the whole world already knows about?' asked Emily.

On the other hand, she felt that, though the Government had been slow in sending out the Women's Committee, the ladies, when they got there, did not spend sufficient time in the camps. The speed of their operations precluded them, in Emily's view, from entering at all into the life of the camps as felt by the people, for the Boers, as Emily put it, are not a race inclined to open their hearts to strangers of a day's acquaintance'.

Boer supporters were no more complimentary about the Ladies work. 'In the whole of their report,' said one article, 'there is not a word of pity for the misery they witnessed . . . no-one would dream of charging Mrs Fawcett, or any of the ladies forming her Committee, with "hysteria" or "sentimentality".' Pro-Boers, who used formerly to be among Dame Millicent's friends in England, cut her dead after she got home. They overlooked the fact that the report, if written in the style they would have liked, would have carried far less weight with the Government. It was a symptom of the prevailing bitterness that had now grown up over the issue, for although as we shall see, the death rate in the camps was at its worst in October, the attacks on the good name of Britain and her Government reached their full fury only in the months that followed.

I I

What the World said

At home, the Liberals' Autumn campaign against the concentration camps and against those who ran them, began with a letter in the *Times* from the Bishop of Hereford dated October 19th 1901. It ran :

Sir,
Every month brings us the dreary record of the enormous death rate among the children in the South African Concentration Camps, and today you publish one of the worst that we have hitherto received.

According to your tabular statement there are 54,326 white children in these camps, and of these 1,964 died during the month of September. As men read these dreadful figures they cannot but ask; How long is this fearful mortality to go on. . . ? Are we reduced to such a depth of impotence that we can do nothing to stop such a holocaust of child-life? . . .'

Ten days later Charles Trevelyan, Member of Parliament for Elland in the West Riding of Yorkshire, added:

'Many of us who were responsible as representatives refused to join in the outcry which followed on the publication of Miss Hobhouse's report. It was not that the mortality did not alarm us even then. But it seemed not unreasonable to suppose that such an operation carried out in time of war, and under such hurried conditions, must almost necessarily lead to a considerable loss of life. When the Government freely expressed its determination to attend to the question, when they appointed a number of admirable ladies to proceed on their behalf to South Africa, with injunctions to make application for whatever was necessary, and when we were led to believe that Lord Milner himself was fully alive to the danger, we

197

rested in the hope that a better condition would be realized within a month or two. The fourth month, September, has been reached and the mortality is enormously higher. Among the whole population it has risen since August from 214 per 1,000 per annum to 264. Among the children from 355 per annum to 440. . . .'

From Paris, Paul de Villiers wrote, again in the *Times*:

'May I, as a Boer, be permitted to doubt some of the facts assumed in your leader . . . Your statement that "the Boers, and not we, are properly responsible for keeping Boer women and children alive" is, you will admit, not true at all. . . . These women and children are, as Mr Brodrick admits, prisoners seized in the operations of war. The Minister of War has been good enough to explain that it was necessary to capture them since they "represented the intelligence department of the enemy". "The formation of concentration camps," wrote Lord Milner, a little over a month ago, "has been adopted on purely military grounds as a means for hastening the end of the war." The procedure, as you are perfectly well aware, Sir, is generally about as follows: Orders are issued for the clearance of a district; farmhouses where families are discovered are destroyed and the families brought into camp. The owner of the farm may be hundreds of miles away and may return months afterwards to find his family gone and his home destroyed. Now, who is properly responsible for keeping this family alive? How can you say that the responsibility is not yours when you have seized the family by force and keep it by force?'

That autumn the South African Conciliation Committee was equally active and, at a meeting held in the Memorial Hall at Farringdon Street, London, E.C., Mr Courtney assured the audience, which included Mr Keir Hardie and Mr Lloyd George, that the Conciliation Committee had *not* helped the enemies of their country—they had waged eternal war against them. But what enemies? The enemies that were within their own gates . . . The Cabinet, he said, was no longer trusted by anybody and a breath would cause it to crumble to pieces.

Kitchener, as usual, was unrepentant and wrote in characteristic fashion to General De Wet:

'Army Headquarters, Pretoria, South Africa, December 1st 1901

198

Sir,

I observe from a communication which His Honour Schalk
Burger has requested me to forward to Lord Salisbury, and
which I have so forwarded, that his Government complains
of the treatment of the women and children in the camps
which we have established for their reception.

Everything has been done which the conditions of a state of
war allowed to provide for the well-being of the women and
children; but as you complain of that treatment and must,
therefore be in a position to provide for them, I have the
honour to inform you that all women and children at present
in our camps who are willing to leave will be sent to your
care, and I shall be happy to be informed where you desire
that they would be handed over to you.

I have addressed a reply to His Honour Schalk Burger in
the above sense.

I have the honour to be, Sir,'

In his report to the War Office of December 6th 1901
Kitchener mentioned that at the request of General B. Viljoen,
he had permitted his nominee, Captain Malan, to inspect the
camps and ask if there were any complaints. Captain Malan
afterwards 'expressed his entire satisfaction with the arrangements which had been made on behalf of the Boer women
and children.'

Lord Kitchener added, 'I take this opportunity of stating
that I would make no objection to Commandant-General Botha
himself, accompanied, if he likes by General Delarey and Mr
Steyn, visiting these camps, provided they undertake to speak
no politics to the inmates, who, as a rule, appreciate the general
situation much better than their husbands or brothers.'

The Liberals were unconvinced.

Early in December the General Committee of the National
Liberal Federation held a meeting in Derby to consider their
attitude towards a settlement in South Africa. Their misdeeds
led to another thunderbolt in the *Times* leader column:

'To hold out vague hopes such as those encouraged by the
resolution passed at Derby can only do mischief by helping to
persuade the more ignorant Boers that this country is waver-
ing. We are unable to understand how Mr Birell can imagine
that the foundations of lasting peace are to be laid by "ex-
hibiting a spirit of negotiation" at a time when the end of the
war is visibly in sight, if we are only firm enough not to be

diverted from the plain object before us by captious criticism or factious clamour.'

The same meeting gave the same leader-writer the chance of another swipe at Emily. The leader continued:

'It is rather remarkable, that Mr Charles Hobhouse, MP for East Bristol, in submitting a motion calling upon the Government, at any cost, to remedy the present condition of the concentration camps, admitted that he could not agree with a great deal of what his kinswoman Miss Hobhouse had written on the subject, and regretted that she had not taken pains to verify some of her statements. This candour was resented by some of those present; by one lady, in particular, who marvelled at the moderation of Miss Hobhouse's report, though it does not appear that she had herself any personal knowledge of the facts entitling her to give an authoritative opinion.'

Meanwhile, Sir Henry Campbell-Bannerman, the party leader, was locked in a bitter exchange of letters with Lord George Hamilton, at that time at the India Office, who wrote as follows (with a copy to the *Times*):

'Dear Sir Henry,
You asked for proof of the assertion that you have calumniated and vilified the conduct of our troops in the field. I will state shortly the facts upon which I base my charge. . . .

On June 14, in addressing a portion of your political followers, after denouncing the military measures recently put in force in South Africa, you ask: "When is a war not a war? When it was carried on by methods of barbarism in South Africa." There are only two belligerents in South Africa, the Boers and the British Army. As your words could not apply to the Boers, they necessarily attach themselves to the British soldier. . . .

You may consider it your political duty to continue this form of oratory, but, if you do, I earnestly hope that for the future you will try to hold the balance a little more evenly between the practices of our enemy and the methods of our countrymen.

Believe me, yours very truly,
George Hamilton'

The *Times* added:

'We have received from the Patriotic Association, of 28 Millbank-street, Westminster, a copy of a pamphlet which they have recently issued under the title, "The Truth about the Conduct of the War". This pamphlet is an excellent exposé not only of the real facts of the case, but also of the shameful tissue of gross and baseless calumnies which has been fabricated by enemies of this country. According to the authors the objects of the pamphlet is "not to defend his Majesty's Ministers, who are well able to hold their own, but to refute false charges against British soldiers and officials, and to make the truth known to the English people at large, and, so far as possible, to the vilifiers of England abroad." The witnesses who are quoted, in evidence of the unvarying generosity which has been shown towards the enemy and of the unselfish humanity displayed by the British troops, include foreigners and pro-Boers as well as officials whose veracity is above all suspicion; and the testimony thus put forward on behalf of our soldiers is more than sufficient to convince any honest reader.'

By now, however, there could be little doubt that the most effective campaign among the Liberals was coming from David Lloyd George, and the famous occasion at Birmingham on which he was shouted down and had to escape disguised in a policeman's overcoat, only served to increase his reputation, even though not a word of his speech was heard.

He was prominent in the House of Commons debate of March 20th 1902 when Mr Chamberlain quoted the Boer General Vilonel as having told the Boers that the enemies of their country were those who, like De Wet and Botha, were continuing a hopeless struggle. Then tempers flared. After a violent altercation between Mr Chamberlain and Mr Dillon, an Irish Nationalist member, which ended in the latter being ordered out of the Chamber by the Speaker, Lloyd George entered the fray, stating that there was not a single war correspondent at the front who contemplated the conclusion of the war within two years.

'Much fuss had been made about Majuba. But during the war we had been defeated in eighteen battles in which we had sustained greater damage than we had suffered at Majuba,' Mr Lloyd George said.

'Sir C. Cayzer (Barrow in Furness): "And pro-Boers rejoice at it." Mr Lloyd George: "Mr Speaker, I do not know whether I am in order, but I say that is a perfectly insolent remark." (Loud Nationalist cheers.)

'The Speaker: "The interruption seemed to be aimed not against the hon. member himself, and in that case it was not a disorderly one." Sir C. Cayzer: "I did not mean the observation as a personal one. I made it against the pro-Boers, who, I consider, are traitors to their country." (Opposition cries of "Withdraw" and Ministerial cheers.)

'The Speaker: "The hon. member says he did not make the observation against any member of this House. That is sufficient." '

Lloyd George, continuing, said that after two and a half years' fighting, the Boers were in occupation of more territory in South Africa than at the beginning of the war. (Ministerial laughter.)

This speech in turn goaded Mr Brodrick into coupling Mr Lloyd George's name with that of Sir Henry Campbell-Bannerman and attacking them both. If Sir Henry wished to know why he was misunderstood he should refer to the speeches of 'his friend and follower the hon. member for Carnarvon'.

'Then he will understand why the country regards him as the leader of a party whose action has actively helped the enemy in the field. (Loud cheers.) If the right hon. gentleman wishes to know how his action is viewed by a large number of people in this country, I would refer him to the description by Southey of the Opposition at the time of the Peninsular War. He will find these words: "The Opposition consisted of heterogenerous and discordant materials. (Cheers and laughter.) From the beginning of the war, through all its stages, they had uniformly taken part against their country. (Loud cheers.) Consistent in this and nothing else, they had always sided with the enemy, pleading his cause, palliating his crimes (Opposition cries of 'Oh' and Ministerial cheers), extolling his wisdom, magnifying his power, vilifying and accusing their own Government, and depreciating its resources." And Southey adds: "In future ages it will be thought a strange and almost incredible anomaly in politics that there should have existed in the Legislature of any country a regular party, organized and acknowledged as such, whose systematic course of conduct, if it had been intended to bring about the fulfilment

202

of their own prophecies, could not have been more exactly adapted to the object." (Loud cheers.)'

But the feelings expressed by both sides in the House of Commons were mild compared to those aired outside Britain.

An awkward and embarrassing situation had already arisen when Mrs van Warmelo, a 'Dutch' lady living in Pretoria, decided to complain to the Diplomatic Missions still stationed there about the conditions in the concentration camp nearby at Irene. She first approached the Consul General for the Netherlands, Mr Domela Nieuwenhuis, and, later, Mr Cinatti, the Portuguese Consul who was Doyen of the Diplomatic Corps, to whom she presented a petition signed by nine leading women.

Armed with this, the Consuls called a meeting, had the petition translated into French and sent a copy by mail to each of the ten powers they represented, as well as to Lord Kitchener. General Maxwell, the British Military Governor, tried without success to discover the names of the signatories.

When a month had passed without any reply from Lord Kitchener, Mrs van Warmelo presented a second more strongly worded petition, asking the Consuls to intercede on behalf of the victims in the camps, since the death rate there threatened the Boer nation with extinction.

Whereupon the Consuls appointed an investigating committee of three of their number which found that the death rate in the camps, including those at Bloemfontein and Kroonstad, was fourteen times the normal rate for Pretoria, and that the death rate for children in the camps had increased to an alarming extent.

The Consuls concluded that the abnormal death rate was due to privations which the Boer families suffered after having been taken from their farms, to the shortage and poor quality of the food rations, particularly those given to the children, and to the cold from which neither the healthy nor the sick were protected. They pointed to the scarcity of clothing and blankets and criticized the lack of proper medical facilities and sanitary staff. Nor was this all.

In December 1901 a cartoonist showed a British Santa travelling over the veld, heavily laden with little coffins. *Lustige Blätter,* the German equivalent of *Punch,* devoted a special number to the Boer cause. King Edward VII, though new to the scene, was often attacked, and one weekly showed him preparing for his coronation by polishing his crown with a handkerchief dipped in a basin of Boer's blood. A prayerbook smirched with blood lay beside the basin.

In the United States, William Jennings Bryan, the famous Democrat orator from Nebraska, was reported as saying that he was glad the war had cost England so dearly and that he considered it a disgrace that no official expression of sympathy had been sent by the US Government to the Boers. The Governor of Illinois went further and issued a public appeal to the citizens to subscribe for the relief of women and children in the British concentration camps which were now coming to be known as 'Death Camps'.

All this was the dark side. But one redeeming feature of the camps was too often overlooked in this welter of criticism, namely the efforts made to provide an education for the children.

The way in which this was to be accomplished was set out in an official document, Command Paper 934, which read:

'English teachers do not teach, nor do they try to teach, the Boer children to be English, but they teach them to know the English as their friends and they sow in the young and susceptible hearts the seeds of an affection and respect which will hereafter bear fruit of good will and lasting peace. . . .'

Even more explicit were the instructions issued in December 1901 by the Director of Education for the Transvaal and Orange River Colony to new teachers who came from Britain to teach in the camps.

'Dear Madam (or Sir),
'As it is unlikely that I shall have the opportunity of welcoming you personally before you begin your duties in the schools of the Concentration Camps, I wish to express in the only way open to me my apprecation of the motives which have led you to offer your services for educational work of a kind as difficult as it may be fruitful of results.

'You have come to share with teachers, who are largely Dutch, the responsibility of educating Dutch children.

'During this prolonged war almost the first common ground which we have held with those opposed to us, is the school; and in my humble opinion the reason that both races have put aside their differences, even while the struggle still continues, and stand shoulder to shoulder in the cause of education, is that the teaching has been made non-political in character.

204

'We use the English language in all subjects of secular instruction because the Dutch as well as the British Afrikaner population recognize that the material advancement (to name no other form of advancement) of the children in these colonies is bound up with an adequate knowledge of the English tongue.

'The religious instruction of Dutch children we leave to be given in their own language lest we should produce a feeling of spiritual alienation between father and son. To my thinking the State should not stand indifferent in matters of religion, but should give all encouragement to children to become full members of the Church to which their parents belong. In the Concentration Camps the parents are nearly all members of the Dutch Reformed Church and use the Dutch Bible. You will see, then, that to introduce the English Bible into camp schools—unless, indeed parents desire its use would be to divide a house against itself.

'Your success as a teacher under such novel conditions must depend largely on your willingness to learn from those who have already borne the heat and burden of the day. Amongst the teachers now in camp you will find some who are fully trained in the best methods of elementary school work, and others whose natural aptitudes are such that they have conquered the difficulties of engaging the attention of a large class of children. Others again are without training or extra-ordinary gifts for teaching; in such cases you should remember the spirit of devotion which must have compelled the assumption of a burden that there was no-one else to carry. Seek out, then, those who know the children of the land, and spend many of your hours out of school with them. Try to learn something of the *Taal,* that expressive language of the Dutch Afrikaner population, which measures and describes everything through the experience of farm life. Offer to talk of your own home occupations, and to read with your new comrades the works of English literature that you value most. Ask them to lead you to the tents of those among their countrymen with whom you can gain the deepest insight into the Boer character. In a word, come among your fellow workers as friends and equals, as messengers of peace.

'As regards the children themselves, I have little to say to you that your own knowledge will not suggest. You will probably be struck, as I was, with their charm of manner and docility; you cannot fail to notice their perseverance and eagerness to learn. If you observe other traits less admirable, these only give scope to your powers as an educator. In cases in which you find apparent stupidity, and a depth of ignorance to which you are unaccustomed, remember that the difficulties of comprehension in a foreign tongue are very great; remember, also, that many of your oldest scholars have never been within reach of a school until they were brought into these camps.

'In conclusion, I would ask that, if you have any gift of writing or sketching, you should lose no opportunity of putting on paper your impressions of camp life. All diaries, or notes of events that may seem humdrum at the time, all drawings, or hasty pictures with the brush, will be welcome to me and my colleagues. We wish to have records of a time so unlike other times, and to be able to give to those who succeed us some idea of the new birth of education in the newest of British Colonies.

E. B. Sargant'

This was not the language of tyrants.

And now perhaps at this point it is permissible to ask how much Emily had really accomplished in her campaigns to improve the conditions in the camps and where she succeeded or failed.

In many senses she failed. She failed to stop Kitchener from herding the fighting Boers in one direction and their families in another. She antagonized British officials to the point where she was banned from carrying on her work. She failed to convince most Britons that their Government was callous towards the women and children of their foes or indifferent to their fate. She could not convince her fellow countrymen that her sympathy for the families in the camps was unconnected with the political attacks made by the Liberals in the House of Commons and she failed to clear herself of the charge of being a pro-Boer, that is one who magnified the virtues of her country's enemies and the faults of her own people.

On the other hand, it was Emily who discovered that the concentration camps really existed. People at home might eventually have come to hear of them through some other agency (despite the strict British military censorship) but without Emily enlightenment would have not come until later, after more lives had been lost and the problem had grown even more intractable. Also she had the power of expression, the ability to write vividly about what she had seen. She had written and spoken powers of persuasion; she was a resourceful advocate; she possessed charm which was all the more effective because of the sincerity that lay behind it. She had the influence needed to get her stories publicized. At home she gave the Liberal Party a cause to fight for, and leverage to force the Government to publish some, at least, of the truth about the camps and to improve the food, clothing, accommodation, medical facilities and sanitary arrangements. Above all she helped to convince the Boers that it would be possible to do a deal with the Liberals—a fact which influenced them towards making a peace earlier than they would otherwise have done—while there was still a Boer nation to be saved.

Perhaps, too, her presence helped to heal the scars of war even while the conflict lasted. Mrs Charles Murray with whom she stayed at Kenilworth near Cape Town once told her : 'We small party of English South Africans owe you perhaps the deepest gratitude of all, for you have helped, more than you can ever imagine, to restore the old ideals of English character which it has been so painful to see shattered.'

Another South African friend, Mrs Purcell, told her at an early stage of the war: 'As time goes on and we feel oppression creeping ever nearer and nearer till the inevitable crisis comes —though it may be that we see our best and dearest snatched from us and we ourselves pass through pain and suffering, England must still have a claim on our love for the sake of men and women like you who deprecate the awful misery inflicted by your countrymen even upon helpless women and children— our very own flesh and blood.'

Yet, on balance, it was, after, rather than during the war that Emily's name became really well known to the people whose lives she had tried to save.

I 2

The Sadness of Peace

For Emily, the surrender of the burghers and the signing of the Peace Treaty at Vereening on May 31st 1902, represented the triumph of the Ungodly over the Righteous, and a falsification of her hopes that those who were inspired by love of independence, by world public opinion and, of course, by the words of the Bible, would triumph over the forces of Mammon.

Nevertheless, the dawn of peace in South Africa conferred two benefits on her. Firstly, she was able to return there to help her friends, and secondly she was able to do so without being thought a traitor to her own people.

Her book *The Brunt of the War,* to be published by Methuen, was now finished, and still bears witness to Emily's capacity for retaining, arranging, co-ordinating and presenting the mass of information she had received from many different sources.

It was a book of some 355 pages, to which Emily had added several formidable Appendixes dealing with the Scales of Rations, the Rates of Mortality, the Farms burnt, and native camps (which Emily confessed that she had neither the time nor the strength to investigate). It contained a map in three colours showing where the camps were set up and seven photographs.

The Preface, chosen from verse published in 1587, ran :

'Go little Booke, God graunt thou none offende,
For so meant hee which sought to set thee foorth,
And when thou commest where souldiours seem to wend,
Submit thyselfe as writte but little woorthe:
Confesse withall, that thou hast bene too bolde
To speake so plaine of Haughtie hartes in place,
And say that he which wrote thee coulde haue tolde
Full many a tale, of blouds that were not base.'

The introduction showed the views which Emily had formed and from which she was never to vary:

'This book is designed to give an outline of the recent war, from the standpoint of the women and children. There is no fear of aggravating a controversy amongst the Boers by its publication, for it will add nothing to their knowledge; these facts and many more are already well known in South Africa. But, so far, little has been heard in England of the farm-burning and the camps, from the side of those most concerned. The story is therefore largely told in the letters of women and in descriptions written by their friends. On them fell the brunt of the war. More adult Boers perished in the camps than fell in the field of battle, and over four times as many children. A sketch is given of the history and extent of farm-burning, to demonstrate how wide was the eviction of families, and how powerless they were in the grasp of circumstances. The comments put forward by all parties on this policy and on that of concentration are recorded. My own connection with the movement is shortly described, as well as the opposition aroused by my efforts to lessen the hardships and save the lives of the women and children.

'I take also this opportunity of publicly denying the accusation so widely made in the Press and elsewhere, that I have slandered the British troops. No one has yet substantiated this accusation from my words or writings. I have, on the contrary, done my utmost to uphold the honour of the army. . . .

'In these pages it is no part of my object to cast blame on any individual, but I have striven simply to portray the sufferings of the weak and the young with truth and moderation. . . .

'The deaths of the Boer children will not have been in vain if their blood shall prove to be the seed of this higher rule of nations. Their innocent histories ought to become fully known and widely understood, and so implant a hatred of war and a shrinking from its horrors, which shall issue in a ripened determination amongst the kingdoms of the world to settle future differences by methods more worthy of civilized men.'

'The book is dedicated to The Women of South Africa
    Whose Endurance of hardship
      Resignation in loss
      Independence under coercion

Dignity in humiliation
Patience through pain and
Tranquillity amidst death
Kindled the reverent appreciation
of the writer, and has excited
the sympathy of the world.'

Within, Emily followed the principle that, wherever possible, she should give chapter and verse for her statements and, in consequence a large portion of the book is devoted to quotations, some in officialese and others in broken English, which destroy the continuity of style and impart a disjointed character to the work.

Nevertheless, for the historian the book contains treasure trove. There is the letter of Dr R. P. McKensie, Acting Chief Medical Officer at the camp at Johannesburg, who wrote to tell the Military Governor of Johannesburg that 'In my capacity as Chief Medical Officer of the Boer Camp, I have to report that I consider the rations served out to the refugees to be insufficient to keep them in health...' There is the research by State-Attorney (later Field Marshal) Smuts early in 1902 into the treatment of women and children in the country districts of the Transvaal. There is the personal narrative of Mrs Barry Hertzog, wife of Commandant-Judge Hertzog, who afterwards became Prime Minister of the Union of South Africa. Mrs Hertzog was compelled to travel for two days in an open railway wagon on her way to Edenburg and to live for nearly a week, without rations, on food begged from the stationmaster's wife.

There was the verdict of Mrs Klazinga of Mafeking, who said: 'As for the camp life, it is in a word slow starvation and defilement. I cannot thank God enough for having been enabled to leave it so soon and come out alive with my two children.'

There are fuller narratives from women running to perhaps three thousand words and an occasional dash of colour from Emily herself who tells how, passing through the wards of the camp hospitals, she would see first one child's head and then another's look up from the pillow calling out 'Poppie' (Afrikaans for doll) and the word would echo down the row of beds when Emily had perhaps only one to give.

Emily refused to accept royalties for herself from the sale of the book. Any profits, a note at the end of the book proclaimed, would go to the 'Re-furnishing Fund' for Boer Homes.

That summer Emily, who had already visited some of her Boer

friends on the Continent, including Mrs Louis Botha in Brussels, returned to England and began to exploit her position. For on July 30th the three Boer Generals, Louis Botha, Koos de la Rey and Christian de Wet, together with various relatives, had embarked on the mail steamer *Saxon* on a mission to England to raise money for relief of their fellow countrymen. And who should be in the tug sent out to meet them when they arrived at Southampton but Emily Hobhouse herself—invited to do so by Percy Molteno, son of the first Prime Minister of the Cape Colony. Emily soon became an unofficial political adviser to the Generals. Unwisely, perhaps, she suggested that they should refuse an invitation to attend the Spithead Naval Review at which they were to be presented to the King. She argued that by appearing they would be submitting themselves to a public exhibition like captives in a Roman triumphal procession. Stories that the Boers had snubbed His Majesty were not long in appearing.

On balance, the British public were favourably impressed by the outward appearance of the Generals. Botha, it was noted, appeared 'refined and cultivated' and was capable of smiling, in a friendly manner. De la Rey, with his patriarchal beard, resembled a prophet from the pages of the Old Testament. De Wet was described as being more like a weather-beaten Admiral in the British Navy (no higher compliment possible) than a stockrider. Those who met him noted that, though not yet fifty, his face was furrowed with innumerable lines. Others concluded from looking at him and his more stately companions, that the Boer pony must be a very good weight-carrier. Some Boer leaders could not be present to plead their cause. Kruger was in exile in his villa at Utrecht. Marthinus Steyn, the last President of the Orange Free State, was convalescing at Scheveningen, that sea-side suburb of the Hague, having refused to set foot on British soil en route, and Lucas Meyer, one of whose last acts had been to look critically at the manes of the cream-coloured horses to be used at King Edward's coronation, had died suddenly.

On the day of their arrival, Emily went with the Generals in their train from Southampton to Waterloo, sitting between Botha and De Wet, and she travelled with them on a horse bus to their hotel in Norfolk Street, off the Strand. She saw them again after they had been taken in a special train for a private visit to the King. Next day they left for the Continent. Thus, the Generals spent only one full day in Britain. This could have been due to feelings of old loyalty towards their former President, since it was known that neither Kruger nor Steyn had been in favour of a peace settlement without independence, or it might have been to placate public opinion at home, or to raise funds as quickly as possible. Their departure may not have been suggested or even supported by Emily, but it created a bad impression in London, particularly as their progress on the Continent was at times accompanied by anti-British demonstrations.

The Generals returned to South Africa in December, soon after a House of Commons Debate, during which Joseph Chamberlain said that if the present grant of £3 million did not prove enough for the restoration of South Africa, he would not hesitate to ask Parliament for more. Emily evidently did not feel called on to follow them at this time. She felt that she needed a holiday. This time she chose Paris, and when she returned to South Africa in May 1903 there were no more camps.

On landing at Cape Town, Emily found she was already a notorious celebrity to the Customs officers (who suspected that she might be carrying firearms) as well as to the clerks in the bank where she called to collect her letters. Also, Boers she had never met called to tell their stories. For a time she stayed with Olive Schreiner, whose views on war and on women (she was a feminist) were akin to her own. In the Cape they complained to her that no-one could get cooks. 'It is one of the effects of the war—the complete demoralization of the coloured servants,' Emily wailed in characteristic Edwardian style. But she made her friends admit that they would willingly do without the best cooks in the world if they could get rid of Milner.

Then the old medicine began to work once more. In Bloemfontein she re-visited the Fichardts, where once more she began to hear complaints of muddle and delay by the British in re-instating the Boers on their farms. It seemed in fact that the hopes which the Boers had been encouraged to hold in good faith when peace was signed were remaining unrealized. On impulse, Emily decided to see for herself, and chose as her guide an ex-prisoner of war named Enslin. Once he had been a farmer. Now he was a pedlar travelling from farm to farm with goods no Boer could afford to buy. Emily hired his wagonette, which was big enough to hold food and clothes for the needy as well as her own stores and bed. Four mules to draw the wagonette, a Kaffir to look after the party, and the forage was thrown in with the deal. This was the kind of gipsy life that had always fascinated Emily as a girl in Cornwall thirty-odd years ago. Now at forty-two, her dream had come true. Sunburnt, her face peeling, her hair caked with dust, she visited farm after farm collecting details for her case-book of grievances.

There was certainly plenty of hardship, but also plenty of misunderstanding about the agreement which the Boer leaders had made at Vereeniging. The Boers had been told that £3 million had been earmarked under the peace settlement to re-establish them on their farms. It was one of the items to which their leaders had directed their attention in explaining the peace terms, and it was perhaps natural for them to have concluded that the British Government, in naming this sum, had thereby undertaken the task of making good the damage caused by British troops when carrying out Kitchener's scorched earth policy. Not so. And some of the claimants had to live off roots.

Under the terms of the settlement the British Government admitted liability for war damage suffered by British subjects, neutral foreigners, natives and the 'protected burghers', who had laid down their arms in response to Lord Roberts' proclamation of March 1900—in this last case only for damage suffered after the surrender. The British were also prepared to pay for livestock, farm produce etc. that had been requisitioned by the army in the field. But for the Boers who had continued to fight, more especially if they or their families had broken their oath, there was to be no compensation. The £3 million was an ex gratia gift to which no individual farmer had a personal right. It was intended to assist the 'restoration of the people to their homes and for supplying those who, owing to war losses are unable to provide for themselves with food, shelter, and the necessary amount of seeds, stock, implements etc., indispensable to the resumption of normal conditions.' But which people? And how was £3 million to repair damage worth much more? Obviously the money could not be paid out to rich and poor alike without regard to the amount of damage suffered. So 'claims' had, after all, to be submitted. But these could not be paid out until the total 'claims' had been added up and scaled down to the £3 million that was available to meet them. Meanwhile what was to happen to the harvest while the calculations were being made? The solution was to offer money on loan to the Boers (who were not fond of borrowing) and to undertake to deduct from this loan any amounts subsequently awarded as claims. In practice most got a flat payment of £25. Those asking for more were offered about 10 per cent of the extra amount claimed.

So there was no shortage of hard cases for Emily to hear as she went on her rounds. Soon she found the mules were far too slow for her purpose and arranged for horses to relay her from one farm to the next. She drove sometimes seventy miles a day across a countryside bereft of roads, and strewn with heaps of bleached bones in a different carriage every day.

At Hoopstad Mr Bosman handed over to Emily the receipts which the military had given him and which the authorities were now refusing to honour. She found farmers and their families sleeping in stables because they were the only building left standing. Her own reports were written by lantern light while she sat on a rolled blanket.

In July she stayed with General De Wet and his family on his farm. He had come back to find house, outhouses, stock enclosures, all destroyed and even the fruit trees cut down. His rifle, and the white horse Fleur that had carried him through the war, were his only movable possessions. He had had to go himself to fetch his wife from Vredefort camp. Now he was beginning to put the place in order with the help of his two sons. The royalties from his book had not yet begun to come in.

It was De Wet who persuaded Emily to attend the People's Gathering at Heidelberg and to allow herself to be publicly presented to the Afrikaners at their first mass Assembly from far and wide since the end of the war. Emily travelled by train through the night, talking at first incognito to the Boers in her carriage and then revelling in the warmth they showed towards her when they learned who she was. In Heidelberg she saw a procession of solemn silent threadbare Boers, some riding, some in carts, others walking, a few on bicycles, while Emily herself travelled on the way to the Market Square behind a group of Boer Generals in a carriage belonging to Mrs Viljoen. Botha received an address of welcome and made a speech on the steps of the church and afterwards, because the hall taken for the meeting was far too small, a platform of tables was set up under the trees of a garden and those who could not get near enough climbed into the branches and hung there, as Emily put it, like a swarm of bees.

The speeches went on for three hours, after which resolutions were passed, and Botha announced that his audience was invited to attend another garden nearby for coffee and sandwiches, where he was going to introduce them to Miss Emily Hobhouse. Then the audience which had been almost silent cheered 'as though they had been Englishmen'.

They took Emily along and made her sit at the high table with the Generals. Botha introduced her and a Minister began to make a speech in Dutch. Emily by this time was feeling weak and giddy as she always did at high altitudes and clung for support to a little tree in the middle of the garden. In an effort to shorten the ceremony, she begged the Minister not to get the speech interpreted. 'Ek kan verstaan, dankie,' she said and the Boers, catching the sound of her words, knew that she was in sympathy with them and cheered all the louder. There were more bouquets for Emily at Pretoria though the reception had to be held in a private garden because the Government, ever mindful of Emily's influence with the Boers, sought to add to it by refusing permission for the use of the public park for a function in her honour.

It was the same in Middelburg except that she was made to sit in the sitting room of the parsonage instead of being allowed to enjoy the fresh air of the balcony. The only way she could get out into the open was to propose a visit to a cemetery where the children who had died in the camp were buried. And so she went on, staying overnight in ruined farms, sleeping in tents, visiting Belfast. . . . Roos Senekal where it was Holy Communion week for which the Boers gathered from far and near . . . talking to people who were trying to rebuild prosperity out of twenty-zinc sheets and a few beams. Only the police station still stood. Near Dullstroom Emily wrote:

'We passed over break-neck roads through the mountains to Dullstroom. Further on I saw some ruins (in fact I get quite annoyed now whenever I see a roof, it seems so unnatural and well-to-do).

'So with patience and pain we lumbered on. At the very top of the pass was a grave with a big white cross standing against the blue sky. Captain Angus Menzies of the 1st Bttn. Manchester Regiment, who fell near the end of the war. We got out and visited it. We generally do to all the graves, and singly or in groups we pass very many. There was something about this one, lonely and aloft, that struck me as very pathetic. We passed that night close by at the farm of Piet Taute, the Veld Cornet, a fine Boer specimen. He had been very rich and prosperous. His house had been burnt down three times, and he had been trying, himself, to rebuild it. But cash for roof and fittings had failed, and it was, though large, in terrible confusion, awful to sleep in, the holes in the roof blowing blasts on your head all night. His wife was stamped

215

with the Camp look, a look quite absent from her old mother who had kept in the hills all through the war and looked hale. She was a colonial woman and could speak English, and looked on my visit as a godsend. Her confinement is imminent, and no cash. There was a large party of us at supper and so little to eat. These meals are mostly long graces.'

After her trip through the Transvaal in winter, Emily was glad to get back to Pretoria. Here, she first met Smuts. She saw him as a genuine Afrikaner who had cut loose from Cecil Rhodes, the imperialist, in order to serve President Kruger. In negotiations he had tried his best to stave off the Boer War, but when it came, he led a Commando group with such success that the British had put a price of £1,000 on his head. Having studied law in England he was called as legal adviser to the Boers in the peace negotiations and, from the way that Botha relied on him, it was clear that he would become one of South Africa's future leaders. Emily stayed with the Smuts family more than once during this visit and wrote home to her brother:

'I wish you could meet him. He is so cultivated and clever and full of fun, though underneath, of course, he is broken-hearted at the loss of his country. Having been so long in Cambridge and London he is so entirely like one of ourselves. I prophesy a great future for Smuts.'

Next came visits to Nylstroom and Pietersburg where Emily contemplated a scheme by which rifles for shooting springbok would be loaned to those in need of fresh meat.

Finally she handed her case book to Patrick Duncan who was then Colonial Treasurer but who later became Governor General of South Africa. Then, having finished for the time being with the Transvaal, she turned her attention to the Orange Free State again, and went on to Heilbron, Driefontein and Lindley.

'It was late when we got to Lindley itself and the moon was all we had to guide us. The road was bad, and the drift across the river deep with very steep cliffs on either side, but we came through and at last drove into the silent broken village, white in the moonlight. A strange medley it was of ruins and tents with a few new roofs, brand new, rising here and there from the refuse of the past. No one was about, and it was some time before we could find our way or anyone to guide us. Finally I was consigned to old Mr Kok, and Mr Theron got a bed on the floor of an office and our Kaffir boy in the stable.

The Sadness of Peace

The whole of Lindley is too sad and dejected outwardly and inwardly to write about. . . . The Koks are so poor I hardly dared to eat their food; their bed was corrugaged iron, the floor would have been pliable by comparison. The ruins of their nice house stand before the door, never alas to be rebuilt, for they are old and can never earn the money again. He is 74, but the plucky old man saved the Church registers and stuck to them through thick and thin. He is an educated man. From affluence they are brought in old age to dire poverty. But there was no word of complaint; he spent his time telling me of all the poor around while he said no word of his own condition. I had to learn that from others. It is all lamentable in the town and district. I shall never forget the pathos of the meeting when they came to address me. I felt so utterly at a loss what to say to them. Even General Olivier could not speak, but turned away, and they silently melted off, each with his burden of want and debt and barrenness, in face of which one's sympathy seemed a mockery. It is the hardest sort of speech to make, talking to people who are well-nigh starving, whose homes are in ruins, who have no money and no prospects. They have struggled bravely for over a year, but now all is closing in dark around them. I fear hope is waning at last, and I dread lest their self-respect should be lost.

'Our trek from Lindley was a sad one; we drove away from the ruins early, trying to shake off the depression which hung upon the place. About fifteen miles out from town we met a man with a bundle under his arm walking towards Lindley. He had on the green trousers of the Ceylon prisoners-of-war, and there was purpose on his face. Shortly we came upon his little daughter, a child of twelve. She was neatly dressed in a blue print frock and kapje, and she was riding a creature which must by courtesy be called a horse. At least it had four legs and a tail and a sort of bone which supported the saddle. She was leading another such animal which had helped to carry her father to town. We called to her to ask the way and she rode close up to our cart. She had the motionless face of the veld girl with the deep still eyes, and she sat her horse with grace and self-possession. We had some talk with her.

"How goes it with you?" we said.

"It goes well," she replied.

"Have you then food?"

"No, we have no food."

"You mean that you have no meat?"

217

"No, we have no meat."

"But you have vegetables or potatoes?"

"No, we have no vegetables."

"But at least you have bread?"

"No, we have no bread."

"What, no bread nor meal?"

"No, we have no bread nor meal."

"Then what do you eat?"

"Just mealies."

"And have you many of those?"

Some moisture gathered in the child's eyes as she answered "Very few left."

"But your father is gone to town, will he not work and bring you home some food?"

"Yes, my father has found some house building work to do in town, but he cannot bring us home food; he owed money to the store before the war and he must work to pay that off."

"But these horses are your own?"

"No, we had them from the Government and in two years we must pay for them."

"And how are you off for clothes?"

"It goes scarce with clothes."

'We gave the child half a loaf we had with us, and as she took it her lips trembled and a flicker like the shadow of a smile passed over her face as she said, "My mother will be very glad." Then silently she turned and hugging the loaf trotted away over the veld, a solitary blue speck in the vast brown expanse.

Some miles further we came to a place called Plezier; a greater misnomer could not be imagined. A piece of house had been patched up, but there was no smoke or other sign of life. Not a tree or bush or plant or green blade of any sort could be seen near or far. We knocked, seeking permission to outspan. A deadness hung over the place; I felt anxious, I wondered what we should find. Remember, the Boer custom when a cart drives up to the door is for the master or mistress to come out, introduce themselves, and with all heartiness invite you in and make you welcome. After several knocks the door was opened, leave was given us to outspan, but still we were not invited in. I got out of the cart and went to the door. The house was poor but exquisitely neat; there were no chairs, just a table and a box or two to sit upon. Upon the clay walls were fastened the few relics of better days. A good-

218

looking woman and a number of girls, neatly but poorly dressed, were grouped round the room and an equal number of tidy boys in the kitchen in the back. There were eleven children. They sat very silent looking at me, and I introduced myself as coming from well-known men in their town. Mr Theron wanted to take our luncheon in the house, but some instinct told me there was great trouble there and I could not eat with all those eyes upon me. So I only asked permission to boil my kettle on their table out of the wind, and then when we had lunched I said I would come and hear their story. I hated myself afterwards to think I had made my tea at their table. When I made them understand who I was, the women told me all—the same sad tale, of course, as everywhere, but they had nothing left, nothing to eat but mealies, and so few of them that they must eke them out by one meal a day only. There was nowhere to turn for money or for help; the husband had tramped away some thirty miles to seek work on a railway; at best he would get 4s. 6d. a day, and on that no family here can live; it would not much more than feed him. But it might be weeks before she would hear from him; they had been comfortably off, tenant farmers paying £50 a year rent. They had come to the bare land and every improvement on it had been done by themselves, the houses built and all, and all had been swept and done away, no single sheep remained of all their possessions, and now a letter had come from the owner's agent in Bloemfontein raising the rent from £50 to £70 a year. She and her children sat there face to face with starvation, that terrible kind which is combined with perfect respectability. (I had been told about them in Lindley.) Even if there were neighbours the girls could get no work, for no-one can afford to put out washing, ironing or needle-work.

'One of the girls took me into the bedroom and in a whisper told me they had nothing to eat. The woman kept her secret longer. It is so awful to people of this good class to say they are in want, or even seem to beg. They pointed to a house about half a mile off, and said it was just the same there. There was a big lad, and hearing there was a wayside store not far off, I took him there and bought food enough to last them about a week till the bag of meal which I had ordered for them in Lindley should arrive. That may last three weeks, and then they are in the same position again. The Government must feed the people. At the store stood a lamentable vehicle, drawn by animals which might be either horses, mules, donkeys or ponies. I can't say which. The lad asked the driver if he could take for him the half bag of meal I had given him and leave it at the farm. The man said he was sorry, the animals were borrowed and so was the cart and harness and they were so weak they could hardly crawl along, and he dared not add to the weight. This man was a very fine young Boer with well-cut features. His young wife was with him. Mr Theron introduced me to them; they belong to a good family, as indeed was apparent by their dress and bearing. The woman put her arm through mine and whispered she wanted to speak to me. She drew me out of earshot of the men on the stoep. Then her courage failed her and she could not speak. Her face was very white with blue shadows round the lips and eyes. I said, "Are you hungry?" I am getting experienced now and begin to understand. She said for months she had eaten nothing but mealies, not meal, not meat, nor coffee, nor anything else. They had borrowed the cart and come to the store to fetch the last half bag they could buy. She put her hand on my arm again and said, "I have nothing, we have nothing, don't you understand?" And then at last I did understand, her baby was coming, the first baby, and she had not even a shawl to wrap it in. I understood her Dutch perfectly, but she was too shy to speak openly. She said she had a frightful craving for a bit of fresh meat, but none was to be got in the shop. A baby's shawl and a bit of flannelette made heaven open for her again, and I gave her a tin of Australian mutton and a few groceries. She had a good face. Six of her brothers and sisters had died in Kroonstad Camp.'

When she got back to Heilbron, Emily organized appeals in London, the Cape, Johannesburg and the Western Transvaal, thereby raising more than £8,000, which was spent partly on food and partly on teams of oxen for re-ploughing the land.

Emily was of course by no means the only researcher to discover poverty and starvation on the veld. Mr Ramsay MacDonald, Britain's first Labour Prime Minister, who had been forced out of the Fabian Society because he opposed the war in South Africa, toured South Africa in September and October 1902 and recorded his impression in the *Leicester Pioneer*, published in the constituency in which he was then interested. He, too, referred to 'ruined men who find only white crosses instead of families. 'For three days we drove about 150 miles,' he wrote. 'The country was as waste as the edge of the Sahara. Almost the only cattle we saw were carcases rotting on the wayside. And,' he added, 'I found no well-informed sagacious person, whether he took his stand with the conquered or the conqueror, who shared what is the general but mistaken opinion here that the war has established the supremacy of British ideas and the permanency of the British Empire in South Africa. Only the flags,' he said, 'had changed.'

MacDonald too noted the many failures and misjudgements of British bureaucracy in its attempts to repair the ravages of war. In particular he held that the British Military Compensation Board was not the right body to decide whether a given property had been damaged by Her Majesty's forces or by those of the Boers. In short, things dragged on so long that as one Boer put it: 'Die pap is nou zoo deur makaar gebrouw, dat ons hom nie meer kan eet nie.' (The porridge is now so overcooked that we can no longer eat it.)

The *Northern Whig* described South Africa as 'a country despoiled of everything save the useless wastage of war, ruined towns, burnt homesteads, barbed wire and block houses, disorganized, depopulated and literally destroyed.' The *Review of Reviews* accused Britain of making a solitude and calling it peace.

That year Emily stayed again with Smuts and his wife in Pretoria and in December 1903 they invited her to pay them another visit at the Strand, near Gordon's Bay. She seems quickly to have attained a certain ascendancy over him and as early as February 1904 felt confident enough to rebuke him for paying more attention to watering his garden than to keeping her regularly informed about events in South Africa. She preferred to address his daughter by a name she had chosen herself rather than by one the Smuts had provided, and not long afterwards she felt so certain of her status with him that she published part of a strongly-worded personal letter that Smuts had intended for her eyes alone—a protest against Milner's plan for importing Chinese labour. 'Lord Milner's heart,' the letter said, 'will be thumping with holy joy. For he has dreamed a dream of a British South Africa—loyal with broken English and happy with a broken heart and he sees his dream coming true.' In his letter Smuts spoke of the 'spoliation of our heritage' through the importation of Chinese Labour. He alleged that the major part of the mining industry was bogus and sham and that it would be better to let the 80 per cent of the mines that had no

221

reasonable chance of working at a profit go to the bankruptcy court for then there would be enough labour (without the Chinese) to work the other 20 per cent. Smuts was worried because he had written other letters to Emily which might, he feared, get him expelled from the country if they were published. As it was, he lost legal briefs and was suspected by industry and the mine-owners of being 'unsound'.

A semi-romantic exchange of letters followed, with Smuts confiding to her that whereas he felt like giving up the political struggle for the quiet life, she seemed made for battles and high endeavour. In return Emily sent pages of womanly inspiration. Happily her writing was bold and easy to read, her choice of words attractive and appealing and her style concise and emphatic, with many dots and dashes. She wrote from the peace of a garden at Shiplake, a village on the Thames between Maidenhead and Reading, and urged Smuts not to give up the fight. She denied his assertion that she belonged to the conquering race and said that, on the contrary, she was half-Celt whose ancestors had been driven away to remote Cornwall by the Romans, Anglo-Saxons and Normans. She admitted that even when fighting for ideals, one loses some of one's finer nature, but surely this was better than dreaming without doing, which was what she had had to do in her youth in Cornwall. Then inconsequentially she confided that she was thinking of settling down herself somewhere, in a cottage in the country.

That summer she asked Smuts to look her out a site for a cottage near Pretoria. It was time to make a home for herself as there was no one else to make it for her. She was torn in two directions, she said. One part of her, the materialistic side, clung to the familiar comforts of 'home' (she was writing from her uncle and aunt's house in Bruton Street) where, if she became sick there were relatives to turn to. But her other side, the more romantic one, yearned for the country and the people with whom she had become so unexpectedly linked and she might even without a companion be able to afford to live in South Africa. In July Smuts was writing to her, for once at least, as 'My dear Friend', and is skittish enough to end his letter 'Tata, totus tuus', of which a free translation might be 'Goodbye, totally yours'. But he wonders whether it would be right for her to settle permanently in South Africa. In old age, he said, which would come to Emily as to others, people return to the scenes of their youth and relive those days. In youth we long to leave the scene of our childhood, in middle age we smile at it, and in old age we return to the scene of our own memories. He went on to say that he would prefer to retire to the hills where he herded sheep and cattle as a child. He added that land was falling in price so there was no hurry to buy and he concluded that in any case South Africa might not be a good land for anyone but Boers and Kaffirs to live in. But in the end Emily had her way and, when later she sold the cottage, she made a profit.

Emily spent nearly seven months of the year 1903 in South Africa but bad news about the health of her uncle and aunt brought her home despite the prospect of an English winter. She sailed two days before Christmas. In Lisbon, out of sorts from the motion of the ship, she decided to make the rest of the journey overland, without however having brought enough money to do so. Her battles with the British Consul, the bank, and the Portuguese authorities, who wanted to fumigate her underwear because she had come from a plague area, made vintage Emily stories when she reached Bruton Street again.

That winter she took up the cases of the Boer widows and orphans for whom—but for the Government promise to look after them (unfulfilled)—she would have been able to collect more money. She attacked the Government for not honouring the receipts given by the British forces for goods and livestock commandeered. She campaigned for pensions for the dismissed Boer police force and complained that, though there seemed to be no lack of money for war, peace seemed to be different. She lobbied the Liberals too and instructed them on the facts of life in South Africa so that when they came to power, as they were expected to do in the near future, they would know where their duty lay. Her main influence was exerted over Campbell-Bannerman, though according to one candid observer, he was weak, vain and too easily led by pro-Boers.

In the spring she had a new idea—to encourage the less affluent Boer women to take to lace-making and needlework—since they seemed to like staying at home and had time on their hands. It was to be a cottage industry which could be pursued at home as part of farm life. She studied collections of old lace in private houses, museums and antique shops. She decided that her aunt would not mind being left for a few weeks, if she stayed north of the equator, and this made it in order for her to visit Venice, which she considered to be the birthplace of European lace-making.

There was also time on the way to visit Mrs Steyn at Cannes and ex-President Kruger at Menton; time, too, to lose her purse on the way to Venice, and time to discover after spending weeks in Venice that she ought also to go to Bologna and study technique there as well. Instead, she preferred Brussels and then went on to stay with her uncle and aunt at Crowsley Park in Oxford- · shire. Then, the lease of her flat being up, she settled at Bruton Street amid an atmosphere of near-luxury.

She could certainly have stayed there in comfort for as long as her aunt had lived, but, restless as usual, she soon began to ask herself whether her presence in Bruton Street was really necessary, seeing that there were so many servants to look after her uncle and aunt. Not realizing that it was her company and nothing more that was needed, she went to Ireland to study spinning and weaving, for it had been pointed out to her meanwhile that lace would hardly be bought by anyone except the richer families in Johannesburg whereas blankets, rugs, tweed coats and the like were needed in the countryside and could be made on the farms from wool locally grown.

Soon afterwards she wound up the South African Women and Children Distress Fund and formed instead the Boer Home Industries Aid Society.

In December that year her uncle died and her aunt was so distressed that she could not bring herself to attend even the memorial service held in his memory at St Margaret's, Westminster, and her diffidence prevented her from asking Emily to stay with her, though she needed her as never before. Emily was in a quandary. She had already booked her passage for South Africa, raised the funds for her new venture and recruited one expert and an assistant, Margaret Clark, who became a friend for the rest of Emily's life. She remembered that her aunt had often before been in poor spirits in the winter and had recovered when better weather came in the spring. She persuaded herself that it was her duty to leave England.

In January 1905 she set sail from Antwerp in the *Kronprinz*, travelling out with Margaret Clark and ex-President Steyn to whom she insisted on reading out passages from Roper's *Life of Sir Thomas More,* Boswell's *Life of Johnson, David Copperfield* and other English classics. And so, in February, Emily was in the Orange River Colony, getting weekly letters from her aunt, who comforted her by saying that she would rather think of Emily doing useful work in South Africa than sitting by her bedside. Towards the middle of May, when Emily had planned to be on her way home, the letters suddenly stopped. Emily had lost the woman who had been a mother to her for more than twenty years. She decided then to stay abroad.

The first of Emily's schools was set up with the help of ex-President and Mrs Steyn at Philippolis in the Orange River Colony in March 1905, with a class of six girls. Tuition was free and the girls were able to learn to spin competently in six to eight weeks, after which they each bought a spinning wheel, or had one made, and took it home. The school paid three shillings a pound for spun wool, less a shilling in the pound for expenses. Of Philippolis the Official Railway Guide for 1906 says,

'Before proceeding north the tourist should visit Philippolis (by post cart, daily service, Sunday excepted), beautifully situated on the Otterspoort River, the centre of the sheep-farming and horse-breeding district of that name. The town has a population of 568 whites, and 241 coloured persons, and the district 1,988 whites and 1,046 coloured persons, making a total population of 3,843. Just above the town there is a beautiful park, where three excellent tennis courts, and a croquet ground are laid out. To the Sportsman, few districts in the Orange River Colony offer greater attractions than Philippolis. Springbuck are very numerous, and good sport can always be had. The Commercial is the only hotel in town, but there are also two private boarding houses. The distance from Philippolis to Fauresmith, Jagersfontein, and Colesberg is 36 miles in each case [most towns in South Africa were about a day's journey by ox-waggon from the next], and to Bloemfontein 98 miles. The road between Philippolis and Colesberg crosses the Orange River by means of a fine steel bridge, which, however, cannot be used at present. The bridge was blown up by the Republican forces in their retreat from the Cape Colony in the early part of the late war. It is hoped that before long it will be repaired, and once more available for the heavy traffic which formerly passed over it.'

The guide did not however mention that despite its river, the town of Philippolis was perpetually short of water and that the area was remote from supplies of coal and timber.

Nevertheless Emily possessed the drive, resource and imagination needed to overcome the difficulties of the environment and also the knack of inspiring the enthusiasm of all connected with the project. Above all she realized that the best way to save money was to get into production without loss of time. At first the woven cloth looked amateurish and the colours wrong. Emily

225

H

believed that the strong light, the dry air and the character of the water were to blame. Dust and grass seeds permeated the wool and were hard to get rid of, farmhouse dyes faded badly. But some of the cloth was good enough to be sent home, with an appeal for more qualified instructors.

Later the evenly spun thread, the finely matched fast dyes and the woven cloth had a professional touch. Emily herself designed some of the tapestries. A second school was set up near Johannesburg in a zinc shed with a mud floor and, as production increased, wool was handed out to be cleaned and teased into straight fibres by the elderly or the children in the surrounding villages. A women's organization in Switzerland sent some spinning wheels so that the yarn could be spun at home too, and other wheels were bought cheaply in Scandinavia. Eventually a new industry brought satisfaction and self-respect to the Boers after years of disappointment and disillusion.

In some ways, however, Emily failed to live up to her image among the Boers as a heroine. For her own staff there were poetry readings, picnics and English songs, accompanied by Moses the black boy and his guitar, but she could not join in the time-wasting gossipy coffee parties beloved of the Boer families, nor was there anyone who could represent her at these gatherings. Her work exhausted her and she needed her evenings for rest. Nor did she take pains to cultivate friendships with the British community, by whom she felt she had been misjudged and misrepresented (although quite possibly they would now have been won over by her undoubted charm, vivacity and good humour). Thus, to many she remained a remote, unapproachable and lonely woman.

At the end of a year Margaret Clark went home and Emily found herself spending Christmas alone with her black servant Joanna, eating boiled rice and sleeping by herself in an open summerhouse on a friend's farm. No wonder her friends sometimes raised eyebrows and threw up their hands.

In time, Emily was able to leave the day-to-day management of the schools to assistants. In May she took another holiday in Switzerland and then spent a week with her brother Leonard in Normandy, after which she sailed once more for South Africa to arrange for her schools to be taken over by the provincial Governments of the Transvaal and the Orange Free State.

By this time, there were weaving and spinning schools in Bloemfontein, Philippolis, Winburg, Fiksburg, Bethlehem and

Smithfield and spinning schools at four other places. The Transvaal had weaving schools at Pretoria and four other towns, with spinning schools at ten centres. (Government Ministers and their wives bought coats and lengths of cloth at an exhibition in Cape Town held in 1908.)

Even Smuts wore a suit made from Emily's material, though he was reported as saying that he felt like a female ostrich in it. Others—feeble men in Emily's view—found the tweed rough and uncomfortable but bought it and wore it either because it represented something which South Africa had made for herself or because Emily told them they looked very handsome in it.

In due course all the schools that Emily had helped to set up were taken over by the Governments of the Transvaal and the Orange Free State (twelve of them were still in use when she died eighteen years later) and were maintained with grants. But, in the Transvaal at any rate, increased mechanization became the order of the day, and the original ideal of an independent rural cottage industry vanished as more and more of the impoverished white workers moved to the cities. The style of management, too, was changed, and Emily disengaged herself, somewhat disillusioned, from the schools in both states. In Hugo Naudé's portrait of her painted about this time we see a tall, slim woman with a fair complexion, oval face, blue-grey eyes (they were noticeably pale), and grey hair swept back. She wears a dress of dark blue material with green tints, a long skirt, three-quarter-length sleeves and a discreet V-neck. She looks directly at the artist with the hint of a smile. Beside her stands a spinning wheel. Naudé has succeeded in capturing an expression of warmth, sympathy and affection.

Now, once again, she returned to England—in mid-October with the winter before her and no new cause to champion. Her health had deteriorated. She spent Christmas with her friends the Ellis's and New Year with Sir Edward Fry and his family. Earlier, in April 1904 when she was still in Venice, she had complained that it hurt her arm to write, and, in November that year, we find her depending on a secretary to finish a letter to Smuts which she had started writing. Like many people possessed of charm and apparently inexhaustible vitality, she had spells of depression, and although her enthusiasm helped her on occasions to face considerable hardships, there were times when she felt unable to contemplate cold, heat, altitude, a sea voyage, travel (although for most of her life she had a maid), immobility, inactivity or—as her arthritis got worse—activity. Her friends thought she needed someone to look after her, yet she hated to depend on anyone. Sometimes she consulted friends or relatives but rarely took their advice, and they had to stand by while she made plans which could be carried out—if at all—only with the greatest difficulty. She took strong likes and dislikes to people as well as to their policies and found it difficult to make allowances for their limitations. Yet she herself had the limitations of ill health.

The story of her flat in Rome became a family joke. She had chosen it because it had a splendid view of the Forum and its only disadvantage was that it was at the top of seventy-two steps (some accounts said 100). Some of Emily's more active friends had no objection to undertaking the climb but she herself could not manage the journey and had to hire two men to carry her up to her eagle's nest. Her cottage in South Africa had a magnificent view of mountains but the high altitude area continued to give her giddiness and nosebleeds.

All her travels, staying in rich private houses, hotels, boarding houses, and at times mere hovels failed to suggest to her the kind of house she needed for herself. She kept in touch with some at least, of her relations—especially with her brother Leonard and his son Oliver, who came out to stay with her in Rome. She had as we shall discover later, little difficulty in making friends of good standing in the Italian capital. In January 1910 we find her staying with the Marchesa De Viti de Marco and writing her letters from the Palazzo Orsini, Monte Savello. But she did not relinquish her hold on her friends in South Africa.

Advice to Smuts came readily that year (1910) from Emily—it included disapproval of some members of 'his' Cabinet; warnings to Smuts about others who already in 1910 were thinking of picking a quarrel with Germany; disquiet over England's naval building programme; disenchantment at the way the South African officials were over-expanding her weaving schools; dismay at Sir Henry de Villiers accepting an English peerage; disgust at her own Liberal Government and dismay at her own weak heart which forced her to endure solitude and seclusion in the heat of a Roman summer.

A year later she was in touch again, adjuring Smuts to give up the new motor that he had just bought on the grounds that the saddle was healthier than the driving seat and because motorists in Europe were becoming inhuman and a pest to the poor of all classes with their noise, dirt, danger and smell.

Cabinets earned her displeasure as well. They were guilty of plotting secretly against the people and should be done away with. In Rome's monuments she saw a warning of the fate of all Empires. 'Some day Pretoria too will be as Zimbabwe, as Palmyra, Nineveh, Thebes, and Rome, and perhaps the bombs of aviators will bring it about! Madness to make the air a battlefield. Much love . . .' she wrote.

The same year Emily sent an S.O.S. from Rome asking Smuts, whom she now called 'My dear Oom Jannie' (Oom being the affectionate Afrikaans for uncle), to lend her £50 at 6 per cent for use as a reserve against increased medical expenses. (Smuts at once sent her his personal cheque for £100 as a gift.)

She explained that her treatment involved inhaling specially prepared iodine vapour to give elasticity to her arteries and to liquefy her blood, and also baths in carbonic acid. This treatment, Emily pointed out, had been followed in ancient Rome and unlike the Empire must have been good. Her doctor, an Italian married to an American, practised in Florence and specialized in the treatment of hearts and lungs, she said, and had had great successes with diabetics and asthma patients. He was also an expert on the herbalist doctors of the 15th and 16th centuries.

But her arthritis remained and in September 1912 we find her having to apologize for using pencil in a letter to Smuts because this was the only way she could write lying down. She chided him for inviting the King and Queen to open South Africa's Union Parliament buildings. She claimed that Smuts would not have taken the same line in the days when he and Botha and all the others were much nicer people.

Restless as ever, she refused to take her doctor's advice to remain in Florence and went back to her flat in Rome. She was convinced, however, that she could no longer survive in England and must get a cottage in Italy facing south with a hill behind to shelter her from the wind, that she must do no bodily work and not mix too much in society. She was sure that she had been snatched from the brink of eternity.

So by November 1912 she had let that flat of hers at the top of those steps and was staying in an unpretentious inn while seeking around for a cottage to rent—one without stairs and a garden to sit out in at about half the rent she had been paying.

About this time her sister Mrs Hebblethwaite came out to Rome and wrote home to say that although Emily's mind was as active as ever, and she was eating better, she would never be well. She would never be able to climb upstairs and could not walk more than a hundred yards without having to sit down on a camp stool which she carried about with her.

In 1913 there came one last opportunity for Emily to visit South Africa, when ex-President Steyn invited her to Bloemfontein to unveil the monument which she had helped to design in memory of the women and children who had died in the South African war. But could her health stand the journey, Emily wondered? Was this really a national monument erected with the full support of the South African Government or was it rather a local enterprise to be frowned on? Would it arouse old animosities between Boer and Briton?

Without waiting for definite advice from Smuts on this point (she had made up her mind to come and had even booked her passage) she returned for part of the summer to England, staying even for a while at Hadspen. It was the occasion of another slightly malicious note from her to Smuts, whom she regarded as a miniature Czar. Referring to the recent labour troubles in South Africa, she said that all the developing countries of the world had labour troubles and asked Smuts why should South Africa be free of them? Besides, strikes might benefit the kaffirs who at present not only suffered themselves from phthisis contracted in the mines but went home and gave it to their families. 'And also it is well that plutocracy as well as aristocracy should learn the power of democracy. Don't you agree?'

By the first week of October she had disembarked in South Africa from the *Garth Castle* and was resting near Capetown with friends.

Womanlike, having talked herself into the trip, she now upbraided Smuts for having urged her to risk her life by coming so far. She was as usual fighting her doctor, who had urged her to turn back. But she agreed to stay in the Dutch Reformed Church Parsonage at Beaufort West to see if her heart could get accustomed to the altitude.

Without heroics, she tells Smuts that she believes the doctor when he says that another heart attack like one she had already had might prove fatal. She tells him where to find her will and assures him that there is enough money at the Standard Bank in Pretoria to pay for her funeral.

In the end she turned back for home but copies of the speech which she would have made were distributed to the vast audience and her words still survive.

'Alongside of the honour we pay the Sainted Dead, forgiveness must find a place. I have read that when Christ said, "Forgive your enemies," it is not only for the sake of the enemy He says so, but for one's own sake, "because love is more beautiful than hate." Surely your dead, with the wisdom that now is theirs, know this. To harbour hate is fatal to your own self-development, it makes a flaw, for hatred, like rust, eats into the soul of a nation, as of an individual.

'As your tribute to the dead, bury unforgiveness and bitterness at the foot of this monument forever. Instead, forgive, for you can afford it, the rich who were greedy of more riches, the statesmen who could not guide affairs, the bad generalship that warred on weaklings and babes—forgive—for so only can you rise to full nobility of character and a broad and noble national life.'

At the time the whole affair was a cruel anticlimax for Emily. But her day was not done and in due course she discovered a cause even more controversial and unpopular than that of the Boers.

13

Secret Journey

By now Emily had acquired, as she put it, a public conscience that could not be stilled, any more than her private conscience could be, and, before leaving South Africa, she addressed herself to the problems of the Indian workers in Natal. Thousands of them had originally been brought there in the mid-nineteenth century to work for the sugar planters, and they were now campaigning for unrestricted entry to the Transvaal, having ceremoniously burnt the passes they were supposed to carry when in the Transvaal to show that their presence there had been authorized.

Eventually Gandhi, who had led the Indian community in South Africa since before the Boer War, organized a strike of Indian workers in the coalmines of Natal, and marched them pass-less across the border into the Transvaal—a commando of illegal immigrants.

It was an awkward time for Smuts who, since 1910 (when South Africa became a self-governing Union with its own Parliament), had occupied the posts of Minister of the Interior, Minister of Defence and Minister of Mines. He had had trouble with the miners ever since Milner tried the experiment of importing Chinese labour; a new series of riots was the last thing he wanted. It was at this moment that Emily offered her services to Smuts as a mediator in the Indian dispute. She pointed out that her family had special connections with the Indian subcontinent; that her uncle, Lord Hobhouse, had served in India as legal member of the Government and that he had turned his Mayfair home into a kind of centre for distinguished Indians in London, and that as a consequence Emily herself had developed a sense of sympathy for their susceptibilities and admiration for their abilities.

She said that as a woman without a vote, she sympathized

with other voteless folk such as the Indians. She pointed out that, as a Celt, and therefore as a member of an oppressed race, she was 'agin' all Governments on principle, since she felt that they stood for the enforcement of outgrown laws.

She admitted, with considerable far-sightedness, that the British would not be supporting the policy of allowing unrestricted entry for Indians into the Transvaal, if there had already been say, five million of them in Britain, and added, 'I tell them "You can't force your altruism on other countries".' But she said that Gandhi had asked her to write and would probably come to see her if she invited him.

Nothing seems to have come of Emily's efforts as a go-between, and a spell of ill-health diverted her attention during the months after her return from South Africa. In April 1914, writing from a lodging-house in Oxford, she told Smuts, 'They wheel me out in a chair every day to relax against a background of trim English lawns ringed with flowering shrubs and bird-song.' She was still interested enough to read Gandhi's latest book on Home Rule for India but added that in some ways it was nice for her to be able to criticize and sympathize without taking responsibility. That was one of the compensations of old age and weakness, she reflected.

She returned to the subject of her health again in the beginning of June 1914 and told Smuts how she had to hire a wheel chair to bring her to the river's brim when her nephew Oliver took her on the river in his punt:

'I begin more and more to regard death as a most desirable friend. To us, whose freedom and independence was our all in all, and which we have lost either through sickness or old age, the feeling that death liberates—literally bursts our bonds —is very attractive. I like to think of cremation and then the scattering of one's ashes to the four winds, the confined spirit free to join the universal spirit of life and keep up the sum total of things. I, who live now in perpetual imprisonment, feel all this very strongly.'

Already perhaps she recollected the moving lines of Charles Wesley's 'Burying tune' that she must often have heard sung in her childhood in Cornwall.

> 'Ah! Lovely Appearance of Death!
> What Sight upon Earth is so fair:
> Not all the gay Pageants that breathe
> Can with a dead Body compare:

With solemn Delight I survey
The corpse, when the spirit is fled.
In love with the beautiful Clay
And longing to lie in its Stead.'

And then, of course, there was the outbreak of the Great War
in August 1914. Emily was dismayed in more than one way.
She felt that it would ruin England (and was not far wrong
in this prediction). She visualized the British isles being cut off
from food. She watched Oxford's beautiful colleges given over
to the soldiery with their 'odious' greenish brown khaki uniforms.
Lloyd George, she thought, had ruined his life's work and she
added that it would be some satisfaction if she could put Sir
Edward Grey, the Foreign Secretary, and the Kaiser each by
himself in a separate battleship and let them fight it out. Three
Ministers, Lord Morley, John Burns and Charles Trevelyan,
friends of the Courtneys, mollified her somewhat by resigning
from the Government. And there were Belgian refugees to look
after.

She cavilled at Britain's choice of allies—the Russians, 'semi-
barbarians' and the Serbs, as she put it 'said to be about the
lowest set in Europe', and came to the conclusion that 'we must
all be Labour now to rule those who get themselves into trouble
and send others to fight to get them out of the mess.' And indeed
on the Sunday after war broke out Labour and Trade Union
leaders with George Lansbury and Keir Hardie among them
organized a big anti-war march from the East End and a
demonstration in Trafalgar Square.

Emily begged Smuts not to let South Africa get dragged into
the war since he had quite enough to do to manage the natives
without taking on the Germans just across the border in their
colonies of South-East and South-West Africa. Smuts and Botha
of course disappointed her. She found comfort in her friends.
From South Africa there was Olive Schreiner, who found difficulty in getting rooms in London because of her 'German' name,
and at home there were stalwarts like Ruth Fry, who became
Secretary of the Friends' War Victims' Relief Committee, which
operated in France, often in cities like Rheims under German
bombardment; and Margaret Clark (now married to Arthur
Gillett, a successful banker), who confided to Emily that she
did not believe that Britain could really care about the rights
of poor little Belgium after what she had done in South Africa,
—and many others.

234

Several other Hobhouse relatives were deeply stirred by the tragedy of the war. The Courtneys, of course, and Leonard Hobhouse, who was at one time a member of the British Neutrality Committee. But the Hobhouse who caused most heart-searching within the family was Stephen Hobhouse. He was Emily's cousin, the eldest son of the Rt Hon. Henry Hobhouse and his wife Margaret, and heir to the family estate at Hadspen. Stephen had been a scholar at Eton and was equally successful at Oxford, where he joined the University Cyclist Corps, an auxiliary body for those with military ambitions. He was converted to pacifism partly by reading Tolstoy's 'Confession' and partly by talks with Emily about the wickedness of the South African war. He renounced his inheritance and joined the Society of Friends, but, having found the Yorkshire Quakers 'complacent and luxury-loving' he set himself up in a workmen's tenement block in Hoxton, where he felt those around him could benefit more directly from his welfare work and pacifist connections. He married another Quaker, Rosa Waugh, daughter and biographer of Benjamin Waugh, Founder and Secretary of the National Society for the Prevention of Cruelty to Children. Rosa had come to the Passmore Edwards settlement as superintendent and story-teller at the Children's Play Centre. In the summer of 1916 she started a 'pilgrimage of peace' through Bedfordshire and Northamptonshire and was tried and sentenced to a term of imprisonment in Northampton jail for 'prejudicing recruiting'.

Stephen's fate, the result of the Conscription Bill introduced in 1916 by Mr Asquith, was more dramatic. He became one of about 16,000 conscientious objectors, who, between the passing of the Bill and the Armistice, refused to perform military service. He declined to argue that the work he was already doing with the Quakers on behalf of enemy aliens trapped in Britain at the outbreak of war, having been approved both by the Home Office and the War Office, was therefore of national importance. He decided not to appeal for exemption from military service on medical grounds though, he probably could have done so; and he refused service with the Quaker Medical Unit, which he considered to be an appendage of the Army.

The sequel was a period of four months in Wormwood Scrubs, another sentence in Exeter Prison and other spells in the Guard Rooms of various military establishments.

He was released, unrepentant, at a time when it looked as though he might die on the Government's hands (Emily insisted on thanking Smuts) but he survived to write *An English Prison*

235

from Within and to collaborate with a fellow-prisoner, Mr Fenner Brockway, in *English Prisons Today*. Stephen's mother, Margaret Hobhouse, was strongly affected, the more because her younger son Paul had volunteered to fight. He was wounded in August 1915 and again in July 1916 but returned to the front a third time to be killed in action in the last year of the war. The two brothers remained friends till the end but Margaret, the imperialist of Boer War days, was converted to pacifism and set her beliefs in a book, *I Appeal unto Caesar*. It put the case for the Conscientious Objector, maintained that obedience to conscience is a primary duty of Christian ethics, and achieved a ready sale.

Emily, for her part, concentrated especially on supporting the efforts of women to mitigate the effects of this man-made catastrophe. In March 1915 she set off via Dieppe to Paris with some members of the Quaker Relief Detachment.

Pacifist women were in a difficult position. They wanted peace, and sought to enforce it by encouraging public opinion in the United States and elsewhere to press for a conference of neutral nations who would mediate in the conflict. But these tactics threatened to put them in direct opposition to the belligerent governments, the ones who were in the best position to give them their other heart's desire—votes for women. Worse still, militancy for peace might even split every suffragette organization into two sections hostile to each other.

Nevertheless in February 1915, six months after the war had got under way, Dr Aletta Jacobs, the Netherlands' first woman doctor, assembled an unofficial gathering of women delegates from Belgium, Germany and Britain in Amsterdam and arranged for an International Congress of Women to be held in April at the Hague to protest against the war and to suggest steps for preventing its recurrence in the future. The Governments involved in the fighting were, on the whole, uncooperative. Some of the German suffragettes who wanted to attend the conference were stopped at the Dutch frontier. Others —about twenty-eight—including Germany's first woman judge Dr Anita Augsburg, were allowed through but were arrested on their return. No French or Russian women were allowed to attend. Britain assembled a delegation of about one hundred and eighty (Emily had attended one of the recruiting meetings at Caxton Hall) but only twenty-five passports were granted and the North Sea was closed to shipping on the day they had planned to sail. Margaret Bondfield, Sylvia Pankhurst, Eva

Gore-Booth and Maud Royden were among those who had to stay behind. Three Englishwomen, not including Emily, managed to reach the Hague independently as delegates but Emily may well have been present in the body of the hall. Some twelve countries were represented with more than a thousand voting delegates. Twenty resolutions were passed and provided, amongst other things, for continuous mediation by neutral powers and a voice for women in the ultimate peace settlement. An international Committee of Women for a Permanent Peace with headquarters in Amsterdam was established, in which Emily, as the British counter intelligence service later became aware, played a part.

That summer Emily decided that her task should be to mobilize the women of Switzerland and Italy as part of a great crusade against man-made war. She felt more than ever that men were unprincipled, and motivated by fear, greed and envy and that they were incapable of governing the world without woman's civilizing influence. She and Oom Jannie Smuts now had nothing in common as she told him in a letter written on March 9th 1915. For she and women of her persuasion recognized no enemies, and all humanity as their friends, since their interests everywhere were one and the same. Preach this, she told Smuts, and you will be a great statesman.

The activities of Emily and her companions—described by Asquith as the twittering of sparrows—did not pass unnoticed by the Foreign Office. Sir Rennell Rodd, British Ambassador in Rome, wrote on June 18th 1915 from his post to Mr Eric Drummond:

'I have seen in the Italian newspapers that there is a group of English Pacifists who are said to be raising a cry for coming to terms with Germany. This reminds me to mention if I have not already done so that there is a Miss Hobhouse here (or quite lately she was) who is trying to make propaganda in this sense in Italy. She appears to have the Boer War especially in her mind and apparently endeavours to persuade her hearers that we behaved in the most monstrous manner in South Africa. I don't suppose she will do much harm, but these people are a great nuisance and I get letters about her which I would rather not. I have it in my mind that she was very active during the South African war and very much in the press.

'It is all right at home but it would be much better if these people remained there. . . .'

So once more, officials showed their 'affection' for Miss Hobhouse by wanting to keep her close to them.

Their desires could not be accomplished at once but as a result of Sir Rennell's letter, Sir Robert Cecil's Private Secretary sent a note to Mr Harris at the Home Office suggesting that, if Miss Hobhouse returned to England and wished to go abroad again, permission should be refused.

Mr Harris replied with caution, saying that, while nothing could be done by the Home Office so long as Miss Hobhouse remained abroad, the Foreign Office letter would be borne in mind should she return to England. At the beginning of September, the Foreign Office, ever watchful, was able to tell Mr Harris that Miss Hobhouse had left Rome a considerable time ago for Holland although her maid was still in Rome and that if she did return to Italy she would probably have to pass through the United Kingdom en route. It was a stirring call for the Home Office not to flinch from doing its duty.

But in the meantime, the Home Office, moving with the speed of the Imperial Cavalry during the South African war, had not been idle. Its officials had discovered that they themselves had already let Miss Hobhouse out of the country by giving her a visa dated July 17th to travel to Amsterdam. This permit had been granted *after* they had received the warning from the Foreign Office but *before* a reply was sent saying that the matter was out of their hands. They stated furthermore that Emily had said that she was going to stay with Dutch friends and that she might be away for two months. But now, after the quarry had safely fled, Mr Harris did go so far as to say that the Aliens Officers had been asked to notify the head of their section when Miss Hobhouse returned.

Later it was discovered that, while in Holland, Miss Hobhouse had acted as temporary secretary of the International Committee of Women for a Permanent Peace. At this point it is worth mentioning that on July 5th, twelve days before she was able to leave the UK, Emily had applied personally to the Military Permit Office for permission to return to Italy, but they refused to grant her application or to support a recommendation to the French authorities for her to travel across France. The Netherlands, being neutral, was outside their sphere of authority.

The next move in the Foreign Office campaign to keep Miss Hobhouse at home came on October 24th when Mr Ernest Maxse, British Consul-General in Rotterdam, telegraphed from The Hague that Miss Emily Hobhouse, the noted pacifist, would arrive at Tilbury from Rotterdam on October 23rd. The telegram was dispatched at 3.27 that afternoon, was received at 5.50 p.m. and examined the following day at 12.30 by a Foreign Office official who duly informed the Home Office.

A direct confrontation then took place between the Home Office and the Foreign Office over the future of Miss Emily Hobhouse. On October 28th 1915 Mr Haldane Porter wrote from the Home Office Aliens Inspectorate to Harold Nicolson, a comparatively junior official in what was then called the War Department of the Foreign Office, to say that 'Sir John Simon (at that time Home Secretary) had decided that in the absence of any detailed information as to Miss Hobhouse's conduct in Italy, no steps should be taken to prevent her leaving the United Kingdom.' If the Italian authorities found her presence obnoxious, it was, he thought, for them to see that she did not enter Italy. Mr Haldane Porter's letter was on a 'Yours Sincerely' basis to Nicolson and did not say what had led Sir John to take such a decision, but we do know that about this time Emily made two or three further applications to the Military Permit Office for a visa to proceed to Italy and was refused and that the Military Permit Offices at Bedford Square and Downing Street had been notified that she should not be granted permission to leave the United Kingdom. But of this Sir John was either ignorant or else he was contemptuous of the judgment of the Military (he later resigned from the Government when conscription was introduced). It would not be too much to assume that he might have been influenced in his judgment by some of Emily's eminent Liberal friends whom she might have button-holed after her application for a permit had been refused by the Military in the previous July.

The reaction of the Foreign Office on receiving Sir John's communication was noticeably sharp, and was expressed in a note sent on November 8th by Lord Robert Cecil to Sir John Simon. 'Surely with all deference to the Home Secretary it is not a question of Miss Hobhouse's presence being obnoxious to the Italian Government,' the letter said, 'but the possibility of a woman known to have indulged in absurd and undesirable conduct in the past, repeating this behaviour to the prejudice of British interests in Italy (or in any foreign country really) at a time when our relations with Italy are a matter of concern.

'In view of this I should like your opinion as to whether it would not be possible for you to reconsider your decision.'

The Home Office replied with a deafening silence and the

next that the Foreign Office knew about the affair was a telegram from Mr Grant Duff in Berne sent on December 8th. It
read: 'Miss Emily Hobhouse is in Berne. Am I to facilitate her
journey to Italy?' This news, disastrous for the Foreign Office,
was followed next day by a vintage Emily telegram, brought to
the Foreign Office by Arthur Ponsonby, Liberal MP for the
Stirling Burghs: 'Please see Sir Edward Grey on my behalf,' it
said, 'Ask him instruct legation Berne let me proceed to Rome.
Passports for self and maid in order visa'd London and Paris
for Italy via Switzerland. Resting here two days find myself
stopped. No reason assigned. In weak health must get on, wind
up affairs in Rome, cannot afford to keep flat there longer nor
stay here. Emily Hobhouse, Volkhaus, Berne.'

Ponsonby added that he could confirm that Emily was not
well off nor in good health and he assumed that since she had
been allowed to leave England with a passport visa'd for Italy,
there seemed no good reason for not allowing her to proceed.

Similar letters were received from other Emily supporters including Lord Courtney and Henry Hobhouse, who advanced the
view that Emily could not stay in a cold climate like that of
Berne for long without serious injury to her health.

Faced with this impasse, the Foreign Office compromised. Mr
Grant Duff was authorized to give Emily her visa for Italy
provided that she gave an undertaking not to indulge in propaganda, especially peace propaganda, and not to stay in Italy
longer than was necessary for her to settle her private affairs.
The instructions to Mr Grant Duff added that it would of course
be open to the Italian authorities to refuse her admission if they
saw fit. This was accepted by Emily.

What had happened was a typical example of bureaucratic
muddle. For on November 4th, two days after the Military
Authorities had notified their Permit Offices that Emily was
not to be allowed to leave Britain, they received another letter
from Scotland Yard saying the Home Office 'had intimated to
them privately that Sir John Simon did not wish to interfere with
this lady's freedom to go abroad unless some evidence was
received that she was carrying on peace propaganda on her last
visit to Italy.'

For some reason best known to itself the Home Office had
omitted to pass on to the military authorities the evidence that it
had already received from the Foreign Office regarding Emily's
activities in Italy, and, in consequence, the various Permit
Offices were told on November 14th 1915 to take note of Sir

John Simon's decision, which reversed their previous instructions. On November 29th 1915 Emily applied to the military for a passport visa'd for Italy and was granted one.

It may well occur to the reader to wonder what happened to the letter written on November 8th by Lord Robert Cecil to Sir John Simon asking him to reconsider his decision. But this presented no real problem to Sir John Simon, who no doubt dutifully clearing out his in-tray before the Christmas festival, wrote back to Lord Robert Cecil on Christmas Eve, after nearly seven weeks delay, as follows:

'My dear Cecil,

You wrote to me some time back about Miss Emily Hobhouse and I have discussed her case with my people here. The question of placing restraint upon her movements is not without difficulty and indeed I do not know whether she is at present in England or not. But I venture to suggest, in view of Sir Rennell Rodd's communication, that if the Foreign Office think she should be prevented from going abroad, the proper course would be for her passport to be cancelled. You of course know who she is and will be able to estimate whether the circumstances justify this. But plainly that is the best way.

Yours very truly

John Simon.'

In other words, since Emily's trouble-making occurred abroad the Foreign Office and not the Home Office should be responsible for stopping her going there. Cecil's noncommittal reply was that when Emily returned to England 'I think it would certainly be desirable that she should not be allowed out again.'

In other words the Home Office had won the day and had successfully avoided making itself unpopular with Britain's most prominent Liberals.

For some time nothing more was heard about Emily and there were no complaints of her making peace propaganda in Italy. But in May 1916 reports appeared in the Swiss press that Emily was engaging in peace propaganda in Switzerland. And indeed the *Bund* newspaper of May 3rd 1916 printed a story under the headline 'Die Frauen und der Friede' (Women and Peace) with a report of a meeting held on May 1st by the Berne group of the International Women's Union for Permanent Peace. Emily was mentioned as having been present and as having reviewed peace propaganda carried out since the Women's Congress at the Hague in April 1915. What to do about it? The simplest course of action, the Foreign Office now argued, would be to withdraw Emily's passport. But how could they get her to give it up while she was abroad? Obviously that would not be easy.

Nevertheless Mr Grant Duff was at once given authorization to withdraw the passports of Emily (and of a Mrs Holbach who appeared to have sinned in a like manner) and if this meant their leaving Switzerland, to issue them a passport marked for one direct journey to the United Kingdom, and nothing more.

Unfortunately, Mr Grant Duff was unable to discover Emily's whereabouts in Switzerland until early in June, since the Swiss police were strictly forbidden to give information on undesirable foreigners to Legations and Consulates who might be pursuing political refugees. On June 5th however, he was able to request Emily to call at the British Legation any morning between 11 a.m. and 12.30. She replied that she was just leaving Berne but would call on her return.

And when she did return three weeks later her passport bore a stamp showing that she had been in Brussels which was then occupied by the Germans. A stormy interview ensued. 'When she appeared,' Mr Grant Duff reported, 'I first taxed her with breaking her declaration of December 11th that "if I receive the British visa to proceed to Italy, I undertake not to engage in propaganda of any sort, especially propaganda in favour of peace".'

Emily admitted that she had been at the peace meeting at Berne but maintained that this was not in breach of her undertaking not to engage in peace propaganda; this, she said applied only to Italy.

'I do not know whether by a quibble the declaration can be construed as applying only to Italy; but it was intended to cover her proceedings in Switzerland as well. Even if her contention is legally valid, it is a piece of sharp practice showing clearly the kind of woman with whom we have to deal,' Mr Grant Duff added in his report.

The Minister then asked Emily where she had been between June 6th and 24th and she at once confessed that she had been given a safe conduct to visit Berlin by the German Minister for Foreign Affairs 'an old acquaintance with whom she had been in correspondence.'

Mr Grant Duff's report continued: 'I pointed out that for a British subject to proceed to Germany without sanction from His Majesty's Government was a most improper proceeding and that I was by no means certain that it was not an indictable offence. She pleaded ignorance and said that her business in Germany was so important that she considered it her duty to go. She was specially desirous of visiting the Ruhleben Camp for Interned Civilians. She then proceeded to lecture me on the state of the prisoners in that camp, upon which I told her that we already had information at our disposal on the subject and that I would not trouble her to describe her visit. She then stated that she had important information to lay before His Majesty's Government, but what it was she declined to divulge. On June 26th she called at His Majesty's Consulate about her passport. I had in the meantime given instructions that she could have a passport marked "for one direct journey to England to be given up on arrival, not valid for a residence in Switzerland". I impounded her old passport and hold it at your disposal.'

But now at the very moment when the Foreign Office looked likely to be assailed by a flood of awkward questions, officialdom had a stroke of luck. Emily left behind on the Consul's desk an envelope containing a highly compromising letter written by her to Dr Aletta Jacobs. Mr Grant Duff's report does not say whether the envelope was sealed and had to be steamed open in order to read the contents and then re-sealed, but this seems highly probable, since neither Emily nor the Consulate appear to have referred to the text of the letter when Emily called later to recover it.

In any case a copy of the letter had been made for intelligence purposes and, from the copious typing errors in the copy possessed by the public Record Office, it appears highly improbable that the work was carried out by any qualified secretary.

The covering envelope was addressed as follows:

via Deutschland
Dr Aletta Jacobs,
158 Koninginneweg,
Amsterdam
Holland

The letter gave Emily's address as

c/o Dr Gertrud Woker,
17 Riedweg,
Berne
June 24th 1916

Dear Friend,
I *hope*, all being well to leave Switzerland and go home on

243

the wings of the wind, and ere leaving must write you once more freely because from England that will not be possible. Listen—to business; I returned last night from a trip through Belgium and Germany. I have been to Berlin and seen von Jagow, whom I knew in old days. From this, much I hope may develop. I am to keep open a line of communication with him. Will you help—saying nothing.

If you get a letter from me (or a card) from home beginning as above "Dear Friend" and signed by me—but either allusive or with not much meaning for you, will you put it into an envelope, address it to him, but *do not post it*—take it to his Ambassador at the Hague—to forward urgently.

If through the same hand any word or letter should come back to be forwarded to me, will you re-write it, if necessary in your own hand and sign it with your name, unless it should reach you from the Legation in a form in which it could be forwarded. But a postcard is better.

Remember, my address is:

c/o Barclay and Co. Ltd.,

137 Brompton Road,

London S.W.

Gertrud Woker has been such a dear. I am too exhausted to write, but want you to know that Frau Ragaz and Mlle Gobat have returned from Stockholm very disgusted with affairs there—and say Rosika has gone home, for which they are sorry, since she has such capacity. Emily. . . .

Emily Balch is there, and I hope she may pull the things together. Everything is at its worst and this great battle is preparing. Thousands on both sides have to meet death in July—or sooner.

Too tired to write.

I am establishing here also a line of communication—but posts are so uncertain across France that I think a duplicate line necessary.

Best love, Emily.'

As Grant Duff pointed out in his report, Emily's letter to Dr Aletta Jacobs was being sent through Gertrud Woker, 'a militant pacifist, who lives at 17 Riedweg, Berne. Her name is well known to me as one of the most aggressive women in Switzerland.'

The letter also showed that Emily had prepared not only a line of communication with the agreement of the German authorities through Aletta Jacobs and the German legation at the Hague, but was also establishing a second line of communication across France to Switzerland.

The Rosika mentioned was Rosika Schwimmer, the Hungarian pacifist, who had toured the United States with Emmeline Pethick Lawrence in the autumn of 1914 to urge the women of America to support a policy of mediation. Frau Clara Ragaz and Mlle Marguerite Gobat were both Swiss pacifists, and Emily Greene Balch (later winner of a Nobel Peace Prize), was at that time Professor of Economics at Wellesley College in the United States.

It was perhaps consistent with her character that Emily, though departing from Switzerland under an official cloud, should not have left the duty of announcing her homecoming solely to officials of the Berne Legation. Her own telegram, addressed to Sir Edward Grey, was sent off from Southampton at 8.22 a.m. on June 28th (for in those days telegraph offices opened earlier) and was received in London at 9.40 a.m. 'Arrive London about midday,' it said, 'await kind instructions Westminster Palace Hotel.'

The reactions to this telegram at the Foreign Office, where officials began to examine it on the following day, were mixed. 'I do not know whether there is any intention that this lady should be interviewed,' said one. Another commented, 'One would very much like to know what Miss Hobhouse has been doing in Berlin but we have no reason for interviewing her.' A third wrote: 'I think that she should be ignored but watched by the police.'

Later, on July 1st, when Mr Grant Duff's written report arrived at the Foreign Office, someone added: 'This seems quite sufficient to justify interning Miss Hobhouse: even more drastic action might be taken.'

Meanwhile the Home Office, or at least a special branch of it, had not been idle, and Mr Basil Thomson, Chief of the Criminal Investigation Department of New Scotland Yard who was in close liaison with the Counter-Intelligence Sections of the War Office and Admiralty, summoned Miss Hobhouse to New Scotland Yard, from which he wrote an account reading as follows:

'Dear Dormer,

I had an interview with Miss Emily Hobhouse yesterday, and we have now a pretty clear story of her movements in

245

Germany. She has a house in Italy, and on her way home, while in Switzerland, she wrote a letter to von Jagow, whom she had known when Ambassador in Rome, asking whether he would permit her to see the present condition of Belgium, and also Ruhleben Camp. She received permission, and went straight from Berne to Brussels in company with a German Officer engaged on civil duties, and (she says) without the knowledge of the Military Authorities. She visited Aerschot, Cambrai, Liège and Louvain, saw the distribution of soup etc. and formed the opinion that the blockade was responsible for heavy infant mortality etc. exactly the sort of conclusions the Germans desired her to form.

From Brussels she went to Berlin, and had a long interview with von Jagow, and was thence escorted to Ruhleben, where she talked to a number of prisoners, and formed the opinion that imprisonment was affecting a number of them mentally, but that generally speaking, they are well treated. Her conclusions, of course, are quite immaterial, but I gathered in conversation that her talk with von Jagow included the usual discussion about Peace terms, and in that respect I think it probable that the Germans regard her as an unofficial peace emissary, from whose visit some results may be expected. I did not press her on the subject of the conversation, because she evidently preferred to communicate this to Sir Edward himself, or to someone delegated by him.

Up to a point she was evidently speaking the truth. I am expecting today or tomorrow a draft of a letter that she wrote to von Jagow from Switzerland, in her handwriting, which has come into our agent's hands; but what she did omit to tell me (a fact that came into my hands after the interview) is that she was given an address in Amsterdam to which she is to communicate when she wishes to write to von Jagow. Probably it will be possible to intercept the letter, but one cannot be sure, and therefore she ought to be treated with great reserve. At the same time I do think that it might be well for her to see the Foreign Office.
Sincerely yours.'

Later he took a more serious view. 'He (Mr Thomson) has just telephoned to say,' a Foreign Office memo noted, 'that since that letter the Police have information of an address in Amsterdam through which Miss Hobhouse has arranged to communicate with von Jagow. She has also written to him and mentioned

246

our offensive. The Police are now asking the Home Office to intern her, as being in communication with enemy subjects, and in the circumstances he thinks the F.O. should not see her.'

Why Emily was not interned we do not know. Possibly her offence was not sufficiently serious. Or perhaps the intelligence sector wanted her to continue her correspondence and learn something from it. Or perhaps she still had friends at court. At any rate the attitude of the Foreign Office towards her continued to be increasingly remote.

When her telegram of June 28th to Sir Edward Grey remained unanswered—for a whole twenty-four hours largely because of Foreign Office inertia and not as she thought because it might have been delayed by the Censor—she wrote the following day from the Westminster Palace Hotel to Sir Edward Grey revealing that she had been asked to call at New Scotland Yard 'where they have taken my papers' on June 30th, and expressing the hope that it might be possible for her to see either Sir Edward himself or Lord Crewe, Lord President of the Council, first. She said that she would not feel happy until she had told Sir Edward all she had learnt and that she was asking this favour 'only in the interests of our distracted world'.

She added that she would be in the hotel all that day and the evening and all tomorrow morning in case Sir Edward instructed her to come. The Foreign Office reply was that it would be better for Emily to write 'in the first instance' what she had to say. Then came a second letter on July 1st from Emily to Sir Edward. In it she assured the Foreign Secretary that she brought no message of any kind from von Jagow and that she was in *no* way an emissary of the German Government:

'a thing which I am sure would not be acceptable to you. It is simply this—owing to the chance of old friendship I had a long and intimate talk with von Jagow—easy and unofficial in character—of the kind that gives one vivid and deep glimpses—Afterwards it came to me as a certainty that it was my duty—if you permit—to convey to you the gist of that talk—for the day might come when it might be of great use to you.

'One cannot convey such things by letter, therefore I have ventured to beg for the honour of an interview.'

The prospect of being given 'vivid and deep glimpses' from Emily did not apparently modify Sir Edward's attitude and she turned instead to Lord Robert Cecil, who had since become the Minister of Blockade. Here she drew a blank at first but made a second attempt after hearing that Lord Robert had informed Mr Arnold Rowntree that she should apply at once to his office for an appointment to be fixed to talk about 'the camps'. The official who saw her letter minuted however: 'Miss Hobhouse is a mischievous pacifist and I suspect you should not see her. Ask her to write.' To which Lord Robert added the single word 'Please.'

Throughout these somewhat distressing exchanges Emily retained her drawing-room manners and was anxious to avoid being accused of being importunate. What was the truth about the visit and what had Emily seen? Her view of the whole matter was set out in a letter which she wrote from Bude to Lord Robert Cecil on November 3rd and which, on his instructions, was not acknowledged. In this she said:

'In case further questions should be asked about my passport I am anxious to inform you quite directly of the truth of the matter.

'I am not a diplomatist but a very simple direct person. I never tell a lie and have never made a false statement in my life. Neither do I go back from my word when given.

'For seven years I have been "domiciled" in Rome and obtained a passport in the natural order of things to return to my winter home. It has always been my custom to go and return via Switzerland, resting there.

'It was while there in May last that the account in the *Times* of Ruhleben Camp determined me to ask leave to go and see our men interned there—for I know too well what camps can be. Then I thought that I might as well at the same time ask to see Belgium about which I was troubled. Also I hoped that the act of going there voluntarily in the midst of a great war would have a softening influence and be a link to draw our two countries together. I believe it has helped towards this.

'The German Minister von Jagow is an old acquaintance and that probably facilitated matters—for when convinced of the innocuous nature of my proposed visit—in the interests of truth, peace and humanity—they gave me an informal permit bearing the words "with humanitarian object".

'From the first your Government has at my desire been made aware of my visit and much information was (had you wished it) at your service.

'I shall always be glad I went and grateful to our opponents for their noble comprehension of my aims. I have the honour.

Yours obediently
Emily Hobhouse'

Lord Robert's unwillingness further to discuss the matter might have been due possibly to the words used in the last but one paragraph of Emily's screed, in which she claimed that the British Government had been informed 'from the first' of her visit. This was accurate within the literal meaning of the words (Emily was not claiming that she had told the Government of her *intention* to make such a visit) but this interpretation would hardly have been acceptable to Mr Grant Duff.

Nevertheless Emily apparently made little attempt to keep her plans a complete secret and the Editor of the *Morning Post* received a note from a friend of his in Italy which read as follows:

'Dear Mr Clerk,
A friend of mine in Italy writes to me as follows:
"A British MP who was passing through here on Sunday told me that Miss Emily Hobhouse accepted an invitation to luncheon at the German Legation at Berne! She was here during two winters, but spent a good deal of her time at Velletri. Several people here refused to meet her. I was at Oxford with her brother, who was (and probably is) a terrible 'crank'. Do try to prevent her coming out here again, as she will encourage the Italian Germanophiles, of whom there are quite enough already."
Yours sincerely'

Emily's suggestion for a visit to Germany and Belgium was indeed put first to the German Minister in Berne, Baron von Romberg. Permission to undertake the tour came after about a month—about the same time as she was asked by Mr Grant Duff to call at the British Legation. And since she was sure that the British Legation would not have agreed to her visiting enemy-held territory, she decided to depart at once, without even reading the conditions which the German Government had insisted on as her part of the bargain. And here, as on other occasions Emily followed the example of her kinsman Edward John Trelawny, adventurer and friend of Byron, who was quoted by his biographer, Margaret Armstrong, as saying: 'I could long endure annoyance and depression, but, when at last excited, I never tried half measures, but proceeded to extremities without stop and pause.'

While still in Switzerland she was introduced by the German Minister to her courier, Herr von Rosenberg, who arranged to pick her up in a car from the Blaukreuzhaus, a temperance inn in a quiet street in Basle, and to drive her across the frontier into Germany. From there she went by train to the Belgian frontier, where she was handed over to a second young aristocrat, Baron Falkenhausen, Freiherr von Friedensthal, who spoke perfect English. He conveyed her to the Astoria hotel in Brussels. Here she learnt for the first time that she must always be accompanied by her guide, even when going round the corner to buy a stamp, must sleep only in Brussels and that it was considered inadvisable for her to speak to Belgians, even though she pointed out that this was a weakness in the German case and told her more than she could have learned from the people themselves. But the rule stood. The hotel was half shut and there were no books or newspapers to be seen. They had given up serving dinner.

As she journeyed round Brussels with her guide she noted that he invariably travelled on the platform of the trams separately from the other passengers inside. The people of Brussels treated him with the same antagonism and disdain that the Boers showed towards the British, only this time Emily was travelling under the auspices of the occupation powers and was out of touch with her partisans; however she remarked that German martial law did not seem to be any more strict than the British martial law she had experienced in the Orange Free State.

Working out of Brussels, Emily visited Antwerp, Malines, Charleroi, Aerschot and Louvain, which had been reported in some Allied papers as having been completely destroyed. The German case was that on August 25th Belgian partisans in the houses round the city's main square, believing that they were about to be relieved by forces from Antwerp, had, on a concerted signal, opened fire on the German soldiers and, that in the ensuing fighting, during which hot tar was poured from the roof tops, the famous library was burnt, the roof and bells of the cathedral damaged, and the City Hall saved only by blowing up some of the surrounding houses. Fighting continued the next day in spite of the fact that the Mayor and other prominent citizens selected as hostages were paraded through the streets. The Germans maintained that only about one-eighth of the city had been destroyed and that 38,000 out of the normal population of 44,000 were still living undisturbed. It was perhaps unfortunate that Emily, not being allowed to talk to the Belgians, had no independent means of checking the figures she was given but nevertheless accepted them without question. She was allowed to interview the manager of one of the communal kitchens and learnt that the rations were insufficient and that there was an increase in the number of cases of tuberculosis as a result.

Her formal request to go to Berlin was made or possibly renewed through officials of the Political Department of the German Foreign Office in Brussels, although von Jagow doubtless knew already of Emily's wishes. Permission came on June 17th and she was soon installed in the Hotel Furstenhof, a very comfortable establishment near the Potsdamer Bahnhof in the centre of Berlin as it then was. Soon afterwards, she met her old friend von Jagow, but at this point a significant discrepancy occurs in the account of the meeting as related by Ruth Fry and the one given by Emily in her letters. Ruth Fry's account says:

'She had so long determined on her journey to Germany that she records that she felt nothing strange in the experience and they [Emily and von Jagow] had a most friendly talk lasting nearly an hour in which Miss Hobhouse gathered that it was intended for her to take the hint to England that Germany was willing to negotiate a peace if advances were made to her. She endeavoured to convey this to important people on her return but, as might be expected, without success.'

Yet in her letter to Sir Edward Grey Emily stated that she bore 'no message of any kind from von Jagow' and that she was 'in no way an emissary of the German Government', words which, though they may have been true in their most literal sense, could easily have given a false impression.

In any case, Emily's efforts could hardly have borne fruit, for von Jagow himself was jockeyed out of office soon afterwards largely because he was an unconvincing speaker in the Reichstag and was opposed to the proposed policy of unrestricted submarine warfare.

Emily did, however, succeed in getting in touch with a number of those who were carrying on welfare work on behalf of the interned Britons—among them Dr Elizabeth Rotten, a Swiss girl formerly of Newnham College, Cambridge, who was Secretary of the Berlin Committee for the Relief of Foreigners in Germany, and she was able to visit Ruhleben, where the

251

British were confined. Ruhleben was in one respect only, the counterpart of the British concentration camp at Johannesburg: it was established on a former race course. It comprised several spectator stands, administrative buildings and brick stables with hay lofts above. The camp was under the charge of Count Schwerin, a handsome old gentleman of uncertain temper, but the United States Ambassador James W. Gerard, who was looking after British interests in Germany, was allowed to visit Ruhleben and other camps at twenty-four hours' notice and to converse with prisoners in sight of, but out of the hearing of, camp officials. On the whole the German treatment of British prisoners seems to have been based on the principle of reciprocity. On the outbreak of war, British subjects were locked up in Spandau Gaol from which they were transferred to Ruhleben when it became clear under what conditions Germans were being interned in Britain. At one time John B. Jackson, former United States Minister to Greece and Cuba, was sent to Britain to visit camps there in order to be able to allay rumours that German prisoners were being ill-treated. On the whole Ruhleben was by no means a hell-camp.

Two independent accounts of Emily's visit to Ruhleben have survived. One was sent to Lord Robert Cecil by a correspondent from Hatch End, Middlesex, whose son wrote: 'I was sitting alone in the Italian room reading "Paradise Lost" as a comparison with the "Divina Commedia" (and curiously enough had just reached the curse of Eve) on the 22nd inst. at 12.35, when the door opened and in entered Graf Schwerin, other officers and a *lady*. I stood up. The others went upstairs. The lady who was tired, sat down. After the first words she spoke I knew she was English. She had been seven years (? months) in Rome, was now on her way to England and was very nice to me. She said I looked very well and asked if she could do anything for me. The officers came downstairs. The lady asked my name, shook my hand and departed (I presume) for London. She did not explain what she was doing in the middle of Germany but I have no doubt she knew—of course the others all ragged me to death about this and they all say that she is probably—(well you know about Roger Casement?)—but I do not believe it. I had not spoken to a lady for 20 months.'

The other, signed 'Returned Ruhlebenite', appeared in October in the *Times* and read:

'Sir,

It was with feelings of regret that I read in your issue of October 18 a letter from that ardent propagandist, Miss Emily Hobhouse. As stated in her letter, this lady visited Ruhleben camp and Dr Weiler's sanatorium, where I was then interned, in the month of May or June this year. She was escorted by a German officer, and travelled under the auspices of the Berlin War Office, who made every effort to suppress her identity. During her visit she commented on the excellence of the Kriegsbrot, of which she ate a minute portion in public, and pronounced it most beneficial for the indigestion—a remark which I cannot believe even Count Reventlow himself would have endorsed. She described the dingy villa, where we were packed like sardines in a tin, and which made a mockery of the word sanatorium, as a delightful spot, and declared it almost made her wish to be ill that she might dwell in such a place. She made several more equally fatuous and disingenuous remarks, such as that the British Government was to blame for the small number of civilian prisoners exchanged; but I hope I have written enough to show how little credence should be placed in the statements of a witness who can arrive at such very definite conclusions after a wholly inadequate examination of the facts.

I am, Sir, your obedient servant'

Emily's visit to Ruhleben was not however entirely fruitless for it suggested a scheme for an exchange of all British and German civilians over military age and the internment of the remainder in a neutral country. But the Foreign Office had other ideas of its own and discovered in addition a number of difficulties which the transfer of some 22,000 Germans of military age to Switzerland across France would involve.

By this time Emily's trip had become public knowledge. Indeed she had written about it in a report published in the *Daily News* of September 4th 1916:

'Externally all is so fair in the beautiful city of Brussels that it would be difficult for visitors to bear in mind the existing tragedy were it not for the sharp rejoinder that recurs at the sight of the long lines of people waiting to be fed in various quarters of the town. . . . One halted involuntarily as before a passing funeral and then crept past them with a sense of awe and shame. And next day the same sight aroused the

253

same feelings, and the next and the next, till slowly the mind grasped something of what it must mean to stand thus for hours, day after day, week after week, month after month, mounting at last to years. For in those queues one faced a bit of war in everyday garb, stripped of glory—war in its ultimate effect upon a civilian population in misery and broken lives.'

(That week too she had written to Isabel Steyn. 'We pacifists dare not pause—far less than those who make destructive munitions of war.... Fancy our beloved country, fancy France, fancy beautiful Italy and Germany, all given up to making death-dealing instruments, girls and boys hard at it night and day in all our countries. It is ghastly, and twenty millions of men hurling these things at each other, each seeing who can kill the most.')

She referred to her trip again in a letter about Louvain in which she reproduced the facts that she had been told during her visit. It led to an acrimonious correspondence and to questions in the House of Commons and House of Lords which persisted for nearly a month.

The first spirited piece of verbal sword play took place on October 26th. It and subsequent exchanges provide a splendid example of ministerial equivocation:

'MISS EMILY HOBHOUSE

Major HUNT asked the Under Secretary of State for Foreign Affairs whether Miss Emily Hobhouse obtained permission from the Foreign Office to travel to Belgium?

Mr PENNEFATHER asked the Under-Secretary of State for Foreign Affairs whether he is aware that a Miss Emily Hobhouse, a British subject, has been enabled to travel hundreds of miles through Germany and Belgium; by whose permission Miss Hobhouse went to Germany and Belgium; whether it was with the knowledge of the British Government; and, if so, were they aware of Miss Hobhouse's object in going?

Lord R. CECIL: His Majesty's Government are aware of Miss Hobhouse's visit to Germany and Belgium, which evidently took place with the permission of the German authorities, but His Majesty's Government had no knowledge of the matter until after the lady's return to Switzerland.

Mr ASHLEY: Surely the Foreign Office had to issue a passport showing where this lady was going to travel?

Lord R. CECIL: I can assure my hon. Friend that the Foreign Office certainly never issued a passport to enable any British subject to go to Germany.

Major HUNT: Did they issue a passport to allow Miss Hobhouse to go abroad?

Lord R. CECIL: I should like notice of that, but I presume she had a passport before she went abroad.

Sir W. BYLES: May I ask whether the visits of the lady to high officials in the German Foreign Office might be of great service to this country?

Lord R. CECIL: No, Sir; I think it is very undesirable that any British subject should pay visits to German high officials.

Colonel ALAN SYKES: Is the Noble Lord going to take any action in the matter?

Mr PENNEFATHER: Are we to infer from the Noble Lord's replies that if Miss Hobhouse obtained a passport to leave this country she must have done so under false pretences?

Lord R. CECIL: No, Sir, I should not like to say that. I do not know that the facts in my possession warrant any statement of that kind. No doubt she obtained a passport to go to an Allied or neutral country. What she did after that I do not know. I have no reason to suppose that she made any false statements to us.'

Lord Robert engaged in a further exchange of questions and answers on October 31st:

'MISS EMILY HOBHOUSE (PASSPORT)

Mr PENNEFATHER asked the Under Secretary for Foreign Affairs on what date a passport was issued to Miss Emily Hobhouse; if any particular destination was mentioned therein, and, if so, what destination; were there any limitations; whether Miss Hobhouse gave any reasons for requiring a passport, and, if so, what were the reasons given by her?

Lord R. CECIL: Miss Hobhouse was given a passport on 5th March 1915, to travel to Italy, where she stated that she wished to go for the benefit of her health. The lady having returned to this country, her passport was, on 29th November 1915, furnished with a visa by the military permit office entitling her to proceed once more to Italy. She made a stay in Switzerland both on the outward and homeward journeys, though she appears to have made no mention of any such intention when applying for the visa to leave this country.

There was no limitation on the use of the passport specified in the document itself, except in so far as the mention of destination amounts to such.

Mr ASHLEY: May we assume then that this lady obtained the passport under false pretences?

Lord R. CECIL: Everyone must draw his own conclusions from the answer I have given.

Colonel ALAN SYKES: Is the Noble Lord going to take any further action on this matter?

Lord R. CECIL: I imagine Miss Hobhouse will not be allowed again to leave the country.

Mr OUTHWAITE: Has the Noble Lord's attention been drawn to a report in the *Times* yesterday that six Russian ladies have been received by the German Empress, and is there any particular reason why an English lady should not go to inspect camps in Germany?

Mr BUTCHER: Is there no means of bringing to justice a lady who goes abroad for the purpose of betraying her country?

Lord R. CECIL: My hon. and learned Friend will see that that is not a question which it is possible for the Foreign Office to answer. He may, if he desires, put it to the legal advisers of the Crown.

Mr TREVELYAN: Is it not the case that immediately on her return to this country Miss Hobhouse offered to give every possible information she had to the Government?

Lord R. CECIL: I do not know anything about that, but I know that the general opinion of the House—and I believe of the country—is that Miss Hobhouse's activities have not been in the interests of this country.'

On a further occasion an MP suggested, on November 1st that Emily might have been guilty of a punishable offence in making her visit. In answer to one such question the Attorney General, Sir Frederick Smith (afterwards Lord Birkenhead), conceded that if Miss Hobhouse had 'conceived the idea' of going to Germany at the time she applied for her visa, her failure to inform the Home Office of that intention might be punishable. But getting into contact with the enemy from neutral territory and thereby entering enemy territory was not, the Attorney General said, a criminal offence as the law stood at present unless aggravated by other circumstances. However, it was proposed to make a Regulation under the Defence of the

Realm Act to make this an offence in future. The Attorney General added that whatever Miss Hobhouse might or might not have said while in Germany, since she would not be allowed to leave the country as long as the war lasted, she would not enjoy any similar opportunity in the future of disparaging the cause of the Allies.

But on November 4th the pace hotted up. Major Hunt asked the Under Secretary of State for Foreign Affairs if he could now say whether Miss Hobhouse had a passport from the Foreign Office and, if so, whether she stated for what purpose she was going abroad. When told that a passport was issued to Miss Hobhouse in March 1915 to travel to Italy and that she stated that she desired to visit that country for reasons of health, the Major was ungallant enough to pursue the matter. 'In view of the fact that her statement was not correct,' he said, 'can the Rt. Hon. Gentleman say whether she is going to be prosecuted like any ordinary woman, or is she going to be protected by high personages. . . .'

At this point the Speaker jumped in to say that the Hon. and gallant Members must give notice of that question. In the Lords, Lord Courtney of Penwith (was he perhaps one of the high personages referred to by Major Hunt?) argued on Emily's behalf that his impression was that 'the intention of going to Germany did not exist in her mind at all when she started for Italy. If it did exist it lay there very dormant all the winter and through the early spring months.'

(Here again there is a slight conflict of evidence between Ruth Fry's account—quoted above—which said that the trip had long been in Emily's mind and the interpretation of her thoughts by Lord Courtney.)

Emily, in a letter to the *Times,* dated November 8th but not published till five days later, flatly discounted the possibility of dormancy:

'Sir,

As your paragraph in today's issue of the *Times,* following upon erroneous statements in both Houses of Parliament and in the Press in regard to my movements, will give rise to misconception, will you allow me to state definitely, what indeed is now known to Ministers, that my Foreign Office passport was issued to me early in 1915, to journey, as usual, to my winter home in Italy—that this was visa'd last winter for the same purpose—that I passed the entire winter in

257

Rome—and that no idea of visiting Germany came to me
until I was in Switzerland on my return journey this summer.
I went to Germany quite simply and openly, contravening
no law; I went under my own name with a "humanitarian
pass", in the interests of truth, peace and humanity; and I
am proud and thankful to have done so.

I am, Sir, yours faithfully,
EMILY HOBHOUSE'

The truth was probably that she did not perceive until she
was in Switzerland that a way could be found for her to visit
enemy territory although she had long hoped to do so.

From now on Emily was permanently disillusioned. She realized that this had become a multi-lateral World War and was
no longer a conflict which could be halted or curtailed by any
single individual striving for a reconciliation between the rulers
who began it—as might have been the case with the Boer War.
An overwhelming sense of melancholy and self-doubt led to her
return to Bude, the Cornish 'village' where in happier times her
mother had taken her on family bathing parties.

Already, she had become a mortal without a home. She saw
herself as the woman who had once hoped for too much idealism
from her own countrymen and who was now identified by them
as a persistent advocate for their enemies. More and more her
superficial gaiety and humour was submerged beneath the seas
of melancholy.

But in Whitehall the conflict had still to end. General
Macdonogh of the Military Permit Office wrote to Lord Robert
Cecil to complain that Lord Robert's answer in the House had
given the impression that the Military Permit Office had been
responsible for allowing Emily out of the country, whereas in
fact they had persistently refused to give her the permits she
asked for, until they were obliged by Sir John Simon's directive
to alter their policy.

Accordingly, Sir Edwin Cornwall was induced to ask a question on November 16th of a nature that allowed both the
Military Permit Office and the Foreign Office to pay off old
scores. The question was whether the permit granted to Miss
Hobhouse, in consequence of which she obtained a visa, was
granted on the advice or with the approval of the military
authorities.

Lord Robert Cecil was able to say with assurance 'No, Sir;

258

I understand that neither the military authorities nor the Foreign Office gave any such advice or approval.'

Mr Ashley then asked: 'Has any other Government Department given approval?'

Lord Robert Cecil replied: 'I understand that the permit was issued on the direction of the then Secretary of State for the Home Department.'

But the blame accorded to Sir John Simon was merely a reflection of the public disapproval of Emily's latest adventure.

Already on November 1915, at the time she was endeavouring to return to Italy, Lady Courtney had written in her diary an entry to the effect that the Womens International League had had two meetings to discuss a rather difficult question relating to EH. 'Her personality always excites extremes of feeling,' Lady Courtney added.

Her old friend Jannie Smuts did not allow himself to show extremes of feeling but did from time to time exhibit a certain acidity. He had received more than one highly emotional letter from Emily and it cannot have been pleasant for him to have been given well-meant advice on how to handle the rebellion staged by De Wet and other of his own Boers in 1914. ('Keep them in prison if you will till the end but do not execute them, do not, *do not, do not*. Only once more I beg and pray you to *spare those men* for in opposing a war of aggression [against German South-West Africa] they were surely right, even if the means they have taken have been wrong.') Mrs Smuts afterwards told Sarah Gertrude Millin, 'She was very unkind to the "Ou-Baas" and I never wrote to her again.'

In March 1917, however, when Smuts was expected in London, Emily wrote once more to him to tease him about the honours that were being showered on him for following the imperialist path and wondered whether there was still enough of the old Jannie left to associate with a pacifist, anti-imperialist like herself. She tried to persuade him to spend his Sunday on a visit to her in Bude. If not, though frantically busy with many engagements to fit in, she would come to London. Soon after seeing her on March 21st, he wrote home to Mrs Smuts that Emily was all for making peace by negotiation but that she was 'a little troublesome and, of course, as always, tactless, so that her whole family, even her brother, is against her'.

Emily called again to see Smuts that week, after which he wrote home: 'Miss Hobhouse was here again yesterday and will write to you. She is quite sweet and her letters are much exaggerated. But she is, of course, a little mad.' And two weeks later he wrote to tell Margaret Clark Gillett that Miss Hobhouse had moved to town in order the more effectively to labour for the salvation of his soul.

To his wife he was less guarded. 'Miss Hobhouse has now come to London to be nearer to me,' he complained, 'she is a pacifist of a very troublesome kind.' However, to Margaret Gillett he writes more tolerantly, referring to her as 'the dear Auntie' whom he had taken to see her brother Leonard Hobhouse.

By November 1917, she had moved back to London to St Dunstan's Road, Baron's Court, from which she was complaining to Smuts about the 'odious shrapnel' with which London was being defended from the German air-raids while at the same time praising the mass desertion of the Italian soldiers during and after the battle of Caporetto.

But on the whole the later war years were not propitious for the pacifists. A neutral committee composed of international lawyers, economists, parliamentarians of the various countries continued to discuss peace throughout most of 1916. Their work came to an abrupt halt early the following year. On January 31st 1917, Germany, in retaliation for the Allied blockade, declared unrestricted warfare against neutral shipping around the British and French coasts. Within four days three United States ships with food for Belgium were torpedoed and the United States severed diplomatic relations with Germany. On April 2nd President Wilson changed course and took the United States into the war. 'I, too, want peace,' he declared 'but I know how to get it and they (the pacifists) do not.' On the other side the Germans had already reached the stage when the slogan 'Gott Strafe England' (God punish England) was stamped on envelopes and even on paper money (the United States was added later), and Ernst Lissauer's 'Hymn of Hate' expressed the feelings of many German families.

In Britain, Lord Milner aroused a storm when he said a few good words on behalf of the German people and when, on Armistice Day, Lady Courtney took along the banner she had been embroidering—a large blue silk one with a dove and olive branch in the middle, to Chelsea Town Hall, hoping that it would be displayed there with the other flags, she was told that it was quite unsuitable and that 'we are not Germans here.' 'Nor Christians either apparently,' retorted the outraged embroiderer as she walked out.

But, all the same, the war to end all wars was over at last.

14

Envoi

At sixty, a portrait of Emily shows her face almost unlined, her expression alert. The nose is delicately pointed, the high cheek-bones add that faint trace of acidity which saves a woman's features from the complacency of middle age, and the eyelids, hooded above the eyes like Gothic window blinds, suggest the power to express emotions ranging from affectionate approval to distant hauteur or even overpowering distaste.

Emily is dressed in a fur coat and a dress of dark tasselled material. There is a touch of delicate lace round the throat and a veil behind the dark wedding-cake hat.

In short she is ready to be invited to take a drive in a smart brougham or to attend a pre-view of the Royal Academy summer show.

And so once again it might have been if the world had been able to manage its own affairs.

In fact, however, there was much to be put right. The League of Nations, forerunner of the United Nations, was a subject on which Emily was prepared to give lectures, even before the war was over. And, when it ended, she threw her energy into three new tasks. One was to raise money for the Swiss Relief Fund for Starving Children which brought children from Austria, Germany, Czechoslovakia and Hungary to private houses and nursing homes in Switzerland for rest and recovery. Emily and her friends paid all the expenses of collection, and reduced railway fares cut the cost of holidays to about £4 per child. The fund was eventually merged in the very much more extensive work of the Save the Children Fund.

Then there was the Russian Babies' Fund (of which Emily was Chairman). This was founded in July 1919 to send milk,

261

baby clothes, soap and other necessaries to Russia to be handed out there by the Friends' Relief Fund workers.

Finally, there was her own work, which she carried out in the field, for the Save the Children Fund.

In September 1919 Emily left England as the representative of the Fund in Austria and Germany, and collaborated with Dr Schwytzer, a Swiss doctor, in preparing reports on conditions in Vienna and Leipzig, two of the worst-hit centres. In Leipzig they saw the faces of the people had turned yellowish grey from under-nourishment, and the children were thin and rickety. There were no public feeding kitchens to make up their rations. Emily as usual was able to browbeat the Leipzig city authorities into co-operating, and by January 1920 had succeeded in starting up a school feeding system. It covered 11,000 schoolchildren in the eastern part of the city, the remaining schools being supplied by the American Quaker Relief organization.

Here once again Emily found happiness, and her large-scale enterprise did not prevent her from making friends of individual children or from helping them in cases of personal suffering. Her sympathy and charm were as effective in Germany as in the veld. Children wrote poems for her and the staff at her hotel treated her like an Empress.

Her flare for detailed organization was impressive, and she continued to collect funds from England, Switzerland, Denmark and even from Mrs Steyn in South Africa. The South African Government gave £5,000 under their pound for pound grant scheme.

In April she finished her spell as representative of the Save the Children Fund, but, without an office or any paid helpers, she was able to continue her work independently, largely through the loyal support of her German helpers. In addition to providing supplementary meals she was able to organize her own holiday scheme by which children were sent from Leipzig to the Black Forest, or Switzerland or even to the sea to regain their strength.

Emily was decorated by the German Red Cross, honoured by the city of Leipzig, but was pleased most of all by the letters that she got from children she had helped.

Emily had to leave Leipzig in 1921 owing to ill health; but the work that she had begun was carried on by her 'staff' until March 1922.

It was hardly to be expected that Emily would end her life in a state of luxury. She was an impulsive spender and though good at managing other people's affairs did not consider it necessary to organize her own on any systematic basis. Back in 1887 she had received a legacy from her Aunt Elizabeth who lived in style with her own garden and greenhouse in Grosvenor Place, but little of this remained. Dividends in the post-war slump became less and less generous, and Emily was compelled to sell first her jewellery and then her fine lace shawls and veils that she had inherited from her aunt Lady Hobhouse. Her South African paintings were the next to go and this was followed by a Canaletto with which she had been presented in the good old bygone days. Finally Emily had to part with her beloved piano.

No doubt in those days her family was too hard hit to offer much help but, in 1921, her friends in South Africa raised £2,300, collected in half-crown subscriptions, to be spent by her on a permanent home for herself.

Emily chose a small Victorian house at the Cornish seaside artists' resort of St Ives and was indeed happy and contented for a while. That Christmas (1921) she wrote:

'For all that surrounds me and gives me a feeling of comfort and rest and security the warmth of my little room—the feeling of being at home—for all this I have you to thank. As I look back on the year that has passed I am more and more amazed at what you and your people have done for my happiness and well-being.'

But, as time went by, she missed the company of her family and her intellectual friends. Also, it was hard to get servants in St Ives. She therefore sold the house and, after borrowing money from the bank on the strength of her securities, was able in 1923 to buy a small house in Tor Gardens on Campden Hill, London, where many of her relatives and old friends were able to visit her.

In 1923 she published *Tant' Alie of Transvaal*, her own translation of the diary written during the Boer War by one of her friends, Alida Badenhorst, *née* De Wet, a farmer's wife who wrote in true vernacular Afrikaans. In fact Emily felt that she should really have translated the diary into Cornish dialect.

Tant' Alie was by no means a pacifist, but the story of her life, after her husband had been taken prisoner, typified the hardships of war as experienced by the non-combattant women and children.

During the last few years of her life Emily also completed a work which she had begun some twenty years earlier, called *War without Glamour*. It was a book without glamour as far as appearances went; it had neither index nor list of contents. Its unadorned blue-grey mottled cover with black title letters and the cheap paper on which its 158 pages were printed could have had little sales appeal. (The introduction from Mrs Smuts for which Emily had appealed was not forthcoming.) Moreover the subject was hardly suited to the mood of the twenties. It was a mere six years since the British had emerged greatly shaken from the Great War—and they needed no reminder of far-off battles or of the hardships suffered by others.

Published by the Nasionale Pers Beperk (National Press Limited) in Bloemfontein, *War without Glamour* is now rarely to be found outside private collections. True, the book contained reproductions in colour of three of Emily's water-colours—two burnt farms in brick reds, greens, ochres and purples, and a Boer war cemetery by moonlight—but it needs no art teacher to discern from the lighting and composition of these works that Emily painted with charm but with limited perception and sense of perspective.

In essence, it contains the case histories of some thirty Afrikaner women, several of them wives of 'Dutch' pastors.

In her Preface Emily wrote:

'Besides their value as historical records, these accounts are, in my belief, a real aid to the cause of permanent peace, for they depict war in simple unvarnished language, with complete unconsciousness disclosing its squalid and ghastly details, thus making clear to unbiased readers its effects on the children, the old and the sick. The universality and similarity of experience is striking. Had every woman of the two Boer Republics (apart from the few big towns) recorded her experience, the result would have been but a general repetition of these statements with minor variations of detail.'

This remains true; but some details, trivial in themselves, nevertheless help to reconstruct the atmosphere of bitterness and resentment which existed and still exist in the minds of the older generation of Afrikaners even today when they think back into the past.

As, for example, the feelings of Mrs Viljoen wife of the Pastor of Reitz in the Orange Free State, sent as an 'undesirable' to the concentration camp at Harrismith in the Orange River Colony when she was invited (and refused to accept) invitations to the British officers' tea parties and dances. Her distress as her servants left her because the British offered them more than she could afford; her indignation at the British nurse who went out to a military dance at five in the evening leaving her patients uncared for till eleven the following morning.

There was Mrs Gezina Joubert of Klerksdorp whose friends were ordered to stop preparations for the funeral of her son who had died in the camp until his ration card had been found and returned to the Camp Commandant.

There was Mrs Johanna Rousseau who on her journey from Reitz to Kroonstad had to battle with cattle for the foodstuffs that had been thrown on the ground, and who reported that a Mrs Akkerman had felt compelled to carry her eight year-old son, who was dying, out of her tent to one where there was a light so that she could see him die.

The book showed, too, glimpses of Emily's sympathy for the more well-to-do, cultivated families akin to her own class at home, who suffered all the more because of the sharp contrast between life in camp and their previous existence.

A passage in the last few lines of the book concerning the case of Mrs Neethling explains without equivocation Emily's final thoughts about the concentration camps. Mrs Neethling whose husband was Chaplain to a Boer unit, was held in detention at Balmoral about 60 miles from Pretoria till she died, despite the pleas for her release by friends and relatives who would have looked after her.

'Who is responsible for the death of this woman?' Emily asks:

'That naturally enough is the question asked by the relations and by her six children. We, in England, ought to answer it also, each according to our lights. No doubt many were in part responsible from the Minister of War downwards. But in war it would seem impossible to fix blame upon any one individual, not even excepting the Commander-in-Chief himself. It is the System which is responsible. Once a government has abandoned itself to the arbitrament of War, its members would seem by that fatal act to have lost responsibility and all in authority are caught up and whirled along by the iron law of Military Necessity. So long as the system of War is maintained and practised by civilized nations, so long will these tragedies happen; for under that system anything and everything is justified. The attempt to "humanize" war by Hague, Genevan or other regulations has not succeeded, for all these paper rules are broken by each nation in turn as it goes to war. Neither women nor children are spared, neither the aged nor sick; the Juggernaut of war crushes all alike who have the misfortune to be in its path. The one and only hope is the abolition of War that is itself a condition of lawlessness which renders cruelties a "necessity" and indemnifies all who commit them in its name.'

Even during her last few years Emily continued to take a close interest in South African politics, and welcome the victory won in 1924 by Dr Hertzog's Nationalist Party in alliance with the Labour Party over General Smuts, who, she felt had been placing imperialist interests before those of South Africa.

She was critical however of Hertzog's policy towards the coloured community, and declared in letters to Mrs Steyn, (April 27th, July 13th 1924) that it was not possible for South Africa to treat the colour problem as a water-tight affair that concerned South Africa only. The world had become too small for that, and the problem was one that was pressing in on us from all sides. 'Personally I believe segregation of any of either race or colour and class the wrong policy and one which can only lead to discontent and ultimate disaster,' Emily proclaimed.

So Hertzog, too, would have disappointed her, for she was a hard woman to please.

Yet as a woman who had saved the lives of thousands of South African children and laid the foundations of reconciliation between Boer and Britain she had surely the right to advise.

In 1925 once more restlessness gripped her, and at the beginning of the last winter of her life she moved to a rented bungalow near Chichester, close to the Sussex coast. Her friends, as ever, bewailed the choice that Emily had made and did not hesitate to condemn Emily's new dwelling as unsuitable. It might be all very well for a summer holiday home but was not designed to keep out the cold of an English winter. Moreover Emily was now an invalid and often bed-ridden. She suffered from asthma, angina pectoris and other distressing complaints. She could afford no luxuries and she had only a young girl to look after her. She was far away from most of her friends and her letters to Mrs Steyn show clearly that she felt sad, lonely and apprehensive. And she realized that as she grew weaker and needed more looking after, life would become still more expensive. In bed, from which often she was unable to move for days at a time, she would wonder what was to become of her, and where she would find the permanent home for which she had been searching for the past twenty years. She was beginning to discover some of the drawbacks of a democracy in which the privileged are not after all so privileged.

'Life is filled up with the mere effort to eat and sleep decently,' she wrote to Mrs Steyn. 'That is in varying degrees what our civilization is coming to, the decay of the intellectual life, the impossibility of maintaining the life of mental activity under the grinding circumstances of present physical and financial difficulties.'

At first she had been delighted at the victory of Ramsay MacDonald and the Labour Party in the general election of 1923. 'For the first time in my life I shall to some extent feel "represented" in Parliament and in the Councils of State,' she wrote.

Her old supporter Charles Trevelyan had once again become Minister of Education and she hastened to urge him to abandon militaristic teaching and to encourage the moral teaching of history and the 'right views of foreigners as brothers' and fear and hatred of war as a universal curse. But MacDonald like other politicians eventually disappointed her by refusing to revise the terms of the Treaty of Versailles.

In her last years she had been writing her autobiography, on which Ruth Fry drew extensively. No doubt, as Bernard Shaw said in his *Self Sketches,* 'Very few people know what has happened to them or could describe it artistically,' yet in Emily's case sincerity overcame her occasional lapses into self-dramatization, and at times she wrote for many of us.

For example after looking at a sketch which she had made as a girl of the view from her window she wrote:

'Simple enough, but it moved me to tears, as it brought the sudden re-awakening of my girlhood's aspirations. Yet as I look at it, knowing the dreams are gone for ever, I am sensible of the same aspirations, the same stirring desires and lofty aims, I feel within me the heart of a girl while those around me see only the bowed form and decayed body. As I but rarely look in the glass, I am conscious of this change by the feeling of imprisonment; the burden of a still ardent spirit pent up in a weak and useless frame, which cannot carry out its behests. When the final decay has gone will the torch of the spirit continue to burn, finding some better medium for its expression? I like Maeterlinck's thought: "The dead live again every time that we remember them." If this be true, perhaps the best of me, dear friends, will come to life every time you recall me to your minds. It is a solace to feel that, as I pen these words to you.'

Again:

'As I read over the old letters and papers of 60 years, the FIRST thing that strikes me is the many mistakes I have made—the frequent misjudgement of men and things. Viewing it all in the light of riper experience I see in a flash how much better I could have acted—or written—or spoken. Is this, I wonder, a universal experience?

Waller must have felt this when he wrote:

"The soul's dark cottage, battered and decayed,
Lets in new light through chinks that time has made.
Stronger by weakness wiser men become,
As they draw near to their eternal home."

With so many errors it is strange that one has "muddled through". It could only be because the aims were true, however great the ignorance in trying to attain them.

SECONDLY, I am struck—how pain passes whether physical, mental or spiritual. Gashes may be left, but they DO heal. One can read with surprise the burning words written under pressure of some torture through which one has passed.

And thirdly. How often I have been misunderstood—almost entirely from my inability to explain myself—through lack of ready words, or through lack of courage.'

In this last paragraph Emily does herself an injustice for she lacked neither courage nor the ability to say what she thought. Frequently she expressed herself too well and it was in her reasoning rather than in her action that she 'muddled through'.

Emily's departure from London signalled her recognition of the fact that her life was nearly over. She could no longer do any kind of work; and work, as she once confessed; had been to her what husband and children were to others. Life had no savour for her once the power to work had departed.

But she consoled herself with the thought that the fate of the individual was unimportant so long as human progress continued. There were always compensations to be found in all circumstances of life and it was best to fix one's mind on them. 'I am something like a cat, and generally in falling, fall upon my feet' she said.

In early Spring of 1926 she was well enough to visit the Isle of Wight but once more she prepared herself for death. On March 14th she wrote:

'I have all my life looked forward so greatly to death—the rest, the peace, the greatness of it. Just as I look forward to sleep after the heavy work of a fatiguing day, so I have always (and still do) look forward to death.

> "Death comes to set thee free,
> Oh! greet him cheerily
> As thy best friends,
> And all thy woes shall cease.
> And in eternal peace,
> Thy penance end."

Do you remember these lines from Sintram? I wrote them down in my teens—the whole poem, and all my life they have echoed in my thoughts.'

Again on May 23rd on Whit Sunday she wrote to say how her mind was full of the words and music that she had learnt to sing in the choir at St Ive—'Veni Creator.'

The end came on June 8th before her last letter had reached South Africa. On June 1st she was brought to London in an ambulance, and though she rallied enough to ask her friends to come round to see her in her nursing home in Bedford Gardens and tell her all the news, it was clear that she was on her death bed. Dr J. M. Huey certified that death was due to pleurisy, cardiac degeneration and a form of internal cancer.

Emily departed from the traditions of her family and asked for her body to be cremated, and for her remains to be interred in South Africa.

She would surely have liked to have been present at the ceremony later that year during which her ashes were buried at the foot of the National Memorial at Bloemfontein which she had herself so nearly unveiled. She would have relished the Church with its masses of wreaths and madonna lilies, the procession of schoolgirls, dressed in pale mauve carrying the casket of her ashes. She would have treasured the words of Smuts who, rich as ever in clichés, summarized her achievements.

'We stood alone in the world, friendless among the people, the smallest nations ranged against the mightiest Empire on the earth. Then one small hand, the hand of a woman, was stretched out to us. At that darkest hour, when our race almost appeared doomed to extinction, she appeared as an angel, as a heaven-sent messenger. Strangest of all, she was an Englishwoman.'

Only three people have been honoured by burial within the monument—Emily Hobhouse, President Steyn whose wife had been Emily's lifelong friend, and General De Wet at whose house Emily had stayed and for whose life she later pleaded. Emily undoubtedly would have approved of her fellow travellers in what she would have called the Great Beyond.

To the end of her days Emily felt that she had been misunderstood by her countrymen at home. 'I do wish for justice,' she said in her last letter to Mrs Steyn, 'or at least by some wise strong words for the removal of Injustice such as at present rests upon my name . . . I was in no sense a rebel or unpatriotic. Rather I felt that I laboured for the highest, honouring England in striving to succour and preserve the Boer women and children.'

In this she was unsuccessful during her lifetime, and the *Times* gave her a particularly uncharitable obituary.

'HUMANITARIAN ZEAL', the headline read.

Then:

'Miss Emily Hobhouse who died on Tuesday in Kensington became prominent both in the South African War and in the Great War for her humanitarian zeal which was, however, not always according to the knowledge or the dictates of sound judgement. . . .

When in the South African War the Boers in the field refused to recognize their responsibility for the care of their women and children and these and other non-combatants had to be collected in concentration camps, Miss Hobhouse went out and reported on the camps to the Committee of the Distress Fund for South African Women and Children. The deficiencies which she found there were largely unavoidable owing to the conditions in which the camps were formed while the mortality was in part at least due to the occupants' ignorance of nursing and to their primitive ideas of medicine and sanitation. Unfortunately her report was eagerly seized on for purposes of agitation not only by the Boer propagandists but by those whose sympathy with the Boers was less than their hostility to Britain. It even played a part in the divisions which then rent the Liberal Party.

During the Great War in 1916 Miss Hobhouse visited Louvain and the prisoners camps at Ruhleben. She herself said in a letter to the *Times*: "I went to Germany quite simply and openly, contravening no law; I went under my own name with a 'humanitarian pass' in the interests of truth, peace and humanity and I am proud and thankful to have done so."

She entered Germany via Switzerland although her passport was only for Italy, and a regulation had to be made under the Defence of the Realm Acts to meet such cases in future.'

Emily Hobhouse has often been described as the Florence Nightingale of the Boer War by those who have been called on to explain a complex personality in a very few words. The comparison is inexact. Florence was a trained nurse, and an expert on hospital organization. She was sent out by the War Office during the Crimean War to look after the welfare of British troops in military hospitals. Emily's position was dissimilar. She was self-trained, she had no hospital experience, she was not sent abroad by the Government or with Government approval and the welfare of British troops was certainly not the primary reason for her travels.

Such handicaps and disadvantages could not have been overcome by anyone not possessed of a strong personality and considerable determination. In tactics she was an opportunist, and her impatience with obstructionists encouraged her to take short cuts, often with success, to save time in reaching her objective. And to this should be added Emily's ability, possessed by all champions, of being able to call on extra reserves of power in an emergency.

These were the qualities that enabled her to break through the barriers of official obstinacy and mulishness. But these assets brought liabilities. Emily's impatience offended and estranged officials; they were unused to such treatment from a woman, especially in the days before women had votes. Sometimes, acting on impulse helped her break through obstacles by the sheer momentum of her advance but at other times haste led her to make wrong judgements. Having strong convictions and being intolerant of opposition, she found it hard to exercise the patience and flexibility required for successful committee work.

It was difficult for her to disagree without rancour and she was inclined to view differences of opinion as moral issues. To the end of her life she never lacked the consolations of religious faith, although her regard for the church as an institution had been diminished by the conduct of some of its servants. Separation, years of absence and even at times disagreements did not snap the links with her family and she continued to treat her relatives with tenderness and affection.

Indeed it is probably fair to say that, although her travels, her loneliness, and the hardships which she learned to endure, conferred on her the boon of self reliance, she never grew away from the protective world of her childhood.

Her pacifism was not the political pacifism which considers capitalist wars to be unjustified but socialist wars to be right. Nor did she oppose the war with Germany on the grounds that the Germans were not the guilty party. Her pacifism came nearer to the Quaker view that all men are good at heart, and neither the atrocity stories of Belgian refugees, nor the 'defection' of her brother, who believed that Britain in World War I was defending national existence and international liberty, changed her thinking.

In her will—the probate value of which was £5,621 1s 9d—she remembered, among other people, her niece Dorothea Thornton who lived in Park Walk, Chelsea, and must often have come to see her, her sister, Maud Hebblethwaite and Maud's son Patrick, together with other more distant relatives. The £100 which she had borrowed was repaid to General Smuts, and various possessions went to Margaret Gillett. Emily's residuary legatee was 'my dear nephew and almost son' Reginald Oliver Hobhouse, son of her brother Leonard who, as a boy, had taken her out in his punt on the Cherwell and had then disappointed her by becoming a soldier in World War I. To him she left all monies, securities and title deeds not otherwise disposed of, enjoining him only—and perhaps here she thought for a moment of her days in Mexico—'not to use my bequest in speculations'.

Bibliography

Anonymous. *The Official Guide to South Africa,* issued by authority of Cape Government Railways, Central South African Railways, Natal Government Railways, Rhodesian Railways, The Beira and Mashonaland Railways, and the Caminho de Ferro de Lourenço Marques (Gilchrist & Powell Ltd) 1906.

Barton, D. B. *A Historical Survey of the Mines and Mineral Railways of East Cornwall and West Devon* (Bradford Barton Ltd) Truro 1964.

Bassett, Arthur Tilney. *Life of John Edward Ellis* (Macmillan & Co) 1914.

Batts, H. J. *Pretoria from Within during the War* (John F. Shaw & Co) 1901.

Bell, Julian (Ed) *We did not Fight: 1914-1918, Experiences of War Resisters* (Cobden-Sanderson) 1935.

Bennett, E. N. (translated) *The German Army in Belgium* (The German White Book of 1915) (Swarthmore Press Ltd) 1921.

Bolitho, Paul. *The Story of Methodism in the Liskeard Circuit 1751-1967* (Published by the Author) 1967.

Buchanan-Gould, Vera. *Not without Honour: The Life and Writings of Olive Schreiner* (Hutchinson) 1946.

Bussey, Gertrude & Margaret Tims. *Women's International League for Peace and Freedom 1915-1956* (George Allen & Unwin Ltd) 1965.

Carr, John Dickson. *Life of Sir Arthur Conan Doyle* (John Murray) 1949.

Cronwright-Schreiner, S. C. *The Land of Free Speech* (New Age Press) 1906.

De la Rey, Mrs (General). *A Woman's Wanderings during the Anglo-Boer War* (T. Fisher Unwin) 1903.

273

De Kiewiet, C. W. *The Imperial Factor in South Africa* (Frank Cass) 1965.

De Villebois-Mareuil, Colonel. *War Notes* (Adam & Charles Black) 1901.

De Wet, Christiaan Rudolf. *Three Years War* (Constable & Co) 1902.

Doyle, A. Conan. *The War in South Africa* (Smith Elder & Co) 1902.

Du Parcq, Herbert. *Life of David Lloyd George* (Caxton Publishing Company Ltd) 1913.

Estorick, Eric. *Stafford Cripps* (William Heinemann) 1949.

Fawcett, Millicent. *What I remember* (T. Fisher Unwin Ltd) 1924.

Fry, A. Ruth. *A Quaker Adventure* (James Nisbet & Co Ltd) 1926 and (Friends Service Council) 1943.

Fry, A. Ruth. *Emily Hobhouse* (Jonathan Cape) 1929.

Gardiner, A. G. *The Life of George Cadbury* (Cassell & Co)

Gaskell, H. S. *With Lord Methuen in South Africa* (Henry Drane) 1906.

Gooch, G. P. *Life of Lord Courtney* (Macmillan & Co) 1920.

Gerard, James W. *My Four Years in Germany* (Hodder & Stoughton) 1917.

Graham, John W. *Conscription and Conscience—A History 1916-1919* (George Allen & Unwin) 1922.

Halliday, Frank E. *A History of Cornwall* (Gerald Duckworth) 1959.

Hancock, W. K. and Van der Poel, Jean. *Selections from the Smuts Papers* (Cambridge University Press) 1966.

Headlam, Cecil. *The Milner Papers—South Africa 1899-1905* (Cassell & Co) 1933.

Hobhouse, Emily. *The Brunt of the War and where it fell* (Methuen) 1902.

Hobhouse, Emily (Translated). *Tant' Alie of Transvaal, her diary 1880-1902* (George Allen & Unwin Ltd) 1923.

Hobhouse, Emily. *War without Glamour or Women's War Experiences written by themselves, 1899-1902* (Nasionale Pers Beperk) Bloemfontein 1924.

Hobhouse, Mrs Henry. *I Appeal unto Caesar* (George Allen & Unwin) 1917.

Hobhouse, L. T. and Hammond, J. L. *Memoir of Lord Hobhouse* (Edward Arnold) 1905.

274

Bibliography

Hobhouse, Stephen. *Forty Years and an Epilogue; Autobiography 1881-1951).*
An English Prison from Within (George Allen & Unwin).
Hobson, J. A. and Ginsberg, Morris. *L. T. Hobhouse* (George Allen & Unwin) 1931.
Hobson, J. A. *The War in South Africa, its causes and effects* (James Nisbet & Co) 1900.
Hopkinson, Smith, F. *A White Umbrella in Mexico* (Longmans Green) 1899.
Jackson, Murray Cosby. *A Soldier's Diary, South Africa 1899-1901* (Max Goschen Ltd) 1913.
Jenkin, A. K. Hamilton. *Cornwall and its People* (J. M. Dent) 1932.
Le May, G. H. L. *British Supremacy in South Africa 1899-1907* (Clarendon Press) 1965.
Marquard, Leo (Ed). *Letters from a Boer Parsonage* (Purnell) Cape Town, 1967.
Martin, A. C. *The Concentration Camps 1900-1902* (Howard Timmins) Cape Town, 1958.
Meinertzhagen, R. *Diary of a Black Sheep* (Oliver & Boyd) Edinburgh & London, 1964.
Meintjes, Johannes. *General Botha* (Cassell & Co) 1970.
Millin, Sarah Gertrude. *General Smuts* (Faber & Faber) 1936.
Milner, Viscountess. *My Picture Gallery 1886-1901* (John Murray) 1951.
Nevinson, Henry W. *Changes and Chances* (James Nisbet & Co Ltd) 1923.
Fire of Love (James Nisbet & Co Ltd) 1935.
O'Sullivan Molony, W. *Prisoners and Captives* (Macmillan & Co) 1933.
Parmoor, Lord. *A Retrospect* (William Heinemann Ltd) 1936.
Paynter, William H. *Our Old Cornish Mines* (East Cornwall) Liskeard Borough Archivist, 1964.
Pearce, John (Ed) *The Wesleys in Cornwall* (D. Bradford Barton Ltd) Truro, 1964.
Phillipps, March L. *With Rimington* (Edward Arnold) 1902.
Raine, G. E. *The Real Lloyd George* (George Allen) 1913.
Rankin, Lt. Col. Sir Reginald. *A Subaltern's Letters to his Wife* (John Lane, The Bodley Head Ltd) 1901.
Rosewarne, John N. (Ed). *Bygone Cornwall* (D. Bradford Barton Ltd) 1970.
Rowe, John. *Cornwall in the Age of the Industrial Revolution* (Liverpool University Press) 1953.

Rowse, A. L. (Ed). *A Cornish Anthology* (Macmillan & Co) 1968.

Shaw, Thomas. *A History of Cornish Methodism* (D. Bradford Barton Ltd) 1967.

Steevens, G. W. *From Cape Town to Ladysmith* (William Blackwood & Sons) 1900.

Strachey, Ray. *Millicent Garrett Fawcett* (John Murray Ltd) 1931.

Todd, Arthur Cecil. *The Cornish Miner in America* (D. Bradford Barton Ltd) Truro (The Arthur H. Clark Co) Glendale, California, 1967.

Van der Merwe, Dr N. J. *Tot Nagedagtenis van Emily Hobhouse* (Nasionale Pers Beperk) Bloemfontein, 1926.

Van Reenen, Rykie. *Heldin uit die Vreende* (Tafelberg-Vitgewers) 1970.

Vaughan, Major-General John. *Cavalry and Sporting Memories* (The Bala Press) 1954.

Viljoen, General Ben. *My Reminiscences of the Anglo-Boer War* (Hood Douglas & Howard) 1902.

Williams, H. V. *Cornwall's Old Mines* (Tor Mark Press) Truro. Truro, 1970.

Ward, C. S. and Baddeley, M. J. B. *Guide to South Devon and South Cornwall* (Dulau & Co) 1895.

Webb, Beatrice. *Our Partnership* (Longmans Green) 1948.

Whyte, Frederic. *Life of W. T. Stead* (Jonathan Cape) 1925.

Williams, H. V. *Cornwall's Old Mines* (Tor Press) Truro.

Wilson, H. W. *After Pretoria—the Supplement to: With the Flag to Pretoria* (Amalgamated Press) 1902.

OTHER SOURCES CONSULTED

Published Government Reports

Command Paper 264. Correspondence Relating to Affairs of the Cape Colony. July 1900.

Command Paper 426. Proclamations issued by Field Marshal Lord Roberts in South Africa. 1900.

Command Paper 522. Despatch by General Lord Kitchener dated March 8th 1901, relative to the military operations in South Africa.

Command Paper 524. Return of Buildings Burnt in each Month from June 1900 to January 1901 (Farms, buildings, mills, cottages, and hovels).

Command Paper 582. Correspondence etc., between the Commander-in-Chief, South Africa and the Boer Commanders, so far as it affects the Destruction of Property. June 1901.

Command Paper 663. Further Papers relating to Negotiations between Commandant Louis Botha and Lord Kitchener. July 1901.

Command Paper 732. Correspondence relating to the Prolongation of Hostilities in South Africa. August 1901.

Command Paper 819. Reports on the Working of the Refugee Camps in the Transvaal, Orange River Colony, Cape Colony and Natal. November 1901.

Command Paper 853. Further Papers relating to the Working of the Refugee Camps in the Transvaal, Orange River Colony, Cape Colony and Natal. December 1901.

Command Paper 893. Concentration Camps Commission. Report on the Concentration Camps in South Africa by the Committee of Ladies appointed by the Secretary of State for War. 1902.

Command Paper 902. Further Papers relating to the working of the Refugee Camps in South Africa. 1902.

Command Paper 933. Letter from Assistant-General Tobias Smuts to Commandant-General Botha. 1902.

Command Paper 934. Further papers relating to the working of the Refugee Camps in South Africa. 1902.

Command Paper 979. Returns of Farm Buildings etc., in Cape Colony and Natal destroyed by the Boers. 1902.

Unpublished Official Documents
Foreign Office: Files of internal records relating to Miss E. Hobhouse, 1915-1916. (Public Record Office.)

Books Printed for Private Circulation
Courtney, Kate. *Extracts from a Diary during the War (1914-1918).*

Gillett, Arthur B. *Memories from some of his friends* (John Bellows Ltd) Oxford 1955.

Hobhouse, the Rt Hon. Henry. *Hobhouse Memoirs* (Barnicott & Pearce, Wessex Press) 1927.

Hobhouse, Stephen. *Margaret Hobhouse and her family* (Stanhope Press Ltd) Rochester 1934.

Booklets, Pamphlets, etc.
Anonymous. Mr Chamberlain against England: A record of his Proceedings by a Free Briton (Watts & Co).

Boulton, S. B. Address on the War in South Africa given at a Conservative & Unionist Meeting at Copped Hall, Totteridge, Feb., 15th, 1900 (Barnet Press Office).

Comité de la Jeunesse Française en Faveur du Transval. Record of Proceedings.

Green, James (Member of the Massachusetts Bar). Causes of the War in South Africa—Paper read before the Worcester Society of Antiquity, June 1st, 1900.

Hobhouse, Emily. To the Committee of the South African Distress Fund. Report of a Visit to the Camps of Women and Children in the Cape and Orange River Colonies. (Printed and published by the Friars Printing Association Ltd, 26A Tudor St, London E.C.4.).

A letter to the Committee of the South African Women and Children's Distress Fund (Argus Printing Co Ltd, London).

Howard, Elizabeth Fox. Friends Service in War Time (Friends' Council for International Service Devonshire House) Bishopsgate, 1920.

Hyndman, H. M. The Transvaal War and the Degradation of England (Twentieth Century Press Ltd) 1899.

Kuyper, Prof. A. (Member of the States-General of the Netherlands). The South African Crisis (Reprinted from the *Revue des Deux Mondes,* February, 1900, Translated and prefaced by A. E. Fletcher for the 'Stop the War' Committee, Clock House, Arundel Street, London W.C.2).

MacDonald, J. Ramsay (Member of the L.C.C.). What I saw in South Africa, September and October 1902 (*The Echo,* St Bride Street, London, E.C.4).

Morley, Rt Hon. John. Speech at Oxford, June 9th, 1900 'Liberal Principles and Imperialism' (National Reform Union Pamphlets).

"National Congress." Official Minutes of the National Congress held at Brandfoort on 1st and 2nd December 1904 to discuss Compensation etc. (De Vriend Drukkers en Uitgevers Maatschappy Beperkt, Bloemfontein) 1905.

Petavel, E. (D.D.) of Geneva (late Pastor of Swiss Church, Endell-street, London). The Rights of England in the South African War.

Robertson, John M. The Truth about the War—an open letter to Dr A. Conan Doyle (*Morning Leader* Pamphlet Department, 30 St Bride Street, London E.C.4).

South Africa Conciliation Committee. Much Fallacy, More Fiction and a Little Fact ... according to Mr Fitzpatrick, published in the interests of Truth (Talbot House, Arundel Street, Strand).

Stead, W. T. The War in South Africa 1899-19   How not to make Peace; Evidence as to Homestead Burning collected and examined by W. T. Stead. (Printed and published by Stop the War Committee).

Stop the War Committee. The Candidates of Cain—a Catechism for the Constituencies (Stop the War Committee) September 25th, 1900.

Thomson, H. C. The Supreme Problem in South Africa (Reprinted from the Investor's Review, Norfolk House, Norfolk Street, London W.C.).

Van der Merwe, Dr N. J. Die Nasionale Vrouemonument (Nasionale Vrouemonumentkommissie, Die Sentrale Pers) Bloemfontein.

Wenmoth, Mrs P. M. St Ive Parish Church (Snell & Cowling Ltd) Liskeard, Cornwall.

Other Unpublished Sources

Records of the Episcopalian Church in Virginia, Minnesota

Kriel, Johannes David. Emily Hobhouse en die Nawee van die Anglo-Boereoorlog: Doctorate Thesis, University of the Orange Free State, Bloemfontein, September 1956.

Index

281

Index

Index

Hely-Hutchinson, Lady, 176, 177, 178, 191

Hely-Hutchinson, Sir Walter, 136, 137, 176–7, 180

Hereford, Bishop of, 197

Hertzog, General, 210, 266

Hertzog, Mrs Barrie, 210

Hicks-Beach, Sir Michael, 54

Hill, Octavia, 24

Hobhouse, Alfred, 14, 16

Hobhouse, Arthur, Lord, 14, 15, 46, 111, 185, 232, 263

Hobhouse, Blanche, 14, 15

Hobhouse, Caroline Trelawny, 13, 14, 15–16

Hobhouse, Caroline. *See* Thornton, Caroline

Hobhouse, Edmund, 19

Hobhouse, Emily: birth, 11; childhood, 11–12, 14–15; background and family, 12–15; parish work, 16, 20–1, 23; 'romantic period', 22–3; leaves St Ive, 24; missionary work in America, 28, 30–1, 32–5; engagement, 35, 36; visits to England, 35, 40; in Mexico, 37, 41; character and appearance, 42–3, 227–8, 271–2; return to England, 44; friends and relatives, 45–6; and South African war, 47, 82, 91, 95, 99; works for Women's Industrial Council, 67; and South African Conciliation Committee, 99–111, 112; speaks at Liskeard, 101, 105–8; founds South African Women and Children's Distress Fund, 111, 112; leaves for South Africa, 112; arrives at the Cape, 117; interviews Milner, 117–18, 119; journey to Bloemfontein, 120, 126–7; at Bloemfontein, 127–32, 138; work for refugee camps, 128–38; sympathy with Boers, 137; returns to London, 139; efforts on behalf of Boer women and children, 146–9; the *Times* and, 149, 151–5, 200, 270–1; attitude to Kaffirs, 149; replies to press attacks, 157–9; public speaking on concentration camps, 159–60; correspondence with Brodrick, 162–7; her position on South Africa, 169–71; returns to South Africa, 173; refused permission to land, 173; detained on *Avondale Castle*, 174–83; deportation ordered, 182, 185; taken by force from *Avondale Castle*, 183–4; and the Ladies' Committee's findings, 195–6; results of her campaign, 206–7; *The Brunt of War*, 208–10; meets Boer generals at Southampton, 211; returns to South Africa, 212; travels among Boer farmers, 212, 213–14, 220; stays with De Wet, 214; reception at Heidelberg People's Gathering 214–15; meets General Smuts and family, 216; and Smuts, 221, 259–60; correspondence with Smuts, 222–3, 228, 229, 230, 234, 237, 259; takes up case of Boer widows and orphans, 223; organizes cottage industries in South Africa, 223–6; ill-health, 227, 233, 262, 266; in Rome, 228–9; medical treatment in Florence, 229; final visit to South Africa, 230; and Indian workers in Natal, 232–3; opposition to the War, 234, 237; her pacifism, 237, 238, 272; Foreign Office and, 237–49; travels abroad on anti-war campaign, 237–44, 249–51; visits Berlin, 242–3, 245, 250–3; interviewed by C.I.D., 245–7; parliamentary questions on her activities, 254–7; disillusionment, 258; retires to Bude, 258; returns to London, 260; children's relief work, 261–2; lives at Campden Hill, London, 263; *War without Glamour* published, 263–5; and South African politics, 266; and colour problem, 266; moves to Chichester, 266; her autobiography, 267–8; death, 269; burial, 269; Smuts on, 269–70; The *Times'* uncharitable obituary, 270–1

Hobhouse, Henry I, 13

Hobhouse, Henry II, 12–13

Hobhouse, Henry III, 13

Hobhouse, Henry V, 13, 15, 45, 75, 235, 240

Hobhouse, Leonard, 14, 16, 22, 46, 226, 228, 235, 260

Hobhouse, Margaret (née Potter), 45, 235, 236

Hobhouse, Maud. *See* Hebblethwaite, Maud

Hobhouse, Paul, 236

Hobhouse, Rachel, 15

Hobhouse, Reginald, Archdeacon of Bodmin, 13, 16, 18, 19–20, 21, 22, 23, 24

Hobhouse, Reginald Oliver, 228, 233, 272

283

Index

Index

Norvals Pont camp, 132, 135
Nylstroom, 216

Olivier, General, 73, 217
Orange Free State, 50, 51–2, 58, 65, 66, 74, 80, 84, 94, 211, 217, 226, 227
Orange River Colony, 84, 86, 161, 171, 193, 195, 204, 224
Orange Station camp, 188, 194
Oxford, 159

Paardeberg, 71
Pankhurst, Sylvia, 236
Peel, Sir Robert, 13
Pensilva, 13, 20, 27
Penzance, 26
Pethick-Lawrence, Emmeline, 245
Philippolis, 225, 226
Phillipps, Capt. L. March, 76–7, 88, 91–2
Phillips, Lionel, 63
Philpotts, Henry, Bishop of Exeter, 16
Pietersburg, 216; camp, 187
Playne, Mary, 73, 91
Plezier, 218
Plymouth, 160
Pole-Carew, General, 85
Ponsonby, Arthur, 240
Porter, Haldane, 239
Portugal, 66
Potchefstroom, camp 187, 194
Potter, Beatrice. See Webb, Beatrice
Potter, Margaret. See Hobhouse, Margaret
Potter, Richard, 45
Potter, Theresa. See Cripps, Theresa
Pretoria, 54, 57, 70, 74, 77, 82, 114, 142, 215, 216, 226, 228; Convention of, 57
Pretorius, President, 52
Prettyman, General, 119, 127, 128

Quakers, 160, 235, 236, 262, 272
Quetiock, 17
Quiller-Couch, Sir Arthur, 110, 104

Ragaz, Clara, 244, 245
Raymond, Rev. E. N., 30
Reading, Lord, 186
Reckitt, Sir James, 159
Redmond, William, 161
Reid, Sir Robert, 143
Rhodes, Cecil, 59, 61, 63–4, 65, 74, 75, 216
Rhodesia, 59
Ripon, Lord, 162, 177

Roberts, Field-Marshal Earl, 76, 77, 82–3, 89, 90, 93–4, 95, 112, 213
Robinson, Ellen, 101, 104–5
Robinson, Sir Hercules, 57, 64
Rodd, Sir Rennell, 237, 238, 241
Romberg, Baron von, 249
Rome, 228
Rosebery, Lord, 75
Rotten, Dr Elizabeth, 251
Rowntree, Arnold, 248
Rowntree, Mrs Arthur, 97
Royden, Maud, 236
Ruhleben, prisoner-of-war camp, 243, 246, 248, 251–3
Russel, Rev. Jack, 16
Russian Babies' Fund, 261

St Clear, 17
St Ive, 11, 13, 18, 19–20, 27
St Ives, 263
Salisbury, Lord, 64, 65, 199
Sauer, Johannes, 149
Save the Children Fund, 261, 262
Scarborough, 159
Schreiner, Olive, 96, 212, 234
Schreiner, W. P., 66, 69,
Schwimmer, Rosita, 244, 245
Scott, C. P., 143
Scourey, Mary, 31
Selous, Frederick, 99
Sheffield, 97
Shepstone, Sir Theophilus, 53–4, 57, 65
Shiplake, 222
Simon, Sir John, 239, 240–1, 258, 259
Smit, General Nicolaas, 58
Smith, F. E. See Birkenhead, Lord
Smuts, Field-Marshal Jan, 15, 210, 216, 221–2, 226–7, 228, 229, 230, 232, 233, 234, 237, 259, 266, 269, 272
Society for the Protection of Aborigines, 149
Society of Friends. See Quakers
Somerset, Lord Charles, 49
South African Conciliation Committee, 99–100, 111, 136, 142–3, 198
South African Republic, 50, 53, 58, 59, 60, 62, 66, 94
South African Women and Children's Distress Fund, 111, 131, 148, 162, 224
South-West Africa, 59, 234
Spencer, Herbert, 111
Spion Kop, 73
Springfontein camp, 132, 133–4, 137, 194
Standerton camp, 193, 195

Index

Stanley, Lord, 161
Stead, W. T., 91, 98
Steevens, G. W., 68, 70. 128
Steyn, Mrs Isabel (Tibbie) (née Fraser), 72, 135, 160, 223, 225, 254, 262, 266, 267
Steyn, President Marthinus, 66, 71–2, 83, 90, 199, 211, 212, 224, 225, 229, 270
'Stop the War' Committee, 98, 143–4
Stuart, Mrs K. H. R., 136, 156–8
Suffragettes, 236
Swaziland, 66
Swinburne, A. C., 81

Taute, Piet, 215
Thomson, Basil, 245–6
Thornton, August Vansittart, 15
Thornton, Caroline (née Hobhouse), 14, 15
Thornton, Dorothea, 272
Thornton, Rev. Francis Vansittart, 15
Toit, Rev. S. J. du, 58
Tolstoy, Leo, 235
Transvaal, 50, 51–5, 57–8, 59–66, 79–80, 83, 84, 86, 113, 144, 195, 204, 216, 226, 227, 232
Trelawny, Caroline. *See* Hobhouse, Caroline Trelawny
Trelawny, Edward John, 249
Trelawny, Jonathan, Bishop, 14
Trelawny, Sir William, 13
Trevelyan, Charles, 91, 197, 234, 267

United States, 81, 236

Van Warmelo, Mrs, 203

Venice, 223, 227
Vera Cruz, 41
Vereeniging camp, 195
Vereeniging, Treaty of, 208, 213
Victoria League, 148
Viljoen, General B., 199
Virginia, Minnesota, 28–30
Volksrust camp, 187
Vredefort Road camp, 188, 193, 214

Wallace, Edgar, 68
Ward, Mrs Humphrey, 111
War without Glamour, 263–5
Waszklewicz, Mme, 139
Waterboer, Nicolaas, Chief, 52
Waterson, Dr Jane, 168, 192, 194,
Waugh, Benjamin, 235
Waugh, Rosa, 235
Webb, Beatrice, 45, 73–4
Webb, Sidney, 45
Wellman, Walter, 98
Wesley, Charles, 233
Wesley, John, 17–18, 19
Wet, General de. *See* De Wet, General
Wilhelm, Kaiser, 234
Williamson, Dr, 183
Wilson, H. J., 143
Winburg, 226; camp, 188, 194
Woker, Dr Gertrud, 243, 244,
Wolseley, Sir Garnet, 54
Women's Industrial Council, 67
Wood, Sir Evelyn, 57

York, 97
Yule, Dr Pratt, 189

Zulus, 53